Dear Aunt Dot,

Oh how I've loved you all my days & my mom told me how much I'm, how much you brother loved you.

Much love

His — Geneva Nic

My People's Story:

Is This Why I'm Me?

Geneva Marie Brett

1. FAMILY & RELATIONSHIPS/Dysfunctional Families
2. SELF-HELP General
3. RELIGION/Inspirational

ISBN-13: 979-8-9894165-2-3

Cover design by Chris Horsley

Printed in the United States of America

Dedication

To Big Daddy, YHWH, God - for creating everything

To My Beloved People,

Especially

Mom - for giving me life, leaving me, and finally achieving
peace

Gran - for a home, raising me, and teaching me not to be a pansy

Aunt Pat - for fun, unconditional love, and modeling forgiveness

And to my precious children, for not following my footsteps,
making your own path, and growing beyond me

CONTENTS

A fair understanding makes for a long friendship

As long as there's life in the body, there's hope for the soul

Clean up around your own back porch before you talk about someone else's

God loves a peacemaker

He'd gag on a gnat and swallow an elephant

I may be old, but I'm not crazy

I'm twenty-one years old, I'll do as I please

Nobody's perfect. There was one perfect man in this world, and he was crucified

Nothing beats a trial but a failure

Smart people change their minds and fools never do

That old coon dog won't hunt

The Lord couldn't please everybody so how could I?

There's no rest for the wicked

Tie that old bull outside

Where there's a will, there's a way

You talk like someone who fell out of a well

You'll never learn any younger

GRANNYISMS

My People's Story:

Is This Why I'm Me?

GENEVA MARIE BRETT

Preface

Howdy Friend!

"Danger, Will Robinson!" – What you're about to read is real life, my life, and my people's lives; it might not be suitable for every reader. Be mindful of your limits and triggers before you dive in. Were it a movie, the content might be rated for mature audiences or restricted due to the subject matter, "language, smoking, drug use, alcohol, violence, and sexual content." This was my life growing up, how my people talked and lived. I tried using asterisks instead of cuss words and found the truth got lost when I did so, except no matter who said it, I can't use God's name as a cuss word. So, sorry to the reader for the foul language. It's still worth the read, and I bet you've heard much worse!

As you read my people's story, you may doubt its truthfulness. I assure you that it is factual to the best of my recollection and research. Did my people exaggerate or embellish actual events? I don't know and will never know; I do know they did not need to "flavor" their stories by embellishing.

Most of these stories occurred in a simpler yet more challenging time. Younger folk may be horrified by what you read: how we lived, the things we laughed about, shoot, the stuff we STILL laugh about! Some of you older folk might feel the same way. You don't know what you don't know. People don't criticize others because they used to wear diapers or needed someone to feed them, so people shouldn't criticize others for how they lived when they didn't know any better. It's unreasonable to hold people accountable to today's standards by canceling their yesterdays of decades ago. History must be told truthfully, as it was lived, as it occurred, whether or not we accept such behavior today. We must know the truth (sometimes ugly) of yesterday so we can grow beyond it.

Life was a different kind of hard in my family. Many of us dealt with the repercussions of another's behavior over which we had no control. That was rough on us kids, so I've avoided using names as much as possible. If you know us, you already know the characters and the stories. Well, some version of the story. As hard as it was, I think we're all grateful for the life we had. It gave us grit, understanding of people, incredible experiences, and since we were Kennedys, none of us were ever star-struck.

My people were/are athletic, good-looking, bright, and personable. The older and even youngest generations excel in wrestling, motorcycle racing, drag racing, bull riding, bronc riding, roping, cutting (horse), baseball, boxing, football, and shooting. There are regional champions, national champions, world champions, near Olympic tryouts, and even a Hall of Famer among us. The love and gift of music is now in its fifth generation of Kennedys. Third and fourth generations have served in our military and law enforcement. Educationally, from my generation on, nearly every person is, at minimum, a high school graduate; there are many college graduates, including master's degrees.

When I was nine, I promised my grandmother and aunt I'd write a book about our family. I re-watched The Grapes of Wrath in 1998, which caused me to begin the book *Me Genti, My People's Story*. I didn't get far before I laid it down for another twenty years.

My husband gifted me a massage for Christmas 2020, which evolved into working with a Myofascial Release Therapist and Wellness Coach at Complete Body Wellness here in Los Banos. They heal from the inside out, which has been life-altering. As lost memories and emotions emerged, the need to complete this book began gnawing on my soul until I finally placed my fingers on the keyboard in May of 2022.

The more I wrote, the more my voice changed; instead of just retelling my people's stories as planned, I found myself writing about how that history affected me, which caused me to feel a bit guilty like I was hijacking their stories, taking center stage. Yet the stories were insistent; they had to be heard, and my voice was the one sharing our history. That's when the title changed to *My People's Story: Is This Why I'm Me?* Aren't each of us a product of our raising? Must we remain captive there? I say no. You're free to choose your future at every moment.

Each day, I prayed for guidance about what to write; this is the answer to those prayers. Revised and edited a couple dozen times over a year.

I love my people. I respect their stories; however, I knew at a young age that I didn't want my life to be like the one in which I lived. I determined to learn my way out of it, to live in a chaos-free home where love and communication were expressed in words and deeds. I decided I would rise above my raisin' in every way I could. Shouldn't that be what we all want for ourselves and our children?

I thought so and was proud to watch a family member do so. He moved away from the family, kept his distance from the chaos, and was very successful. He was living proof it was possible; if he could, I could! I was in awe, and then I heard some family voices criticizing him for excelling, for thinking he was better than them. The worst among them was my grandmother. She and Grandpa had been very successful in real estate ventures, which she slowly discontinued after Grandpa died. It appears she couldn't manage the real estate ventures, income tax business, and raising all of us kids alone.

Frankly, I don't think Gran could stand one of hers outdoing her. I was young, so I can't say if success changed the one who excelled. I don't know how he treated people, particularly our people. I heard things but had no firsthand knowledge. The criticism from others could have been because he became a "jerk" or due to jealousy, insecurity, lack of self belief, or perhaps complacency to simply live life. Not everyone desires or needs to excel, and that's okay!!

But, if that family member could do it, so could they. But they didn't do it, so they needed to pull him back to their level. Several of my people succeeded and got to the edge of being "very successful/excelling," only to have a string of lousy luck repeatedly bring them down and beat them badly. Some of us couldn't stand the idea of moving away, which was the key to being "very successful and excelling," as one family member proved.

The unspoken message was that if you succeed or excel, you will be somewhat ostracized; we won't feel comfortable around your success, so you won't feel "home" around us. This is still happening today across many cultures and neighborhoods. Frankly, that held me back for a long time. I thought I needed my people's acceptance. I believed I needed their love.

Do you know of ET (Eric Thomas, Ph.D.), the Hip Hop Preacher? He's a very powerful, grounded, and beautiful soul. I was listening to him on *The Ed Mylett Show* a few days ago. Ed asked him what advice he'd give to someone who has a dream, has done the work on character, has taken the steps, and is ready to start on the next phase. What's the next thing they should do?

ET's answer struck me like an arrow piercing my heart. He said, "Start where you quit. Wherever you quit before you got going, go back there and start . . . wherever you quit or didn't finish. Wherever you lost your heart, your drive, your soul, wherever that was, let's go back there and get that right and move forward."

Beloved, I already had this book well in the works when I heard ET. I realized I must go back in time, share my people's story, and move forward. It's fulfilling my little girl's promise to myself, my grandmother, and my aunt. It's standing in front of the story that wounded me instead of being a victim behind it. It's saying, "You're going to judge me anyway. Go on and do it then. Ya'll aren't me. Yesterday me is not today me. I no longer need your approval or acceptance. I can't fit in or be like others. My light's too bright, and I refuse to continue to play small. I must be that bold light on the hill. God has a plan and a purpose for my life. I accept both and am walking into both with him. With or without you. I urge you to break loose of yesterday, join me, and find your best self and your own purpose."

As I introduce you to my people, please keep in mind that I present snippets of their lives and personalities. They aren't just the moments and experiences shared herein any more than an athlete or artist is just one performance: they're all, we're all, complex human beings. You, too, have complex people and relationships within your family; every family does.

It just so happens that my people are legendary, and their stories are epic. I cherish my family and stand on their history. I am proud of where I come from!

So, don't be judging my people; just enjoy this most fascinating ride with me.

Introduction

Written in 1998

As a first-generation Californian, I grew up feeling like a misfit … just never quite finding my place in the world. My first decade was spent believing it was because I was less than others. In my second decade, I thought it was because my family was less than others. Eventually, I tried to accept reality and stop blaming others for where I was and who I was.

Gifted along my spiritual pilgrimage, I watched *The Grapes of Wrath* just a month ago, which made sense of the world around me. Nothing in my life has hurt so deeply as the understanding John Steinbeck so poignantly displayed in that fictional work. You see, *The Grapes of Wrath* is a part of my people's story. It's an impassioned observer's recounting of their exodus from a dying land and their journey to the land of opportunity, where dreams become a reality.

As for me, the juice of those grapes of wrath, I lay here in 107° heat at my private water ski pond in the San Joaquin Valley with perspiration dripping off my body like a tree's drizzling drops after a spring rainfall, and I think of my family toiling the earth's produce in this sweltering heat … and I feel like sobbing until I am empty and dry.

John Steinbeck wrote of my people because their story and plight would not turn him loose until he did so. Indeed, his vocation was writing, but this work was most important to him because the people needed help. My people's story got hold of Mr. Steinbeck's soul and gripped him until he set it to paper for all humankind. Indeed, he told a friend he intended to "rip his reader's nerves to rags." And so it is with me, not that part about ripping your nerves to rags, but the part about setting the story to paper for all humankind.

We, children of migrants/immigrants, have a history unto ourselves. Whether our parents came to this new land from Oklahoma, Mexico, Asia, Africa, Italy, Germany, Ireland, or any other land, our people were not treated with the common courtesy and respect due another human being. Our people were scorned, used, abused, criticized, and accused because our ways were not the same as the residents of the new land. Yet we children were taught to share, never to kick one who is down, to be respectful of all humans, and never give up.

We were taught to have pride in our heritage, to be honorable, strong of virtue and character. And then we met the world surrounding us. My people were laughed at and made fun of because of their lifestyle. It was shameful to be an Okie, a migrant ... even second generation.

I grew up hiding my identity, wanting to belong to the masses but never feeling good enough or worthy. Last year, a friend asked if I came from a "good family." At that time, I said no, for the comparisons between our families led me to that conclusion. Today, my answer is yes, I do. It isn't the wealthy, political background, private college, or travel about the world in which he was raised, but it is a strong family. Courageous enough to move to another land without anything other than the hope and belief in The American Dream.

Today, I am immensely proud of my heritage and my people's pilgrimage. Today, I don't look through the eyes of a society that has long painted the picture. Instead, I look through the soul of a human, and I hold my head high. I aspire to achieve the greatness of my people, and to own their courage and tenacity. I dare to dream and know I have a place as an equal in society. I believe in this land of opportunity as my kinfolk once did.

My life has been what it has been; of course, the past is not changeable ... but the future is another story. It's yet to be written. And the point of this writing. The children of this earth may have been brought forth from other biological parents; nevertheless, they are all OUR children, OUR responsibility. They are OUR future. They deserve to know all they can from our past and present to prepare them for the most incredible future they can create. And they must know the true stories of yesterday, "warts, wrinkles, and all" (as my friend Corky says) unfiltered by today's societal standards. It's absurd to think we should rewrite or erase history to conform to current beliefs. Yesterday was, and must be, unchangeable. You don't have to like or agree with yesterday; just accept it was what it was.

I share Dr. Martin Luther King's dream that someday, little children AND adults will go to school, work, and play together in harmony and joy. Discovering our human behavior patterns toward "different" is a step to that end. Frankly, learning our sameness will heal and unify our society and nation. Constantly shouting, "I'm different; treat me special!" hurts inclusion and acceptance. Under our circumstances, beneath our skin, we are all the same and want the same.

So, I shall share *My People's Story* for OUR children in hopes they will never treat as their ancestors were treated. Seems like we've been treating newcomers poorly for centuries. It is time for a change yet again, and that change must come from the hearts of humans, not from ordinance or code. United States history has proven that ordinances, codes, or laws don't change hearts.

Every family, except our Indigenous, immigrated to this land. Just because we believe we've moved toward the top of the heap gives us no right to treat as we were treated.

I hope your heart and soul are touched by *My People's Story*, for that is its purpose. I want you to look others in the eyes, "the mirror to the soul," and see how they're like you. Instead of searching for the difference, search for sameness. We're all wounded; it's just the depth that varies. We're all imperfect. Putting someone else down doesn't truly lift you up. It's not your place to judge; that's God's job. Look in the mirror and judge yourself, where you are.

John Steinbeck and I are both from Salinas, California; people are drawn from all over the world to "Steinbeck Country" because of how he portrayed the landscape and its people. Yet the migrant's story is still relatively unchanged. With the success of *The Grapes of Wrath*, Steinbeck was able to do many things for migrants. He donated time and money to improve the deplorable way those hard-working people were treated.

People tend to shun those of what they consider to be of a lesser quality of life or ability, believing they would not, could not, "live that way." People fear looking too closely, "There but for the Grace of God go I." Folks don't want to see themselves in the reflection. We categorize and rationalize so we don't have to face that part of ourselves. This tendency is easily recognizable by the way most able-bodied people avert their eyes from someone with a physical disability. Most humans do the same with the homeless. Folks don't want to look into the eyes of someone "different." They don't want to read or be read by the "different" one.

Dear reader, it's time we face our own selves and rejoice in our findings. The heart and soul of every human being on earth want the exact same thing. Love.

My People's Story is written to empower the reader to break away from our protective facades and encourage all people to draw strength and faith from the lives others have lived. My people, your people, are the same as all other humans. They live, love, laugh, and cry. Their lives sometimes present seemingly insurmountable challenges they must somehow deal with. They succeed, they fail, they quit, and they conquer. They live, and they die.

There exists only a societal difference in humans. A world leader, star athlete, entertainer, and field worker face the same human challenges mentioned above. What makes the most significant difference is how they're treated; it often causes people to become locked in a role they believe they cannot change.

Former President Bill Clinton is a prime example; his biological father married five times, his parents' marriage was bigamous because his father's divorce from wife number four wasn't final when he married Clinton's mother, his grandparents raised him the first four years of his life, and he grew up with an alcoholic stepparent. Clinton's stepdad regularly physically abused his mother and his half-brother. Clinton once witnessed his stepdad shoot at his mother. All this in "hillbilly country."

Yet Bill Clinton reached his highest goal and became the leader of the world's greatest nation. Could it be that the personal problems that plagued his life stemmed from his childhood belief that he was less than others because of his circumstances? Did he unwittingly sabotage himself to prove the words society thrust upon the young lad? Who, from such a beginning, could ever amount to anything? He got to the top but couldn't sustain it. Same with OJ Simpson.

OJ's folks split up when he was five; his mother raised him in the projects, and his father was a well-known drag queen who eventually came out as gay. OJ scalped tickets to Kezar Stadium, was a teen street gangster, and did a brief stint in juvenile hall. He had successful careers in football, broadcasting, commercials, and acting. He was America's darling, but he couldn't sustain it.

Another scorned by society at large. Perhaps it stems from the identity society placed upon them during their youth, whether overtly or covertly. Maybe no one ever spoke a negative word about the individual; the general comments, the belief about their people, and their circumstances could have been enough to harm a child's fragile self-esteem.

"Those people," "that kind," etcetera, are enough to enslave a human to a perceived role, the role of "her people." Every human has experienced being "different" at one time or another.

I can remember being an observer during my youth, taking in the sights around me and trying to make sense of my world. It wasn't so much that others had more; it was their inherent pride of ownership. They believed they were worthy and deserved what they had, that it wouldn't be taken from them somehow.

Once I started school and got out into the world, I became ashamed of my family. They weren't totally domesticated people; I mean, they didn't conduct themselves like those I saw on television shows of the 1960s, in which people talked through issues instead of fighting out of anger or frustration. In my mind, my people were more like feral creatures that had been tamed; the wildness would always be there just under the surface. I don't mean to say they acted like animals; they could and did get along with others and acted appropriately in most social situations. However, you didn't know when they'd revert to their wildness.

Admittedly, I remember feeling some of that wildness within myself, which is one of the reasons I married young and married someone who wasn't like my people. I recall my brother asking, "Sis, why are you dating him? He's not like us.", referring to my former husband. I responded with, "That's exactly why I'm dating him." Frankly, I wanted stability and what I considered normalcy. My former husband seemed quiet, smart, and safe from a chaotic life.

My people were who they were and lived how they knew to live. I accept that now.

I remember Gran once took my cousins, brother, and me to a restaurant where my mom was waitressing. It was a rare occasion for us to be in a restaurant; it might have been my first experience. My mother was embarrassed by our inadequacies and openly told my grandmother so in our presence. Gran was angry and vowed never to bring us to Mom's work or go around her again. I was humiliated because I was so clueless. If I allowed it in today, I could still feel the burn in my cheeks and the hurt of rejection of being "less than" in that moment. I didn't think of my future children at that moment. However, I made sure my children had good manners.

Although they were treated poorly, less than others, my people mattered. Their lives were no less important than the "haves" and deep-rooted townspeople. Same with all the other migrants and newcomers; their lives matter. I love my people. However, I made considerable and deliberate efforts to improve myself from whence I came.

Are you ready to meet my people and glimpse what happened to folks like the Joads after they settled in California? You will find my people were much tougher than the Joads. Not one of them were weaklings or pansies; every single one had grit. My people didn't fit in; they stood out and became legends within their community.

Okay then, prepare your reading space with a beverage (hydration is important) and a snack; you might need a tissue. I won't think you a pansy if you cry, and it won't hurt my feelings if you laugh.

CHAPTER 1

Circling the Wagons

The memory is vivid . . . Grandma's kitchen, with her beloved pink linoleum, white walls, cabinets, and tiled counters, and a seemingly ever-present and tantalizing aroma wafting from her stove. The windowless wall was adorned with her treasured framed print of *The Last Supper* and the gifted longhorn serving platter on which she'd written, "Tie that old bull outside."

Nine-year-old me sat unnoticed at the table as Grandma and Aunt Pat discussed the latest family drama. As she shared the saga, Aunt Pat shook her head and said, "Someone needs to write a book about our family."

As was typical, they were so engrossed in their conversation that they didn't realize I was in the room until I butted in with, "I'll do it! I will write a book about our family."

Grandma turned toward me, her blue eyes bright as she smiled and said, "Good. You do that, honey."

Aunt Pat said, "It'll be a bestseller, but it'll have to be fiction because no one will ever believe it." (Um, this is where you come in, dear reader; gotta sell lots of these books to honor Auntie's words!)

They both laughed, and my nine-year-old self felt encased in the lock of the promise I'd just made. It's fifty-nine years later, and I still feel the encasement of that little girl's contract. Gran and Auntie are gone, yet my promise and I are alive. I've thought about it, talked about it, and even started to write it. Still, I've been so busy wandering around in circles like the Israelites that it has remained incomplete until now. *My People's Story* picks up where Steinbeck left folks like the Joads in *The Grapes of Wrath.* It's about much more than my people; they're just the best vehicle for the message.

According to a tape measure, Mom's mother was just 4'10" tall; however, to those who knew her, she was a giant of a woman. She was our matriarch, our rock, even when Grandpa was alive. Grandma had drive, determination, and grit. She didn't always know how, but she knew she would. And she did.

Like Jesus, she was always there. There was always Mama's/Grandma's house to go home to. She quoted scripture, sang church songs around the house, and as she worked in the garden.

Sidebar: Gran was always early to rise; she'd drink her coffee and then go out to tend chickens or garden . . . most always singing. A cousin visited once; he liked to sleep late into the morning.

One afternoon, he said, "Man, I sure wish Grandma could find her sheep so I can sleep." We had no sheep, so I asked what sheep he was talking about. He said, "She keeps singing, 'We will all come rejoicing, bringing in the sheep.'"

I replied, "Cousin, she's not singing about sheep. She's singing a church song. It's bringing in the sheaves, a bundle of ripe grain. There's no sheep around here."

"Hmm. I wondered where those sheep were, 'cause I never saw any. I was going to offer to help look for them, so she'd quit singing about finding them!"

Gran raised us on what I call her "Grannyisms." "You'll never learn any younger." "Nothing beats a trial but a failure." "As long as there's life in the body, there's hope for the soul." "Smart people change their minds, and fools never do." "Why he'd gag at a gnat and swallow an elephant."

She was not perfect, which I couldn't see for many years. Well, that's not true. My eyes and ears heard the truth; my mind and spirit didn't allow me to accept it because it was too overwhelming. That, and I had nowhere else to go; there was no one else to love me, to provide me with a home. My father died in Korea before I was born. Five days later, my mother told her mother, "I have a dead husband and two children. I need a job." Mom walked out the door and didn't come back for three months.

She was married when she returned. She didn't take my brother and me home to live with her and husband number three. This scenario was repeated throughout my childhood. At most, I lived with my mother for a total of five years; she visited and communicated with us sporadically. Therefore, I believed I had to hang on to my grandmother for dear life.

Shortly after I turned thirty, my husband of ten years and I divorced. I later got involved with a new man (now my husband of three-plus decades) who wasn't a local and didn't know of my people. I had a fresh start and made the best of it. I distanced myself from my grandmother, mostly because I was so involved in my life. Plus, I didn't want to deal with our family's drama.

One middle-of-the-night phone call from my mother in September of 1994 changed that. Mom's words shook me like the Loma Prieta earthquake shook California's Central Coast in 1989. She said, "Mama's in the hospital." That was a call to action! (I'd been hospitalized as a child and hated being alone in that foreign institution that never slept or comforted a frightened soul. From adulthood, I stayed with my loved ones in the hospital so they wouldn't have to feel like I did as a child.) Heeding Mom's call, I quickly dressed and raced out the door, practically flying the thirty miles from Hollister to Salinas to be by Gran's side.

From that night until she passed a year and a half later, I kept close to Gran. I clung to her like a newly born babe clinging to its life force. I wasn't emotionally ready to have the symbolic umbilical cord cut. I guess I felt like no one loved me as she did. She didn't give birth to me; however, she was my mother, my mommy. My father and grandfather had died, and my mother abandoned me. Grandma was the only one who stayed. There'd be no one to love me as she did once she left. For example, in all the years we slept together, she never once refused to let me place my ice-cold feet between her legs to warm them, nor did she ever complain. My husbands did allow me to warm my feet between their legs a few times in our beginnings. However, they both yipped. I think you can understand where I came from about how greatly Gran loved me.

For the first time in my life, I acknowledged to myself that she would die. No pleading, no prayer, would prevent it … it's something we each must do. Gran was eighty-two years old; it was apparent her days were numbered. I wasn't ready for her to die! But she would, and I'd be left with what I did and didn't do from now until then. I resolved to face the truth and go through the process with her. I would be her rock. I would help her face the steps of leaving this world. I would enjoy her life while she lived to minimize my regrets to just her actual death. From that night until her death, I spent as much time with Gran as possible, trying to show her how much I loved and appreciated her.

I wanted to gather her children around her to lovingly say goodbye. Her relationship with each of them was complicated, and their relationships with one another were complex. As I write those words, I realize complex is a definition of most families. Humans and relationships are complicated and quite messy.

My goal was family unity, which was quite lofty considering that a bitter dispute between two of Mom's siblings had shattered our family over a decade before. We didn't achieve family unity during Gran's lifetime. However, her children did gather around her, one by one, sometimes two by two, to say their goodbyes. Some got closure; some didn't. Again, that's family, people. During that last year and a half, I faced the bittersweet reality of who my grandmother truly was. Like you and me, dear reader, she was flawed. Grandma used to say, "Nobody's perfect. There was one perfect man in this world, and he was crucified." I won't dis my grandmother or any of my people … I'm just telling the story as promised.

Back to that night in September of '94, my mind raced as my car sped through the night. All the above spun through my mind, and landed on a thirty-one-year-old promise to write a book about our family. I resolved to capture my people's stories with audio recordings while I still had most of my older people.

I bought a new cassette recorder and blank tapes and told my family I was recording stories for the book. I have eight to ten hours of my people's stories told by my grandmother and her sister, my mother, and her sister, with pop-ins by one of mom's brothers, three of my cousins, and #10. I'm not a gambler; however, I would wager that the stories my people chose to share for this book are unlike your family stories. That was the basis for my promise when I was nine.

These aren't all the stories; there are many more, some entertaining and some much deeper and more brutal than what you'll read. Some of them may never be shared because they hurt so badly the first time; I can't hurt my family again with the retelling. I love my flawed and imperfect family. Every single one of them.

As I mentioned, Gran's children gathered around her, those who could, visited her during her hospital stays during that last year and a half. She didn't always make it easy. I remember one of her sons flew his private plane over six hundred miles to visit her during a hospital stay when the OJ Simpson mess dominated television. Gran and her sister were captivated by that story. Uncle had flown hours to see his mother; they were in the middle of a conversation when something about OJ flashed on the screen. Gran turned up the TV and ignored her son. Meouch. I don't understand why people have the TV on when conversing with someone in person or on the phone. Don't do that. It's rude and hurtful.

I faced the fact that family unity probably wouldn't happen; too much life had been lived. But an uncle had mentioned a family reunion in passing. We'd had family gatherings for Easter and Thanksgiving but never a family reunion. I could host a family reunion, and miracle upon miracle, we'd all get along for a few hours one day to honor Gran and remember Grandpa! (I'm sometimes amazed at my brilliance.)

My people and outsiders said I was nuts to consider such an event. Some laughed, some scoffed, some winced, some rejoiced, and some outsiders said they wanted to buy tickets because it would surely be a show!

The location was the most important of all details; it had to be on neutral territory. O'Neill Forebay (near San Luis Reservoir in Los Banos) seemed to be the perfect place. Not too far from Gran, we could water ski, fish, swim, picnic, and play. Gran had always cooked for our family gatherings, so I decided our family would feed her potluck style.

The last significant detail was the invitation; I desperately wanted the day to be glorious for Gran. I couldn't stand the idea of it being marred by a fight, a drunk, or someone hopped up on dope, as had happened at more than one gathering. So, it said something like, "You're invited to the First Kennedy Family Reunion. No drugs, no alcohol, no weapons, not even a sharp tongue." Oh yes. I said that to my people.

Was it rude? I still don't know. It was real, and I'm about being real. If they got mad because I told the truth we all knew, they could just be mad. The invitation challenged us to "out nice" one another for a friendly family day. I wanted a fabulous event for our matriarch and for each of us. I invited every one of her children and grands I could find, no matter how I felt about them, how they felt about one another, or how they felt about me. Again, the day was about Gran.

Gran and Aunt Rita (her sister) showed up with fishing poles and wearing matching dresses Aunt Rita had made for them. My heart melted at their cuteness. It wasn't a big turnout (go figure with that invitation), but about 30 people came and brought food. One of Gran's sons, six grandsons, four of us granddaughters, ten great grands, some of our spouses, and Mom's sister came. Oh, and then my mother showed up, so drunk she could hardly walk. Auntie gave her a piggyback ride across the sand to our picnic site. I included a photo of that in the album along with the "Footprints in the Sand" poem, exchanging Auntie for Jesus.

Mom was the only one who broke the rules. I was furious when I saw her, but again, I couldn't let that ruin the day. I didn't try to make her leave; she was being Lou, doing what Lou did when she couldn't emotionally handle a situation. She was way more whacked than when she came to my second wedding and "performed" as the photographer. Once Auntie got her to our site, Mom pretty much slept the rest of the day.

It was indeed a friendly family day; the love was palpable. Throughout the day, most of us shared our thoughts about the first Kennedy family reunion in a blank book I'd purchased for Gran. We all had a fabulous time doing everything I mentioned we could do in the invitation. It was awesome.

I doubt any of us realized we were circling our wagons around Gran, not so much to protect her because she had to die at some point. I think we were circling our wagons to protect our own hearts.

Language has always been important to me; early on I learned the power of words and have strived to carefully choose words to express my exact meaning.

We live so much of our lives alongside one another, not totally connecting as we truly can. Most people don't hear the exact, specific words spoken to them. People translate what was said to what it means to them based on how they interpret life. People interpret a look as something harmful if that's where they're coming from.

Look, and I mean really look, at your people. Be honest with where you are with them. I challenge you to accept that each of them will die, and so will you. How will things be left between you?

Are you nurturing an ancient wound, a grudge perhaps? Are you saying and showing your people that they matter to you? Why not? Because someone hurt your feelings or insulted you? You, and you alone, are responsible for YOUR actions and inactions. On judgment day, God won't care what someone else said or did to you. Your judgment is based on what YOU said or did. Period. Full stop.

We're all flawed. Love God. Love people. Love YOUR people. Forgive them so you can be free. One day, you will stand for judgment in front of The Most High, The Everlasting King of the Universe. You're going to want forgiveness. Forgiveness you don't deserve. Why should you be forgiven if you won't forgive another? You won't be.

There's not one set of rules for you and a different set for everyone else. Beloved sister, beloved brother, it's the same rules for all human beings as we stand before God for judgment.

CHAPTER 2

Fiddle, Fight, and Sexy Time ...

Mom and her family (parents and four siblings, two younger and two older) migrated from Oklahoma on the tail end of the Dust Bowl days. While Grandpa was happy to just live, Grandma was the enterprising sort, and California was the land of opportunity for those willing to work.

Grandma's mother owned cattle and a little farm at a young age, which she sold to buy a restaurant after her husband walked out of their lives. Gran and her older sister stood on boxes and washed dishes, waited tables, and did whatever they were asked to do. Grandma was an industrious worker all her days. Now that I think about it, that restaurant's probably where Gran learned customer service, but that's a story for another day, another book!

Grandma's granddad was a hard cattle rancher who once beat Grandma's mother and one of her mother's brothers with a buggy whip for some act of disobedience. Grandma's mom wouldn't tolerate fighting between her daughters; ironically, she'd whip them for fighting.

Grandpa's family, on the other hand, enjoyed fighting for sport. Grandpa was one of seven children, also raised on the rough ranch life. His daddy died when he was just five years old, and my oh my, did his mother have a time trying to keep all those kids of hers in line! They'd fight among themselves out of anger and for sport. If you hurt one of them, you'd best know the rest of the clan would be after you ... probably carrying a pig sticker (knife) and not shy about using it. There was no time, nor excuse, for crying. Not even if you spilled milk:-)

Grandma was tough like that, too; she had a temper and would hold a grudge for a bit. I remember her sister telling me about provoking Gran until she got "fighting mad" and staying mad until she could exact a pound of flesh from her older sister. Sister would hide in a tree until she saw their mom coming home, warning Gran that they better clean up before their mother saw they'd been fighting or they'd both get a whipping.

Their younger brother had been born with encephalitis (inflammation of the brain), which was treated by placing steel bands around his head. He was always a little different and quite a troublemaker as a youth. He'd get himself into a situation, and his sisters would often have to fight his way out of it.

Their mom had married one of her daddy's ranch hands. Their daddy was an orphan, raised by cowboys wherever he drifted. As you might guess from watching Westerns, his skills weren't those of a domesticated man. He enjoyed the drink and loved to gamble. He'd wander off on a drinking-gambling binge and return, except that last time when his wife was pregnant with their third child. He didn't come back, even a decade later, after learning the mother of his children had tuberculosis and was being sent to a sanatorium. (Don't be judging him, you don't know his story.)

Gran's sister got married before their mother died. My grandmother and her younger brother were sent to an aunt's house, who sent them off to their grandfather's not too long after they'd arrived. They weren't well received there either, so Gran took a job working in a restaurant. Her pay was basically room and board for her and her brother.

One day, my grandpa walked into the restaurant and saw the tiny, blue-eyed, black-haired fourteen-year-old. He thought she was the prettiest girl he'd ever seen and decided on the spot that he wanted to marry her. He was eight years older. Now, don't go thinking too ill of him; that was common practice in those days in that country. He repeatedly confessed his love for her and his desire to care for her and her brother on his cattle ranch. She told him she was far too young to know what love was. Nevertheless, she eventually agreed to marry him for the security he offered. They wed two months before her fifteenth birthday.

After marrying and bedding her, he took her to meet his mother. As Gran and her mother-in-law stood on the porch looking out at the cattle roaming about, Gran asked which cows were her husband's. Her mother-in-law scoffed and said, "Cows? Ray don't have no cows. He had one cow, and the damn fool sold that to buy a shirt to get married in!" Oof. Grandma never forgave him for that. And I do mean, not to her dying day as far as I knew.

Turns out he and most of his siblings simply weren't the industrious types. They liked to hunt and fish . . . but wanted to drink, fight, play music, and have sexy time even more. They were content to just live. This caused many problems between Gran and her husband and her sisters-in-law. She was 4'10" and small-framed; her sisters-in-law were close to a foot taller and much bigger boned. She scrapped with them when they came at her, always giving as good as she got.

I don't know when Grandpa first cheated on her, but when she was pregnant with their first child (two years in), he told her he was going to a little dance party at his brother's house up the hill, and he'd be back later. She said, "I think I'll just go with you to get out of the house."

"No, you're too big pregnant to go up that hill. You should stay home to be safe."

"Well if you're so worried about my condition, you should stay home with me."

Grandpa ignored her and went on to the party without her. Not long after he left one of his brothers came along, her favorite, in fact. The same brother who was hosting the party.

Uncle said, "Where's Ray?"

"He went to your party."

"Why didn't you go with him?"

"Well, he said I was too big pregnant to get on up that hill, so he made me stay home."

That riled my great uncle a bit, Gran was his favorite sister-in-law, and she was young.

Uncle said, "I know Ray has plans to get together with a woman, a real big woman, real big. I just found out that my own wife has been allowing Ray and that woman (Uncle said her name, my whole family knows her name) to have their illicit rendezvous at my home while I was working! Now, I don't take to that at all! So, I'm going to take you up the hill to my house so you can deal with that big old cow."

He pulled out a knife then plucked a hair from Gran's head. He split that hair with his knife to evidence its sharpness. He handed her the pig sticker and said,

"Now Geneva, you just walk right up to that fat bitch, hook her in the gut with this knife and just start walking your way around her till you get back to start. I'll be standing on the back side of that big ole cow, and if anyone has a word to say to you or even looks at you sideways, I'll take them on right then. I'll stick them myself, any one of them sons a bitches, including my own brother."

Then he showed her a second knife, his knife, which was equally as sharp.

They went on up the hill, Gran reached the door and tried to open it, but it was locked. Gran reasoned (probably the wrong word choice here) that someone must have seen her coming and told her husband, so he bolted the front door to keep her out. She was already hurt, embarrassed, and mad. That her man had bolted the door to keep her out made her even madder. Banty rooster mad. (Banty roosters are smaller, aggressive roosters that will fight to the death; they don't care what size the opponent is. They're often used for cock fighting.)

So, my big pregnant, 4'10" grandmother's teenage pride is wounded, her heart is hurt, and she's Banty rooster mad. She saw an axe near the front door; it was used for chopping wood, but to Gran, it was just plain convenient. Gran picked up the axe and chopped down the door! Grandpa saw the door dissolve, and his little bride enter the house. He and his paramour booked it out the back door and split up. The woman ran in one direction, and Grandpa ran up the mountain. For an instant, Gran thought about going after the woman; however, she decided against it because it was her man who needed the reckoning. Grandma was too big pregnant to go up the hill after Grandpa, although she wanted to.

Grandpa didn't rush right back home. But he eventually got there, and they continued with their life.

All this information is to help you understand how these folks lived. I'm not passing judgment on them, and neither should you. This way of life is what they knew, right or wrong; it was their reality. Grandma and Grandpa replayed versions of his cheating until close to the end of his life. I can't speak as to why she put up with it for so many decades, and neither can you.

Undoubtedly, you've watched movies and television shows and commented about the characters, their stories, and how you would do things oh so differently. The more people I've talked with, the more human stories I've heard, the less judgy I've become. What I know for sure is that we never truly know what we will say or do until we're in that precise moment in time. We don't know the full stories, the life experiences, of those other folks and what brought them to their moment, which is why they acted/reacted the way they did.

I didn't witness these stories, but I heard them enough times to know them well. I recently listened to an audio of Grandma telling this story. At its conclusion, my mom said, "And you wondered where I got my crazy, insane temper." Truth is, I had wondered, but after rehearing this recently, I no longer wonder.

The telling of this story over the years was accompanied by laughter. My takeaway, at least for most of my younger days, was that your size doesn't matter. You don't let someone take advantage of you or make you look a fool, you stand your ground and fight back. Or sometimes you start the fight. Use an "equalizer" if need be.

CHAPTER 3

Blue-Eyed Baby and California Dreaming

A little more than three years into her marriage, Gran had gotten accustomed to her husband staying out all night partying. Rather than the supportive cattle rancher he'd portrayed himself as, he was a carouser, serial cheater, and wife-beater. I don't have to tell you that she didn't like that, who would?

Aah, but my people don't quit, no matter how hard or gritty it gets. So, there's Gran, barely seventeen. Her husband hadn't come home, so she was alone with their six-month-old child when her mother-in-law came banging on the door and woke her.

Mrs. Kennedy (that's what Gran called her) said, "Geneva, you're going to have to help me. I can't do a thing in the world with Ray. He's lost his mind, and he's tearing everything up! Come on now, go with me."

Grandma quickly dressed herself and her baby and followed her mother-in-law up the hill to her house. Can you imagine what was going through that teenager's mind on that walk up the mountain? Her husband was out of his mind, his mother couldn't help him, so she would have to do something. In typical fashion, Gran just put one foot in front of the other and walked into the unknown.

Grandpa was highly intoxicated and talking crazy when they got to the house. He was crying and saying he wanted his baby. Grandma offered him their baby, but Grandpa pushed him away, repeating he wanted his baby. She made the baby offer and he refused several times. Grandma and Mrs. Kennedy exchanged confused looks; he wanted the

15

baby yet rejected him each time he was offered the baby. Grandpa growled, "I don't want that baby; I want my big blue-eyed baby!" Which was even more confusing to Gran because their baby boy had big blue eyes!

It was then the story behind this scene began to leak out of Grandpa and his mother. A lifelong deputy sheriff friend of the Kennedys had fetched Mrs. Kennedy to help with her son because he (Deputy) had received several complaints about Grandpa and was unable to manage him on his own.

Let's let Gran tell this part of the story in her own words, except I will leave out the names of the others involved. Gran knew and told the names.

"Deputy took Mrs. Kennedy down to where Ray and a woman were having their orgy, right in the middle of the road! The public road! They were naked as jaybirds, having sex in the middle of the road! When a car would come by, Ray would jump up and run at them, trying to cut them with his knife for bothering them! Deputy took Mrs. Kennedy down there, but she couldn't make them do anything, so that's when she came and got me."

Sidebar: Do you think The Beatles heard this bizarre Stringtown, Oklahoma story and wrote "Why Don't We Do It In The Road?" as a commemoration or salute? Hey - my people might be due royalties! (I've thought of my people's story, actually Grandpa, every single time I've heard that song. Decades later, another male family member did the same thing, except he didn't have a knife or a wife.)

I digress; let's get back to Gran. With her husband's continued rejection of their big blue-eyed baby and now the knowledge of a woman involved, Grandma realized the big blue-eyed baby Grandpa wanted was his lover! She was not only crushed, but she was also humiliated! His cheating was well known, but in the middle of the public road, this would be fodder for gossip and pity for quite some time. Long before Daffy Duck said, "What a revolting development," Grandma thought it.

It was freezing cold outside, so Gran stood beside the wood stove with her baby on her hip to keep him warm. She also slung a few words at her drunken, dirty dog of a husband who continued to cry out for you know who.

Grandpa was mad he couldn't have his lover, mad his wife kept giving him the wrong blue-eyed baby, and mad she was slinging words he deserved, so he shoved her. His shove caused her calf to be pressed into that glowing hot cast iron stove, searing the flesh as bad or worse than her teenaged heart had been seared by his despicable unfaithfulness. When she could pull her leg from the stove, she took her baby and went home without so much as a tear on her face.

Buckle up, friend, as you'll hear Gran conclude the story sixty-five years later, shared for you for this book. Come join our conversation at her kitchen table, where many of these stories were told.

"So, I just went and got that old shotgun and loaded it. When he come down there, I decided to get rid of him."

"So, you decided to get rid of him or kill him? What were you thinking, Gran?"

"I meant to kill him."

"Why?"

"Because he'd burned my leg so badly. I had that little baby in my arms, so I couldn't do anything."

"You knew where he'd been and what he'd been doing?"

"Yes. He told it on himself. I knew all about it."

"So, you were just going to get rid of him? Kill him?"

"Well. Yes."

"So, you loaded up your shotgun, and he came walking up … and then?"

"I let loose of it."

"Single or double barrel?"

"Both barrels at one time. I missed. Then I put more shells in it. It wasn't my fault I didn't miss the corner of my house. He dodged around the corner of the house, and I got the corner of the house."

"Was he sober?"

"No, he wasn't sober, but he got out of the way anyhow."

YEOWZA people! I'm still not sure which slice of that mess is the most bizarre! You've got totally naked sex in the middle of a public road, and Grandpa attacks passersby with his knife for bothering them! WHERE was the knife during sex? Johnny Law can't stop the road sex, and Grandpa's mother can't stop the road sex, so they get his teenage bride to calm him down. My seventeen-year-old grandmother was plotting premeditated murder, and then it was her intended victim's fault that she shot the house! If he'd been man enough to take the shot, she'd have hit him, not the house! Ay, Caramba!

You can't make this stuff up; at least, I couldn't. I told you they were legendary! Oh, and by the way, this blue-eyed lover of Grandpa's was the same woman Gran's brother-in-law had told Gran to "hook a knife in her gut and walk all the way around her" in the last chapter.

Grandma said her husband was a whoremonger throughout their entire marriage.

They moved to California in 1941, had three more children (one passed shortly after birth), and were doing well. Within two years, they were building, buying, and selling homes. In 1946, they took some time off for a trip back to Stringtown to visit family and friends. With seven kids (aged two to seventeen) and two adults and what they'd need for their two-week stay, their car was so jam-packed there was barely room for their thoughts!

It was a great adventure for the kids to meet cousins, roam the hills, see their grandma dip snuff, and that huge pallet on the floor where they all slept was like camping out, minus mosquitoes. Everyone had a great time, and the kids got great insight into their daddy's raising.

When it came time to head home, Grandpa wanted to give a young woman a ride back to California with them so that she could get a job. Grandma had only met the gal once, but she knew the folks she worked for were nice people, so she said sure, they'd help her out. Gran felt sorry for her and said she didn't have a chance there in Oklahoma.

Gran's niece said, "No, she can't go with you, Aunt Geneva."

Gran replied, "We'll make room somehow and help her get a job once we get back to California."

"No, Aunt Geneva. I'll kill her before I let her get in your car. She's not fit to ride in your car! You're too good for that. I'm not going to let her do that."

Such strong words and aggressive attitude were out of character for the niece; it didn't make sense. Grandpa tried to shut her up, which riled the teenager even more.

She practically shouted, "Yeah, Uncle Ray, I didn't want to! I didn't intend to have to come out with all of it. While Aunt Geneva's been out there taking care of that old lady, you've been taking this gal out and sleeping with her all the time. You want to take her to California to continue your affair, and I'm not going to let that happen to Aunt Geneva!"

Woo doggies, Granny went Banty rooster mad for being made to look a fool. She knew him to be the cheater that he was, but this was a new low.

She let him have it, "Ray, you chickenshit bastard. I'm leaving you. The kids and I are going back to California without you."

Sidebar: Gran wasn't one to cuss. So, when she used any of the three cuss words in her vocabulary, you instantly knew she was Banty rooster mad. You just read two of the three; even more rare was when she used the word bitch.

Back to the story, Grandpa was indeed a two-timing, cheating, wife-beating, adulterous philanderer; however, he truly, and deeply loved his wife. Wait. What? How does that make sense?

Gran made up her mind to finally leave her husband. She and their kids would go back to California without him. He could see her resolve and that she meant what she said, much like when a kiddo knows they just got the last warning, and now it's consequences time.

Like that kiddo, in hopes of evading the consequences of his actions, Grandpa decided to go for sympathy and drama; his sweet talking and apologies wouldn't work in this situation. He went outside and literally laid on the train tracks, telling their children he was going to let the train run over him because he couldn't live without their mother. (Low, low, move there, Gramps. Bringing the kids into adult drama puts said adult(s) in the belly-crawling varmint territory in my book. Hey, this IS my book! I adored my grandpa, but that was some low-down, dirty, belly-crawling, varmint business.)

Their kids bought into his show. They cried and carried on, pleading with their mother to please take Daddy with them so he wouldn't die. Gran was a hard case, but she eventually caved. She said she'd have left him if not for the kids and their pleading. Grandpa got off the train tracks, and they made their way back to California sans the girlfriend. My mother said he didn't pull any crap on her after that; well, he got much more careful anyway. He cheated right up to his end.

"Grandpa was a two-timing, cheating, wife-beating, adulterous philanderer; however, he truly and deeply loved his wife." Now I get how paradoxical that sounds; how does one deeply love someone they physically and emotionally abuse? I don't know. Maybe that's what they saw growing up, maybe they think that's "normal," or perhaps they don't have the skill set to live differently. I'm not defending my grandfather's actions here; I'm telling his story and the stories of millions of other women and men who treat their significant other in such a fashion to this day.

One of Mom's brothers once told me, "I didn't know it wasn't okay to cheat on my wife. Daddy did it. The neighbors did it. I didn't know it wasn't okay to hit my wife. Daddy did it. The neighbors did it. It wasn't until I got out into the world that I learned that wasn't acceptable behavior."

My people nor their neighbors assimilated into their new community to learn the ways of its inhabitants. They lived where it was affordable, which was among folks like themselves from Oklahoma. That didn't provide them with the opportunity for growth. They compared themselves with neighbors and "who do you think you are" if you move on up? They remained trapped in the ways from whence they came, as did most of their children, as do many migrants today, as do many from inner-city neighborhoods. Trapped in a seemingly unending cycle of economic and social problems.

Millions never get out into the world; their life is lived in the same environment where they saw such behavior as normal. Our first seven years are THE most important as they set the basis for overall success in life. We learn by watching, listening, and doing. If our parents always fight and yell, that is what we learn to expect from love. If infidelity and domestic violence are witnessed, the children see that as simply how things are among their kind. These years are also essential for society because it's the best chance to influence future prosperity, inclusiveness, and social stability.

The Greek philosopher Aristotle once said, "Give me a child until he is seven, and I will show you the man."

There may be considerable truth to that; however, we don't have to accept that. I didn't. I saw the world around me, didn't like it, and determined I would be different. It wasn't always easy, and I have paid the price for it from time to time. It's work, but it's worth it.

It's said that hurt people hurt people. (Not all of us do.) That's so very sad because I imagine it hurts the souls of those doing the hurting as well. It definitely wounded their souls when they witnessed bad behavior. Even a wounded soul is a soul; all souls come into this world pure and innocent. I don't condone hurting the people you love, and I definitely don't condone domestic violence. Still, I'm not going to judge people for it. I don't know their story. That's God's job; they'll sort it out with him.

I read a story about two middle-aged twins, one an alcoholic, the other sober and stable. When questioned about their lifestyle, both had the same answer. I watched my alcoholic father.

You don't always have control over what happens in your life; however, you ALWAYS have control over how you react and respond to what's happened to you. Choose to thrive beloved, you'll be dead for a long time.

CHAPTER 4

Blame it on the Hogs

The Great Depression caused hard times throughout the USA, even in the hills of Oklahoma. Grandma said, "In the '30s there was no work, no money, people were dying of starvation throughout the land, and others were standing in bread lines." She and Grandpa didn't have it that bad; however, they did need money ... so Grandpa and a friend some twenty years older built a still. They brewed and sold "wildcat whiskey," also known as moonshine. Gran never tasted it but said it looked like clear water.

Interestingly, "whiskey" is a Gaelic word meaning "water of life." It's been said that whiskey was invented so the Irish wouldn't rule the world. (Don't get testy on me here, I've got a lot of Irish heritage flowing through my red American blood!) The "water of life/whiskey" has a longstanding place in world history and lore. Whiskey's been a strong tradition in our southern states/territories, with some of the best coming out of Kentucky and Tennessee to this very day. The government taxed the making and sale of whiskey almost from our beginning as a nation. It seems obvious that the primary reason for making illegal whiskey was to avoid paying those infuriating taxes.

It was against federal law to sell/give alcohol to Indigenous people in "Indian Territory." Of course, that didn't stop folks from doing so. People are people, and money is money. Oklahoma Territory was opened for settlement by non-natives in 1889; saloons popped up along the borders of the Indian Lands like spring flowers and liquor sales were rampant over the next two decades. Grandpa was born in the Choctaw Nation, which became the state of Oklahoma just a few years later.

The 1907 Oklahoma State Constitution prohibited all alcoholic beverages in the state. It goes without saying that the law did not affect the sales, manufacturing, selling, and consumption of moonshine. Even after 1933, when national prohibition was repealed, Oklahoma state law prohibited the sale of anything stronger than 3.2 (alcohol percentage level) beer. Such a law didn't/hasn't stopped the illegal production of moonshine. The illegal making of moonshine has continued to this very day.

Sidebar: That whiskey-making information has nothing to do with our story, but I found it interesting, so now you know too. My kids often tease me that I should write a book of useless facts, bada bing, I've done it! HA! I think I'll make them buy this book with useless facts. HA!

Now let's get back to my grandparents' story. It surprised me that Gran had been aware of the still and Grandpa's moonshining since its beginning. She seemed much more of a rule follower than her husband. Grandpa told her all the ingredients they'd use, which she recited to me decades later. They used malt, hops, cracked corn (moonshine is also called corn whiskey or corn liquor), sugar, apricots, and peaches. They'd assemble their ingredients in great big barrels and let them ferment for a couple of weeks. When it was whiskey-making time (distilling), they'd put the ingredients in huge copper tanks, add water, and put a fire under a burner. The liquid would flow through copper tubing; their peach or apricot-flavored wildcat whiskey would drip out of the copper tubes a single drop at a time into half-gallon jars or gallon jugs.

Once they completed a batch, they'd dump the mash (fermented ingredients) onto the ground. Grandpa's older and experienced friend taught him it was wise to keep the still a distance from the house in case those interfering Revenuers came around. If the still was away from the house, one could deny ownership unless actually caught in the act of making shine.

Grandma said their house was situated in a draw at the "L" of two creeks, with creeks being the size of most rivers in California. There was a mountain behind the house, which was filled with an abundance of wildlife. The still was hidden up the hill a ways. Grandma and Grandpa had free-range hogs who'd go up the mountain daily to forage on acorns, hickory nuts, and such. They'd gotten really big and fat and would come down to the house squealing and screaming like they were crazy. They'd run down the mountain towards the yard, crash into one another, fall over, get up, crash, fall, get up again, and pig squeal some more. (I don't know if you've ever heard hogs squeal, it's loud and creepy because they sound a bit human.)

All that crazy pig action scared Grandma; she feared they'd have to put the hogs down. She'd heard of hydrophobic dogs (dogs with rabies) and wondered if pigs could get the same thing, wondering if their children were safe from the hogs. She feared eating the hog meat because it might be tainted due to whatever was ailing them. Grandma asked Grandpa, "Ray, what's was wrong with those hogs? What makes them squeal and take on like that?"

Grandpa said, "Ah hell, Neva, there's nothing to worry about; the hogs are just drunk."

Seems the hogs would go up to the still every day, eat the mash, and get drunk. The drunk hogs would run down the hill, screaming, crashing into one another, fall over, pass out, wake up, and do the same thing the next day. My grandfather and his wildcat whiskey-making had inadvertently turned regular swine into alcoholic hogs!

Wherever there are stills, there are Revenuers searching for said stills. Back then, it was common for them to break up two or three a day. Both the Shiners and the Revenuers had learned lots of tricks to avoid or capture the other. Grandma thought they must have gotten a tip about Grandpa's still because they came looking around the house. They didn't search the house, but what they did do was notice those big fat hogs. The Revenuers knew hogs didn't get fat on free-ranging, and folks didn't have the means to be fattening up their hogs for slaughter. So, they watched those hogs and followed the sots straight to the still, which they then busted up. Grandpa was quick and lean, so they couldn't catch him or prove the still was his.

I do believe that ended Grandpa's moonshining career.

Have you ever been around an alcoholic or heavy drinker? The smell of booze oozes out of their pores. Those alcoholic hogs must have reeked of whiskey. When I had my pet hog, my youngest once said, "Mommy, I don't want to hurt your feelings, but Petunia smells like pancakes and bacon!" At the time, I was feeding her Omolene, which consists of rolled oats and molasses. So yeah, I bet those piggies smelled like that peach wildcat whiskey.

CHAPTER 5

Did You Just Like Wedding Cake?

Well, that's interesting. Many of the other chapters have flown from my fingertips, but as I start to write more in-depth about Mom, I find some old familiar feelings creeping up on me. The primary emotion is shame, followed by embarrassment. Shame and embarrassment over Mom's actions. Now, I can laugh with family about some of her history because I know that underlying their laughter is love and acceptance for who she was all in all. She was a good soul; they all loved Lou/Aunt Lou.

I expect you will judge her, so I'm feeling a bit protective. And truthfully, I understand your judgment because I judged her for over half my life. It was quite freeing to accept that I can't judge what she did in her life because I don't know HER story, which caused her to act the way she did. It took work, a great deal of soul work, to get to that understanding. I could accept imperfection from others; however, she was my M-O-T-H-E-R and therefore held to a ridiculous standard of perfection she could never achieve. She wasn't a storybook or feel good; let me wipe your tears with my kisses, mother. But she was my mother. I loved her and grew to accept and forgive her.

I recall lamenting over some horror of my teenage life and her not commiserating.

I said, "Mom, I was just looking for a little sympathy."

Her reply was, "Sweetheart, do you know where to find sympathy in the dictionary?"

I knew it was a rhetorical question, but nevertheless, I was aghast when she answered her own question with,

"Sympathy is found between shit and syphilis. Look it up and see for yourself."

I did. She was right. I remained horrified.

Mom married ten different men, was allegedly married to at least three more, and allegedly married one or two husbands more than once. Yeah. I know. That's a lot of marriages, two handfuls, to be exact. Ten marriages, and she wasn't even a celebrity! Not a celebrity, but she did gain infamy within certain circles for her marriages.

Frankly, I'm grateful I can't see your face right now, thankful I can't read the expression on your face. I've never been able to prejudge how another will react when I offer the volume of Mom's marriages. I've seen shock, judgment, disgust, amusement, and many more emotions. There's always a feeling of trepidation when I decide to share that slice of familial history. I always wonder if I'm judged the moment after Mom's judged. I wonder what your thoughts are about me regarding her past. Of all your thoughts, I do NOT want your pity. Mom's life, my life, was what it was. As it is with your life, there's no changing yesterday.

Every once in a while, though, if I'm in a certain mood and the audience is just right, I tell of Mom's marriages for the shock value … and I enjoy the reaction! If I've flippantly tossed it out to you, know that I trust my heart with you, that your shocked look won't hurt ~ it might even cause me to laugh at the absurdity of it.

The volume of Mom's marriages is disagreed upon among two cousins and me. Every time I say she had ten husbands, they quickly correct me, saying their mother told them it was thirteen husbands and that their mom had written their names down. They've yet to produce their mom's list, and I've only documented ten marriages. Well, not exactly. Factually, I've legally documented nine marriages, but I have documentation of her divorce from #9, so I added him to the confirmed marriages. Some of the misinformation may be attributed to Mom changing her last name to match all her husbands' and doing the same with those three almost, but not documented, husbands. Undocumented husbands. HA! Jiminy, I'm a laugh riot!

Having recently spent some time with cousins, and deeper thinking Mom's marriage count, there is a vague recollection that Mom and #10 might have married and divorced and married, and I'd swear she and #5b married. But this IS my story, so I'm sticking with the evidence I've found. If I later find proof of the other marriages, I'll fess up.

Thus far, I haven't found evidence that she was divorced from all the men she married. According to my records, at the top of her game, Mom was married to five men at the same time, four different times. Yeah. Five men at the same time. And she did that four different times! That count doesn't include when she was married to two, three, and four men at the same time as she built up to five simultaneous marriages. Yes, it's illegal to be married to more than one person at the same time. Nevertheless, she did it. Lots of people do illegal things.

Mom's first round of bigamy was when she married my father at the age of nineteen. It turns out neither of their divorces from their first marriages was final. Does that make me illegitimate? Hold on; I'll be right back . . . okay, I just checked Google. My parents wed in Washington. Washington considers a bigamous marriage invalid; however, children of invalid marriages are still considered legitimate. But wait, there's more! I was born in California. Does that make a difference? The whole thing makes my head hurt. They did get their final divorce decrees from their #1s; however, they didn't remarry after they legally divorced their first spouses. Well. This is my story, the US Army recognized me as legit, so I'm going with I'm legit.

I recall Mom's sister once saying, "Lou, you can't be married to two people at the same time. It's against the law. You should divorce a man before you marry another one. Bigamy is illegal, and you're not a bigamist; you're like a quadruplemist!" They both laughed; Mom just shrugged her shoulders and walked away.

As far as I can tell, she remained married to #s 3, 4, 5, and 6. I guess they were keepers, after all! Dang, I wish I'd said that to her before she passed; we'd have laughed. Well, maybe.

I think I was in my early 30's when I asked, "Mom, why did you get married so many times? Did you just like wedding cake?" Oh, I thought I was clever with that line!

She responded in all seriousness, "No honey, I was looking for happily ever after. I wanted to make a home for you and Ronnie. I couldn't tolerate a chippy chaser, so it was over if I caught him cheating. Or I'd give and give and give to a man without getting back, then one day I'd decide I'd had enough of one-way lovin', and that was that."

I wasn't sure I believed everything she said because it seemed brother and I were a nuisance to her lifestyle. It doesn't matter if I believed her; it was her story, her life, we were talking about. It was a massive challenge for me to accept her for exactly who she was, and I couldn't do so for many decades.

She divorced #1 and 7-9, and #s 2 and 10 died. I literally have an Excel spreadsheet of my mother's marriages, divorces, and whatever information I've been able to gather about her husbands and alleged husbands. How bizarre is that? Were I the gambling sort, I'd wager you don't personally know one other person who has a spreadsheet of their parent's spouses! Well, do you?

Neither my brother nor I were ever informed of a soon-to-be; we met her husbands after they'd wed. (Excepting brother had met my father.) There were a couple of husbands I only met once or twice. At least one had children I never met. Oops. That's an undocumented marriage, so he doesn't count.

Mom's multitude of marriages wasn't a family secret but also not something that one readily shared with others. Family friends knew, and I suppose most of the folks who hung out at the same taverns as Mom and many of those in the produce industry. My family was well-known back in the day. Um, legendary, to be exact. (Have I said that too many times?)

Mom's volume of marriages did affect my life, which seems obvious to you. I lived with her briefly when she was married to #s 5 & 8 and visited during her marriages to #s 4 and 7. Number five was my absolute favorite, #4 my least, although I didn't care much for #9. I was an adult and only met him a couple of times.

In my second year of high school, I began hanging out with the rodeo kids and aggies; they were my comfort group. Some of their parents knew my people, therefore some kids weren't allowed to associate with me. It was always a shock when a kid would ask me to confirm my mother's marriages. This also affected my dating; I didn't think I could date a boy from a "normal" family.

In addition to being a very smart and cute cowboy, I think one of the reasons I dated my former husband was because I was told his mom had been married a bunch of times like my mom. (In case you didn't know, two is a couple, three or four is a few, and five or more is a bunch.) Since his mother had been married a "bunch" of times, I thought he'd be able to relate.

Mom was in marriage #8 when I met my former husband. Turns out his mother was only married three times, not a "bunch of times." Three times, pffffft, my mother was married three times before she was twenty-one years old! His mom still had her multiple marriage training wheels on at three marriages! Seriously though, I was quite disappointed with that development. He couldn't really relate.

Mom's marital history affected both my brother's and my marriages. When my brother was nine, he promised himself he'd get married once; he wouldn't put a child through what we went through. He's been married to the same woman for over forty years, having weathered some rough patches but always honoring his promise to his little boy self. (I'm very proud of him!)

I didn't make the same verbal promise but shared the same thoughts and beliefs. Six months after marrying my former husband, I learned something about his behavior before our marriage that devastated me and caused me to question our union. Had it not been for Mom's marriages, my wounded pride would have caused me to divorce him. I didn't divorce him then, but I did a decade later. There've been some very hard and rough times in my present marriage that have caused me to consider divorce; Mom's marital history has been a factor in not quitting. I didn't want to be my mother. (Realistically, after three-plus decades of marriage, I'd have to go on a fairly wild marrying spree to be in her league.) That, and the fact that I've promised two men, before God and witnesses, that I wouldn't quit, no matter what, has caused me to stay to work through the issues this time. I quit one marriage ~ when is my word my word? I would never quit on one of my children. Jesus has never, will never, quit on me. How can I quit?

I never thought to ask her, but now I wonder if Mom's husbands knew how many other men she'd married or that she hadn't divorced a few of them. Do you think it'd be courageous to marry someone who's been married multiple times? I think I'd be too scared to marry someone with such a marital record. If they knew, were they the gambling sort or so sure of their love that they knew they'd be her last love? Most of her "till death do us part" unions lasted about a year.

Sadly, Mom never found the true, safe love she longed for. Every husband disappointed her, including my father, who died days before I was born. When I was younger, I fantasized that had he lived, they'd have remained married, and I'd have had a wonderful childhood. As I matured, got to know her better, and saw her pattern of behavior, I thought they probably would have divorced too. Mom was short on forgiveness, and when she was done, she was DONE!

Given that my father was thrilled as soon as he found out I existed, and Mom didn't want children, had they divorced, I'd probably have lived with Dad. Being a single parent, he most likely would have returned home to New Jersey. My, what a different life I would have had. Frankly, through all the hurts and hardships, I wouldn't change my life; it's caused me to be me. Different experiences would have different results. I also wouldn't have material for this fabulous book you're reading. This book you're going to help become a NYT's bestseller for my Auntie.

In all seriousness, I know she didn't marry any one of them because she liked wedding cake. I thought myself quite clever with that question; in reality, it was probably hurtful. I never asked, but I bet she only had that one wedding cake from her first marriage.

Here's a tip from a kid of a serial marryer . . . a new spouse/partner is not the solution to your discontent. I've married two different men; I divorced one and seriously contemplated divorcing the other. How could I get to the same breaking point with both of them? I am the common denominator between these two seemingly very different men. Meouch.

At some point, it's appropriate to look at yourself. I didn't care to look at that, but I did. And then I quit pointing my finger at all he did wrong because I didn't like the three fingers pointing back at me. I decided to face the three fingers and become a better me, for me, for us, for my children, and for the world.

CHAPTER 6

A Born Fighter

Like nearly every other child my grandmother birthed, Mom was born at home without a doctor. She called herself an eight-month baby; I'm not sure if that's just what country folk called early babies or if that was the general terminology of the day. I've only known them as being premature. Mom was the third child, so there's no "funny" arithmetic between her parent's marriage and her birth; she was indeed early.

As soon as she emerged, my grandfather fetched the doc because his new baby girl was what they called a "blue baby". Her coloring was eerie and frightening; she also had a purple birthmark that covered half her neck and protruded out. The doc told them not to get their hopes up for this little one to survive. Most blue babies didn't live more than 24 hours because their hearts didn't pump the blood throughout their bodies as they should.

So, you see, my mother was literally born a fighter; she fought for her life from her first breath. She was a bit of a sickly weakling for a time, but she made up for it as she grew. Mom loved life and loved to laugh and joke until her last days. She also had a temper, but then so did her parents.

Mom and family hit the migrants' trail (Route 66) in early 1941 with everything they could carry. They didn't have much because their home had been destroyed by fire the year before. It was my grandparents and their five children, ranging in age from a few months to twelve years old.

They slept along roadsides and lived in government camps and section houses on their way to the opportunities to be found in the Golden State of California. They were living in a government camp, a tent camp, with a big main bathroom when Mom was about seven years old. She came home crying one day because some girls had thrown rocks at her, and those rocks hurt.

In such a situation, Mom's mother was not the tender sort. My people believed you had to make your way in this world, and you should not, could not, must not, show weakness at any cost.

Gran told Mom, "You're going to go back there and whip their asses, or I'm going to beat you to death."

"But Mama, those rocks hurt!"

"I don't care. You better jump over the rocks, duck under the rocks, run around the rocks, or run through them. Don't you dare come back here crying to me, or I'll beat you to death."

Yeah, I know. That's harsh language. Just saying those words today would get you thrown in the clink and your kids taken away from you. I've learned people say a lot of things they don't literally mean; they speak phrases they've become accustomed to without really considering the actual words and their meanings.

I'm positive my grandmother wouldn't have beaten my mother to death had she come home crying again. From the stories Mom and her siblings told about Gran's whippings, it would have been a beating, though. Probably a bad one.

So, Mom decided she'd rather face the devil she didn't know than the one she did. She went back and kicked some little girl ass. Mom later told me she learned to fight at the age of seven, and she never stopped.

Sidebar: According to Mom's note in the upper left corner, the cover photo of the family was taken in 1941, which places them living in a migrant camp operated by the Farm Service Administration. I'd seen this photo throughout my young years, but just now it makes sense. It's a professional photograph, taken by someone documenting life in the camps. More investigation into that in the next book. Due to the look on my mom's face, I imagine it was taken after she was forced to learn to fight. Oh, and I wonder if Donald Trump saw this photo and copied Mom's look for his mugshot! HA! I am hilarious!!

Back on track ~ seeing how Mom got some acclaim for her fighting; she grew to like it. Well, I don't know about that for sure. I can comfortably say she was quick to fight and did a lot of it, at least into her early 50s. I don't remember stories of her fighting in her youth other than with the rock-throwing girls, but she was all in during her 30s, 40s, and into her 50s.

Oh my, I just found a newspaper article (online archives) from 1951 where Mom (weeks shy of 18) was in a brawl at the "Big Barn" in Alisal. She charged eleven other youths with knocking her and a 17-year-old girl down and beating them during the fight. Five of the eleven were males in their late teens or early twenties! Imma tell you, I was getting a little irritable over that.

Young men beating girls, Grrrrr. Reading on a bit more, Mom was also charged with battery and disturbing the peace . . . Gran was accused of disturbing the peace too. Well, if my daughter was being beaten by a pack of "yuts" (*My Cousin Vinnie*), including men, you can bet I'd have disturbed some peace too!

The follow-up article a month later was shocking to me, and that's something when my family history shocks me! Are you ready? First, Gran was cleared of any charges, but not my mother. Mom, her sister, and two others were convicted of disturbing the peace. (Some of the others were convicted of battery and disturbing the peace.) Mom, her sister, and the other two were sentenced to 30 days in jail, suspended for two years, and had to pay a $20 fine. No, that's not shocking, but the fact that it was a gang fight, yes, a GANG FIGHT, broken up by deputy sheriffs, shocked me! My teenaged M-O-T-H-E-R in a gang fight. Ay Caramba! There's so much about her I didn't know!

I knew Alisal, East Salinas, has always had a reputation for being home to rough and tough people who would fight as quick as they could blink. I also thought the Okies were kind of a brotherhood who fought each other, I didn't know they had gangs. I thought the gang fights, wars, and drive-bys started a couple decades later, after the Okies moved out and the second and third generation Mexicans grew up. I was way wrong!

Well, the judge warned all thirteen of the "yuts" that any future gang fights would result in a conviction and jail time.

Ay Caramba! My mother was married and two months pregnant with my brother at the time of the brawl! I don't know why I never heard this story; evidently, it wasn't a big deal to my people. Or maybe there were so many similar situations that this one melted into obscurity.

All of you whose mothers were in a gang fight, please raise your hand. Welcome to the club homie! I don't know about you, but I'm in too many clubs I didn't choose to join.

When I was about seven or eight years old, Mom and her sister were visiting Gran's (my home), which always pleased me because I loved them both so dearly. Auntie was like a mother when my mother couldn't be. My delight was cut short when Auntie and Gran got into an argument about something. Although I never liked chaos, it seemed like it hovered above our home like a rain cloud that would drench you at the most unexpected time.

Mom verbally attacked her sister for how she'd treated their mother; her harsh words were returned in equal measure. So, Mom hit her sister, which resulted in a flurry of fists until Gran got between them and separated them.

When we see fights on film or TV, we typically root for one of the fighters, but not in this situation. I didn't like the way Auntie treated Gran, nor did I like Mom thumping on Auntie. Witnessing family violence is rough on a little kid. You don't know how to process it, and no one helps you through it because they don't know how to deal with it themselves. So, we all bury another trauma and just "keep on swimming."

Two years later, I was living the good life with my mom, brother, and #5. Number five was a bull rider and Uncle's friend, so our families traveled to rodeos together. Family, traveling, rodeos, motels, and restaurants. Just when I thought it couldn't get any better, I was allowed to take a friend to the Coarsegold Rodeo. Let me tell you, I was floating with joy! "What you say, Mama? Brother gets to bring a friend too?" My brother's friend was probably the first boy I ever had a press on. (Decades later, my youngest explained she had a "press," not a "crush" on someone because the feelings weren't too very strong. So, I was merely pressing on this boy; it wasn't a crush.)

We had a fabulous weekend, one I thought I'd remember forever for the fun of it … then we stopped for a meal before heading home. I'd only eaten at a restaurant with Gran once or twice, so dining out was always a treat. And then. Dun, dun, dun.

A former girlfriend of #5's happened to be in this same charming family restaurant filled with other rodeo families fueling up for the ride home. I don't remember if it was Mom or the ex who started throwing the stink eye at the other. Throwing the stink eye was followed by hurling comments like, "Who you lookin' at bitch?" Obviously, not well received by the other. I don't believe #5 was truly aware of, nor prepared for, his bride's fiery nature.

Decades before Woodrow Call (*Lonesome Dove*) said, "I hate rude behavior in a man. I won't tolerate it!" My mother lived it. She didn't tolerate rude behavior from man, woman, or child. So, she commenced to thumping on #5's old flame . . . who fought back. Mom throwing hooks and jabs, the other gal grabbing hair and slap-pawing at Mom, eventually yanking Mom's fake ponytail off her head. Mom soundly kicked her ass. A cowboy family friend who'd traveled with us couldn't stand not being part of the fracas, so he upended a table full of trays and plates.

At the time, I didn't appreciate that my mother didn't humiliate her family, or degrade our family's honor, by "fighting like a little bitch" as her opponent did. In my family, if you're going to fight, it's fists and the leaving of evidence you'd been at the other person's face, whether you be a man or woman. My people are tough!

Back in the 60s, fighting wasn't uncommon on the rodeo scene, so the other diners quietly enjoyed the impromptu entertainment. I, too, was quiet; however, my enjoyment was replaced by horror and humiliation. No one needed to tell me that your mother fighting in a restaurant wasn't normal or that further humiliation would follow when this story was spread around the schoolyard like manure.

Number five and Uncle got the two women off one another, they paid for our meal, and we headed home.

Two or three years later, Mom did forty-five days in the county jail for being the winner of another scrap over a man. I rode with one of her brothers to visit her but wasn't allowed in. Now I wonder if it was Mom who didn't let me see her in jail. I'm appreciative that someone made that decision on my behalf. It was rough enough sitting in the car, knowing my M-O-T-H-E-R was locked in a cage like a wild animal for her bad behavior.

I think Mom did a half dozen jail stints for fighting, and those were because Johnny Law got involved. I have no idea of the actual number of fights that didn't get reported or prosecuted. She'd fight a man as well as a woman. She did have a crazy insane temper, going from zero to deadly quicker than you could turn around.

Mom never told me this next story, but #1 did. He was about twenty-one, and Mom nearly nineteen. On his way home after work, he'd stopped at a tavern and gambled away his paycheck. He said he had a gambling habit. He felt terrible about losing all the money, knew she'd be mad, so he didn't go home. The longer he stayed away, the harder it was to go home, so he decided to leave. He went to their house, packed some of his things, and walked out the door. He was a couple of steps out the door when she stabbed him in the back of his shoulder with an ice pick. (FYI – Number one matured and learned that running away from your problems rather than dealing with them in the moment only creates bigger issues. Good info peeps, save that!)

That marked the end of them. Not so much her stabbing him; they didn't get past his leaving that day. My people always blamed Mom for the end of her first marriage, presumably because she ended so many of them. Beloved #1 admitted it wasn't her fault; he walked out on her. I don't know if stabbing him with the ice pick assuaged the stab wound to her heart made by his leaving. Number one said she became a bitter woman after their divorce.

Not too long after the ice pick incident Mom moved back in with her folks. Number one stopped by one day to visit their son. He was caught up in his thoughts when Grandpa caught him walking up the driveway and stuck with his pig sticker before he realized Grandpa was even there. Grampa didn't stab him; he did, however, put enough pressure on the knife to draw blood and ensure his message was heard.

"Boy, you ever hurt my daughter, ever break her heart again, and I'll hook this knife in you and walk it all the way around you. I'll cut you and spill your guts on the sidewalk. You hear me?"

Oh yeah, he heard him loud and clear! Seems like my people had a recurring theme of threatening to hook someone with a knife and walk it all the way around them. Yeowza!

Number one told me that years later, he'd talked to his relatives in Oklahoma, who told him they knew my people. They warned him that my people carried pig stickers and wouldn't hesitate to use them. Um. He'd already been there and experienced it from both father and daughter!

Where were these people before he got tangled up with my mom and her people?

After a time, Mom and #1 became friends and remained friends to her death. When he came to Salinas he'd visit her at her home with her husband of the year, if he liked the man. That or they'd go have some drinks and maybe dance a bit or shoot some pool. Mom and #1 both loved to dance and shoot pool, matter of fact; they'd first met at a dance at the Big Barn in Alisal.

One time Lee, #1, went into Mortimer's in Marina for a beer. He didn't see Mom there with #4, so he danced with another woman. Mom walked up behind him and busted a beer bottle over his head. She and #4 walked out the door before he could get to them. Number one was never a fan of #4. Few of us were.

Sidebar: That story about Mom bashing #1 in the head with the beer bottle was well-known on both Mom's and #1's sides of the family. When #1 was eighty-nine (twenty-something years after Mom passed), he was visiting his daughter in the Salinas Valley. He went to the dry cleaners, mis stepped, and splattered himself on the sidewalk, face first. Woof, his eye was black, and his face was heavily bruised. His youngest son texted a photo of him to our older brother with no explanation.

Oldest replied, "What the hell happened to Dad?"

Youngest said, "We stopped by Mortimer's, and it didn't go well."

Both brothers laughed at the reference to that sixty-year-old story of Dad getting bonked in the head at Mortimer's by his first wife.

Another Sidebar: My mother was not an affectionate person with anyone except my older brother when he was a wee lad. I thought maybe that was because it was pre the many, many heartaches and broken hearts she experienced in her life. Number one said no, she was never even affectionate with him; he couldn't just put his arms around her at the end of the day . . . that was like trying to hug a tiger! She didn't like to be hugged or held on to; she'd give you a hug if she was in a rare mood. Mom never admitted #1 had a special place in her heart from their beginning to her end. However, #1 is the only husband she maintained a friendly relationship with; she'd speak to some of the others, but none were welcome in her home. She never danced with a former husband after they parted ways (I started to write divorced, then remembered she didn't divorce them all) except #1.

Although #1 later married the love of his life, he always loved Mom too. Differently, of course. After his wife's passing, #1 displayed photos of both of his wives in his living room so he could see them daily.

When questioned about that, he said, "Lou was my first love and the mother of my firstborn. She'll always have a place in my heart."

I can relate, as many of you can as well. I'll always love my first husband, the father of our two children. I don't love him so much I want to live with him; however, he'll always have a special place in my heart.

Talking about #4 . . . oh, she really loved him. He was her flame, but he was also a chippy chaser, and she could not, would not, tolerate that. His last bout with cheating was what ended them. Well, not so much what he did, as her response to what he did. He was straddling the sewing machine bench, trying to sweet-talk her again. As he talked, she left the room as many do during a conversation. Mom, however, walked back into the room with her loaded .22 pistol. She quietly, demurely, raised the gun and attempted to end his cheating ways forever by shooting his penis off. She missed, instead, blowing away the end of the bench. Although #4 thought he was a tough guy, he quickly and wisely fled the scene. I'm guessing he decided Mom was serious about her intolerance of his cheating. This, too, was laughed about by my people for decades. I don't know that any of my people, other than Mom, were a fan of #4.

Sadly, very sadly, beloved #5 turned out to be a cheater as well, which broke Mom's heart and made her Banty rooster mad. That story deserved its own chapter, so I won't repeat it here. You'll come across it a little further in.

There was an alleged marriage after #5, but I have no proof of said marriage or divorce, so he's not in my ten count. Mom did use his last name; it's listed as her last name when she married #6, and my cousins have him in their count of 13, but let's just refer to him as #5b for now. Number 5b is the one with kids I never met. He was a good-looking man . . . but he was another chippy chaser. By now, you know Mom didn't tolerate that. She let his infidelity fester, and then she did a drive-by shooting on him long before Salinas gang bangers were making the news with such antics. Again, she missed (I'm very grateful she was a lousy shot!), which gave her no satisfaction. When she learned it was her best friend he'd cheated on her with, she went Banty rooster mad all over again. She decided retribution was deserved, and she was the one to serve it to

#5b.

I don't know why Mom didn't go after him with a gun again. Maybe she finally realized she was a lousy shot and was just wasting bullets. To my knowledge, Mom never shot at another man; #5b has the distinction of being the last man she ever tried to shoot. Instead of shooting him, legend has it that she burned #5b's house to the ground, which again allegedly gave her some measure of satisfaction. I don't know if I buy into that, though. It seems unlikely she'd do that after her baby had died from a house fire. Not my story, and no clear facts, but Mom did have that crazy insane temper, so it's not beyond the realm of possibility.

Sidebar: It's fascinating to see how God weaves us together. Decades later, I learned one of my sisters-in-law (years before we were sisters-in-law) had dated one of #5b's sons, whom I had never met. We were almost family before we were family!!! Wait. Never mind, #5b didn't even get a marriage or his own individual number in Mom's marital lineup.

Mom was thirty-four when she married #7, a big man seven years younger than her. Mom occasionally referred to him as "Baby Huey" ("Baby Huey" was a cartoon character; a gigantic and naïve duckling.). Number seven was the only husband younger than Mom. Turns out he was a woman beater too. Well, he beat my mother anyway.

They lived in Gran's rental next door to us for a few months, which delighted me for a minute. Having Mom close enough so I could see her daily seemed a balm to my heart. Then there came the reality of her day-to-day life, which wasn't stable even though she was married.

I don't remember how Gran realized #7 was thumping on her daughter one day, Mom wasn't the crying out or pleading for help sort. I just have this vision of my Gran grabbing the pitchfork (aka an equalizer) she kept behind her bedroom door and sprinting out the back door like a running back on his way to the end zone. She tucked the pitchfork under her arm like a football, dodging dogs and shrubs as she dashed the 50 yards from the back of our house to their front steps. Her short little legs did double time as she flew up the steps and called him a no-good, dirty bastard. In one fluid moment, she untucked the pitchfork, flipped it around so the tines were facing him (pointed down), and threw it at him like it was a spear, because she absolutely intended to spear him with that pitchfork. Thanks to God, she missed. Gran had thrust the pitchfork hard enough for its tines to stick in the door. Number seven quickly turned tail and booked it out the back door. Last he was seen that day he was running through the strawberry field headed towards town.

Mom was more forgiving of a beating than chippy chasing so she took him back. He did not go to Grandma's house, ever again. He kept his distance from Gran because she was not as forgiving as Mom. It wasn't long after the pitchfork event that Mom and #7 moved to an apartment downtown. They got along; they didn't get along . . . rinse and repeat.

Meanwhile, across town, some neighborhood creep had been stalking and terrorizing Mom's sister, going so far as to hang her children's dog right in their garage. My aunt was a single parent with young children, obviously, that was super scary. The law can only do so much, and restraining orders are just pieces of paper, which don't stop most people with bad intentions. You could be dead by the time the cops showed up after your call, bad guys don't wait on the law to show. (Still true to this day.) So, Mom had my aunt and her children move into the apartment with her and #7 for safety.

One evening Mom was watching one of her sister's children when Mom and #7 got into a loud and aggressive argument. Based on what Mom threatened, I think Mom learned #7 had cheated on her.

She yelled, "Mother fucker, I'm going to fucking castrate you!"

That proved too much for my little cousin. Cousin didn't know what castrate meant, but it did not sound like a good thing. At all. She'd never been around such obnoxious behavior, and it upset her sensitive nature. She nervously locked herself in the bathroom and filled the tub with water, as the closest thing to hiding she could accomplish. Cousin put her tender ears under the water and kept repeating "Lalalalalalala" so she wouldn't hear the horrible fighting.

She stayed in the tub until the water was cold, her skin wrinkled up, and it was quiet in the apartment. When she thought it safe, cousin walked out of the bathroom, only to see #7 holding his crotch with both hands, eyes bugged open wide, mouth agape, and blood gushing down his leg. Years later, when cousin understood what had transpired, she said he was trying to keep his balls inside his body.

Number seven wasn't speaking or moving; he was just holding his private parts and staring. Ah, but Mom was moving. She was in a semi-crouched position, tossing the knife back and forth from hand to hand as she shifted her weight from foot to foot and stared him straight in the eyes, saying "Mother fucker. You mother fucker. Fuck you, mother fucker. You mother fucker. Fuck you.".

All while tossing that knife from hand to hand, like a scene from a B movie.

Someone in the apartment complex must have called the law because they came blazing up the steps and through the door. An ambulance wasn't far behind. Cousin doesn't recall whether Mom still had the knife in her hand when the cops stormed in. The EMTs laid #7 out on a stretcher and worked on staunching the blood flow from the nine-inch stab wound that had barely missed his femoral artery. (Mom was much handier with a knife than a gun.)

The cops were questioning Mom about the evening's events when my terrified aunt raced through the door. Can you imagine her fear as she pulled into the parking lot? She'd moved in with her sis for safety; she came home to cops and ambulances everywhere and her traumatized little child in the middle of it. Cousin was indeed traumatized and terrified . . . but she did not cry. We weren't allowed to cry when we were afraid.

Well, the cops cuffed and stuffed Mom in the back of the cruiser and hauled her off to the slammer. She was charged with assault with a deadly weapon. (Ya think?) She didn't do any jail time because #7 wouldn't press charges, and said he'd refuse to testify against her. He just wanted to be free from Mom and her people! That's not to say they never saw one another again; they frequented the same bars, but he kept his distance. He did not want any further Kennedy justice coming his way.

Somehow, #7 felt it was okay for him to beat Mom, but when she used an equalizer, he exited stage left, and they divorced. Theirs was a fifteen-month marriage; Mom remarried six months later.

Sidebar: Cousin told me that after recovering from the trauma of the fighting and stabbing, she relaxed and felt safe living with mom. She no longer worried about the creep hurting her mom or the kids. She knew Aunt Lou would protect them; she'd seen her in action!

Between #8 and #9, there was a boyfriend much, much younger than Mom, who got too full of himself one day when they were visiting Mom's sister. He started mouthing off to Mom, who'd been drinking. (I can hear my cousin saying, "Uh oh.") Mom was quite short-tempered when drinking and was also getting a bit tired of the youngster anyway.

She looked at the man and said, "Mother fucker, you better shut up. You don't know what you're messing with."

The young man said, "Nah, when we get back home, I'm going to whip YOUR ass."

Mom turned to her sister . . . "After we leave if your phone rings twice and hangs up, call the cops and an ambulance, 'cause I'll have stabbed this mother fucker."

Do any of you older folk remember such a code of ringing twice and hanging up?

Well, later that day, Auntie's phone rang twice and hung up. She immediately dialed her sister, who had, in fact, stabbed the boyfriend in the leg. As Auntie was trying to get details from Mom, she heard Mom yelling at the boyfriend, "Mother fucker, you're bleeding all over my carpet. Get off my fucking carpet!"

Indeed, he hadn't known what he was messing with; Mom clued him in quickly. Remember, Mom did not tolerate rude behavior. I'm not sure if that was the end of their relationship. I was keeping my distance because those were some of her wildest years, and I just couldn't tolerate her life, especially with that youngster who was my brother's classmate.

(Sorry ~ as my cousin Rooster said, "When Aunt Lou got wound up, she used mother fucker as a one-word noun to describe a person, place, or thing.")

Moving on . . . #10 was also a big guy. I'll never forget the night Mom called me and said, "Neva, I just stabbed #10, and I think I might have killed him!"

Just hearing her voice, I knew alcohol was involved.

I incredulously replied, "What? You stabbed #10? Why'd you stab him?"

(We used his name; she never referenced any of her husbands by number. That's me, for you.)

She said, "He was coming at me like he was going to hit me again. I decided I wasn't going to take another beating, so I stabbed the mother fucker."

"Is he breathing, Mom?"

"I don't know, I'm not there."

"Wait. What? Where are you? Why aren't you there?"

"I got scared, so I ran from the house and called you from a pay phone."

"Mom, you need to hang up the phone, call 911 and get back to the house. If you don't do that and the man dies, you'll do prison time, probably for the rest of your life."

Can you imagine giving your M-O-T-H-E-R such advice? Or YOUR mother needing such advice? Yeowza! It was surreal and terrifying. As you might imagine, I was on pins and needles until I talked with her the next day. Imma tell you, it wasn't a satisfying conversation. Number ten was in critical condition; they'd had to perform a colostomy on him, and his survival was iffy. Johnny Law was investigating and was not totally buying her story.

Mom said she told the law, "I was peeling potatoes, #10 walked in the kitchen to talk to me, stumbled, and fell into the knife."

Seriously. How bogus of a story is that? I don't know how coherent #10 was when they wheeled him into the ER because he was liquored up too. I know those folks are trained professionals and have heard uncountable BS stories, so I doubt they believed the tall tale told to them. Thankfully, no charges were made, nor was Mom arrested.

Mom later told me the real truth; #10 was drunk (she didn't mention she was too), she was preparing dinner, and they started arguing. Number ten was getting verbally more aggressive and coming toward her; she knew he planned to wail on her, and she wasn't going to take it.

She turned to him with the knife in her hand and said, "Come on, mother fucker. You think you want to hit me again. Come on, I'll stick this knife in you. You take one more step towards me, you chickenshit mother fucker, and I'll bury this knife in your gut."

Welp. He did, so she did. Mom was a woman of her word in such a scenario.

Hallelujah, #10 survived! I don't know why he didn't press charges against Mom! He wore a colostomy bag for almost a year before healing enough for reconnection. It's alleged they divorced and remarried; however, I have no proof of that. They did split up and get back together several times. One of the times they split up was because #10 paid Mom's friend for a blow job. Now, get this, she couldn't forgive him for that; however, she wasn't mad at her friend. I did not understand that at all, and still don't.

Mom explained, "Honey, she's a whore, a prostitute, and that's how she makes her living. It wasn't personal."

Oh, Mama.

Number ten got to come back and live with Mom again, with a stipulation. He had to live in the garage. (He was a practicing alcoholic until the last few months of his life. He only quit drinking because he couldn't drink and receive chemotherapy.) He was a well-educated, retired Air Force Major, but he'd started drinking as a toddler, sipping what was left from his parents' party the night before. After retirement, he would drink until he passed out. He'd wake up, eat a bite, rinse, and repeat. He stumbled, fell, and crashed into things. Mom had an operative income tax business in her home, so she couldn't have him stumbling through.

Granted, it was a very wonky relationship. But it worked for them. By that point in their marriage, they didn't proclaim love; she'd take care of him, and his pension would take care of her after his death. If I typed dysfunction in all caps, would that add levels to the dysfunction or make it more obvious?

When my oldest daughter was nineteen, she lived with Mom and #10 for a while and told me Mom would walk by #10 and bash him in the head with a heavy crystal ashtray. Mom "911" paged my daughter several times, saying, "I think I might have killed #10. Get home now!"

More than once, this occurred when my daughter was on a date with a very sweet young man who lived a typical family life with zero real-life exposure to the unscripted crime/drama show life of our people. Do you understand why I don't watch those kinds of cop shows?

I don't know if I'll get into all that went on between them from that time until he died of cancer. For now, I'll tell you Mom cared for him at home and let his life end there. That wasn't without drama, either. It was two years after her mother died. She was drinking through the whole ordeal and called my brother and me more than once, thinking she'd accidentally overdosed #10 on morphine. "Honey, I think I might have killed #10."

That was said way too many times! It might seem odd to you, but we still laugh about it and shake our heads at the same time. Oh mama. Our precious mama.

For the record, Mom didn't kill #10 by accidental overdose. He had a peaceful, natural passing. Actually, it amazed me that she allowed him to die at home; she couldn't go to hospitals after my little brother's death. Regardless of all that had happened between them, Mom still had a heart for #10. He experienced a loveless, heartless, upbringing and had nowhere else to go. His alcoholism had alienated those closest to him, as it usually does. Mom was all he had. I'm grateful she was there for him.

Except for the bad grammar, one of Annie Oakley's quotes could easily have been said by Mom, "I ain't afraid to love a man. I ain't afraid to shoot him either."

Thankfully Mom wasn't a good shot like Annie!

Friend, I try to lighten my life up for you, so you get beyond the heaviness, and I get you to focus on the redemptive message. But sometimes. It's light, but there's the gnarly tulle fog. Work with me. Trust me. It's all good; it's all God.

Ed Mylett says we typically "catch" more from our parents than they actually teach us. I accept that as truth. Recently listening to the audio recordings I have of my mother, her sister, my grandmother, and her sister gave me considerable insight into my mother. I'd heard the stories before, but listening to one after the other for hours had a far greater impact on me than hearing the stories sporadically as I grew up.

I don't know if my grandmother ever told any of her children to shoot at their mate. She could have in a particular situation. Welp. Wait a minute, I better rethink that one. Maybe not her kids, but there were daughters-in-law . . .

One of her sons got mad at his wife because she didn't do as he demanded, so he was about to beat his wife in Gran's kitchen. Gran handed her daughter-in-law a nearby meat cleaver, grabbed a knife herself, and told her son he'd best leave his wife alone if he didn't want to get hurt.

Her son said, "You aren't really going to use that knife on me."

Gran replied, "Try me, and you'll see that I will. Don't you dare touch her!"

He lowered his fist and walked away.

A decade later, a different son had been regularly beating on his little wife for not doing what he wanted. For some reason, she was staying at Gran's when they saw her husband approaching the house late one night. It was obvious he was wasted, so who knew what would happen if he got to his wife.

Gran handed her daughter-in-law a .22 pistol and said, "Shoot him! Shoot him!" Her daughter-in-law took the gun and fired a few rounds at her husband.

My aunt told me she didn't really shoot at him with the intent to hit him. She just meant to scare him a bit. It worked; he was scrambling, falling, getting back up, trying to escape the gunshots!

When I was a teen, a bigger kid bullied a seven-year-old cousin. Gran said, "Here, Honey, take this. It's an equalizer. Put it in the basket of the bike I bought you. Walk up to that boy, don't say a word, and hit him the head with it as hard as you can. He'll know what it was for." His parents took that lead pipe from him before he could do any equalizing.

Fast forward a few years, and three teen cousins came home from the Salinas Rodeo complaining about some bigger kids picking on them. The next day Granny was at the front door as they left to go back; she handed each of them a lead pipe, explaining they were equalizers and that if anyone picked on them, they were to hit them in the head as hard as they could with the lead pipe.

My mother and her siblings witnessed the domestic violence between their parents; if they didn't see their mother shoot at their father or their father threaten to do the same, they would have heard the stories. They saw their daddy hit their Mama and saw their Mama throw things at their daddy. So, Mom "caught" that behavior.

I didn't. I broke that generational curse. I have never shot at a husband, which is good because I am a good shot. I've earned trophies and a trophy belt buckle for winning "The Whole Dang Shooting Match" a few years back. I've never stabbed or tried to stab either of my husbands; I never even considered it. It's evident from this book that I saw and/or heard an enormous amount of negative, violent behavior. I CHOSE not to be what I saw.

Crikey, I just realized I'm claiming a badge of honor for not shooting or stabbing either of my husbands! Let me add to that hardware (like on a Veteran's chest) that I was never in a bar fight, nor did I ever throw an ashtray at a husband. Yeowza! Such a life, friends. Just Yeowza. What else can I say? What can YOU say except Yeowza? Maybe Ay Caramba!

I remember being around eight years old, listening to my aunt and grandmother talk about some incident that just wasn't right. I commented to that effect, and my aunt responded, "Honey, that's just how things are.

Wait until you grow up; you'll see." I refused to accept that in the moment, and I refuse to accept it now. Things CAN be different; we are not captives of our past or our people's past.

We are free to be our best and live out the plan God has for our individual lives. Somewhat like the Israelites, I've wandered around in "the desert" for decades, playing small. No mas. There's more time behind me than in front of me, and my soul is hungering for its purpose to be fulfilled before my life ends.

CHAPTER 7

Uncle Stub

That's what some of my uncles called their mother's brother when they were feeling a little saucy. Most of the time he didn't care, but on occasion, he'd get riled when they kept at him, and he'd threaten to dot their eye with his "stub." (His left hand had been amputated, and his right only had a complete index finger and thumb, the other three fingers were amputated at the middle knuckle.) If they got him too riled, he'd threaten to strap on his hook and really give them a beating. Hold on now; they weren't being mean. He, nor them. They treated him like they did one another, sometimes taunting him to the point of a fight just for the fun of a fight. I don't remember which one it was that he did jab in the eye with his stub; they said it was like getting thumped with the end of a pool cue.

Uncle Stub told so many different versions of how he lost his hand that no one ever knew the actual truth. His oldest sister and her husband were eyewitnesses to the removal of the fingers on his right hand. They visited him when he was working as a logger; he wasn't paying full attention to the task and sawed his fingers off.

I don't believe any of us great nieces or nephews were ever cheeky enough to call him Uncle Stub to his face, especially as children. We were a little afraid and a whole lot impressed by him. We never felt sorry for him or considered him disabled. He might have to do things differently than we did, but we never once heard him say he couldn't do something. Our one-handed, two-fingered great uncle was a heavy equipment operator and was alleged to have served in the Merchant Marines. The man had some skills, including BS'ing.

His real name was Cleo Franklin Jones; he was two years younger than Gran and three years younger than Aunt Rita. Their daddy wasn't around when he was born because he'd left on one of his drinking and gambling runs during his mom's pregnancy with him. Such runs weren't all that uncommon; what made this one different was that he never returned.

Gran said Uncle Cleo was born with encephalitis (swelling of the brain). Medical knowledge and procedures were a lot different in 1914 than today. Back then, they treated his condition by placing steel bands around his head. As he grew up, his sisters always felt like they had to look after him. They did so until he passed at the age of seventy-three.

With no husband and three children to support, their mother sold her cattle and her farm and bought a restaurant. Gran and her sister helped wait and bus tables, wash dishes, and do whatever else they could. Cleo was of no help; frankly, he was coddled. I suppose it's not all that uncommon, then or now; having a child with health complications can cause you to hold on a little tighter and perhaps let them play on your already tender heartstrings a bit.

Gran and her sister said their brother was an instigator who couldn't back up the trouble he started, so they'd have to take care of his business. If that meant fighting some bullying boys, that's what they did. They never knew if he instigated things with other kids just to mess with them, but it didn't matter. He was their little brother, so that was that. They backed his play.

Gran was around twelve when their mother was diagnosed with tuberculosis. Her mom's condition weakened to the point where she was compelled to seek treatment in a sanitorium in Texas. Her children had no idea where she was going, nor did they ever know where she went. Gran's older sister, age fifteen, married before their mother was sent away. Their father was not to be found. Many years later, they learned he'd remarried and had another child by the time their mother became ill. (I'm not sure how far we'll venture down that rabbit hole.)

Gran and Uncle Cleo were sent to one of their mother's sister's homes. That auntie had a troublesome marriage with two sides of jealousy and lots of arguing and fighting. Never having lived with such strife, that lifestyle made Gran very uneasy. Auntie didn't tell her niece that she was planning to divorce her husband and wouldn't have a place for them. Instead, she put Gran and Uncle Cleo on a train bound for their mother's father. The same man who'd horsewhipped their mother and their uncle.

No one met them at the train station, so Gran asked a stranger where her grandfather lived; she was told he lived ten-plus miles away. Our weary travelers, aged thirteen and eleven, set foot toward their granddad's place. Somewhere along the dusty trail, they accepted a ride from a man in a wagon, who, after a time, started getting too handsy with Gran. Gran and Uncle jumped off the wagon and set out on foot again. They did not accept any more rides. Hot, hungry, and thirsty, they trekked on. I mean, what other choice did they have? They were effectively orphans. They didn't know if their mother was alive or dead, and ditto regarding their father. Auntie didn't want them, nor did she tell them she hadn't informed their grandfather they were on the way to him.

These two adolescents arrived at their grandfather's place exhausted, hungry, with blistered and bloodied feet and heart hurt. Instead of the hoped-for welcome like that of the Biblical prodigal son, they received a very cool reception. Their grandfather didn't even offer to make them a pallet on the floor. She was only thirteen years old; however, this proved too much to bear for my very sensitive and prideful grandmother.

Before we get too deep into our judgment of Great Grandpa (as I did all my life until this writing), let's recall that he was a harsh father. We know he buggy-whipped one of his sons and his daughters. We don't yet know HIS story or what caused him to believe that was acceptable behavior. So, let's leave great granddad right there and move on.

I don't recall how long they stayed, but I know it wasn't long. Thirteen-year-old Geneva Jones secured herself a job at a restaurant. Her pay was little more than room and board for herself and Cleo. But she made her own way, which she did all her days.

One day, my grandfather entered the restaurant and instantly fell in love with the tiny, black-haired, blue-eyed teen. It took some words and some wooing, but she eventually married him. She told him she didn't love him because she was far too young to know of such a thing. But he promised to care for her and Cleo, which sealed the deal. Cleo lived with them until adulthood. I don't recall at what age he left, nor do I remember how he made his way to California. He settled in San Francisco, where he lived until his final decade.

One of Mom's brothers told me he was eight or ten years old the first time he met Uncle Cleo. My uncle said he woke one morning to find an unknown man in his bed. (Don't go sideways here; back then, folks didn't have a lot of bedrooms, so family sharing a bed was normal. I remember four or five of the boys in my home had to share a bed.)

Anyway, my uncle meets his uncle and, of course, notices the missing body parts. My uncle asked what happened to his uncle's hand. Without a moment's hesitation, Uncle Cleo looked him right in the eyes, making sure he had his full attention. With the lad's rapt attention upon him, Uncle Cleo said, "I shoved my hand up a fat lady's ass, she farted, and it blew my hand off."

Holy moly. Mom's little brother was speechless. I was speechless when my uncle told me, admittedly a little horrified too. You probably are too. Uncle Stub would be pleased.

I'll tell you more Uncle Cleo stories further in; this is just his intro.

CHAPTER 8

Dead Brother Walking

Not too long before the end of WWII, my great-grandfather (who was living in Oklahoma) received a telegram from the Marines saying they regretted to inform him that his son, Major Cleo F. Jones, had been killed in action. Great grandpa was working away from home, so his wife sent the message to Gran's sister. Sister didn't know what to do, so she phoned Gran, who always knew what to do or figured it out if she didn't.

Uncle Cleo's body was to be shipped to Salinas, California, where his sisters lived. Of course, the sisters were distraught; they'd loved and coddled their little brother all his life. They hadn't seen him in years and had no knowledge of his military service. They were very sad but also very proud of their little trouble-making brother. A Major in the Marine Corps, what a great accomplishment! They were determined to give him a final send-off with all the honors befitting his military service, as well as a beautiful Christian burial. The church was ready for the service, and the Honor Guard from nearby Fort Ord Military Base was standing by.

On the scheduled day, the sisters took off work from the celery shed to meet the train carrying their brother's remains. Their Pastor, the Honor Guard, and Grandma's children joined them at the train depot in Salinas. The train came and went without delivering the remains of Major Cleo F. Jones, so they waited for the next train that day and then the next train after that. Still no Uncle Cleo. This scenario was repeated daily for a couple of weeks. Grandma dragged her kids along to meet every train; and let me tell you, those kids got sick of the trek.

The sisters were brokenhearted over their brother's death, and now the military had lost his body. It was torturous to their hearts and downright shameful on the military's part.

This was the mid-1940s, and communication wasn't swift, particularly with the military. There was a great deal of back and forth and "I don't know, Ma'am," but my Gran was tenacious and relentless in her hunt to find her brother's remains. As it turned out, there was no record of Cleo F. Jones having served in the Marines. Gran (whom my Aunt Pat referred to as Dick Tracy, a comic book detective) decided Cleo was the subject of foul play, and the telegram had been sent to throw them off the trail.

She was no *Ace Ventura: Pet Detective*; however, my super sleuth grandmother found Uncle Cleo's last known address, which happened to be in San Francisco. The sisters, particularly Gran, determined to find the truth of Cleo's whereabouts, be he alive or be he dead. At this point, Gran believed there was only one course of action: to load up the husbands and their children and make the hundred-plus-mile trek to San Francisco.

Aunt Rita said, "Now, sister, I know you don't want to hear this, but I have a feeling we're going to get up there and find our dead brother walking around."

Gran was insulted by her sister's callous remark and came close to poking her in the nose over it. Gran was very worried about their baby brother.

Sooo, they piled into their cars: Gran's sister, her husband, and their three kids in one, Grandma, Grandpa, and their five kids in the other. They headed to the hotel where Cleo was last known to live in San Francisco. It wasn't an easy drive; the adults were tired from working, the children were crammed in the back seat, and that was a long car trip. (Mom's sister recalled being scared on the drive home because they had to drive without headlights because of the war. Blackouts required businesses and residents to turn off all lights, which would enable enemy aircraft to identify population centers or specific targets by sight. There could be no lit streetlights, neon signs, flashlights, or car headlights.)

They didn't have much of a plan other than to ask the desk clerk if he knew Cleo and, if so, when was the last time they'd seen him. They decided, or most likely Detective Granny decided, the men would wait in the car with the children while the sisters interrogated the hotel clerk. After all, Cleo was their brother and had always been their responsibility.

Before they went inside the hotel, they decided Gran would do the talking because her sister stuttered when she got excited. This was not the time for stuttering; they needed facts, hard facts. They walked in and approached the clerk.

Gran asked, "Excuse me, sir, do you know a Cleo F. Jones?"

The clerk responded, "Yes, Ma'am, I do."

A look of triumph passed between the sisters.

"Uh huh, and when was the last time you saw this, Cleo F. Jones?"

"Oh, about forty-five minutes ago."

Detective Gran knew she was on to something, but she wasn't sure what. Was someone posing to be their brother for some nefarious reason? She continued her interrogation of the clerk,

"I see. When do you expect Mr. Jones to return?"

I don't know why the clerk was so free and forthcoming with information, maybe folks were more open in the 1940s, or perhaps he thought the two little women harmless.

The clerk answered, "He and his sister and his little nieces should be back pretty soon; they just went out to dinner."

That fired Gran up because she was one of his only two sisters. She started to say just that when her sister poked her in the side and shushed her. Big sister wanted to keep that cat in the bag for now, at least until they got a look at this man claiming to be Cleo F. Jones. As the day turned to dusk, their husbands and children waited in their cars. The sisters hid behind a wall in the hotel lobby for the return of this alleged Cleo and his so-called sister and nieces.

After about an hour of waiting, the door opened; in strutted their brother, alive as could be! Visualize a tall Humphrey Bogart (*Maltese Falcon*) looking quite dapper in his trendy black trench coat and fedora as he escorted a young woman and two little girls into the lobby. The sisters instantly popped to their feet, throwing him visual daggers and accusations without saying a word. The oldest sister felt somewhat validated as she had thought they'd find their dead brother walking, and there he was. On the other hand, Gran was a bit irate because she'd been duped and played a fool.

Cleo walked towards his sisters; as he drew close, Gran spoke, "Hello, brother, would you like to introduce us to this sister of yours?"

Uncle Cleo gave a quick "Ssshhh!" in response, which didn't sit well with Gran. She was not in the mood for being shushed, not one bit.

She fired back with, "All these years, I thought we were your only sisters."

He shushed her a little louder the second time as he guided the woman and children to the elevator and his room.

Once his "other sister" and her children were out of earshot, he explained he had to say she was his sister so she could stay with him. He went on to supply a tale of gallantry in helping the poor single mother in her time of need. The sisters never bought his tall tale; they knew he was shacking up with the gal and lying to the hotel to make it permissible. Respectable hotels didn't allow that shacking up business back then.

Gran fired off at him about the telegram, the fake military service, his pretend death, their meeting trains for weeks with Honor Guard and Preacher only to learn he'd never served. Gran was about a foot shorter than Uncle Cleo, but she whacked him down to her size with the verbal thrashing she provided. Uncle Cleo denied any knowledge or involvement in sending the telegram to their father.

They went around a few times, but it really made no difference. Their brother was alive and well; that was what truly mattered. It would be embarrassing in church, but they'd survive.

Speaking of church … Grandma and Grandpa had built a huge house on Sunrise Street which was often the gathering place for family and friends after Sunday services. Months after the infamous telegram incident, Uncle Cleo popped in to visit his sister one Sunday afternoon. As was typical, the place was packed with adults, children, and food. A grand time was being had by all until a shirttail relative started arguing with Cleo about him being dead and all. Cleo continued to deny any knowledge or involvement in the debacle and asserted his obvious aliveness. I don't remember who separated them before they went to duking it out. Cleo left quickly and didn't show his face in Salinas for a considerable time.

As you may recall, great granddad had left their mother when she was pregnant with Cleo. Great grandpa couldn't be found when their mother was sent to a sanitorium when Cleo was eleven. The sisters believed their brother sent the telegram because he wanted to see if his father cared about him. Uncle Cleo remained steadfast in denying the telegram to the day he died. By the way, he still had two hands that day in

San Francisco when they saw their dead brother walking.

Hopefully, you don't have the personal experience of knowing that children abandoned or neglected by their parents often search their entire lives for the love and acceptance they yearned for as children. If you do have that personal experience, please know that how your parents lived their lives had nothing to do with you. They were acting out their own dramas, lost in their own pain and longings. They didn't know how to give more, to give what you needed. In all probability, you will never know their truest story, their "why," partly because they don't know their own truth or they're incapable of sharing their own pain.

If, like me, you can relate to being abandoned or neglected, I have a tip for you. Have you ever seen a dog shake off excess water after a bath or a swim? (Internet search if needed.) Doggos shake their whole body, and when the water exits their body, it looks like one of those soaker hoses, water flies everywhere. Shake it off, friend, just like doggies. It's not your baggage. Don't carry it. Forgive them for your own well-being because they may never forgive themselves. You will be captive in your pain until you, and you alone, choose to be free.

CHAPTER 9

Holy Rollin'

My people were God-loving, church-going folk from their youngest days. Hmm, now that I think about it, I don't know if Grandpa and his people were faithful churchgoers. His daddy died when he was just five years old, and his mama couldn't control their seven children, so I don't know if she was able to wrangle them to church. She sent them to school every day, but they didn't go; hence my grandpa only had a fourth-grade education.

Grandma and her siblings were raised in the church; both sisters raised their children in the church. I don't recall hearing what brand of church they attended as girls. As adults, they attended a Pentecostal church. Typical for my people, they didn't just attend, sing a few hymns, drop money on the collection plate, and leave. Nah, they were all in, and so were their children.

Grandpa played piano, mandolin, harmonica, and guitar. The guitar was his favorite, so he gifted his guitar playing to church services. Their children sang in the choir, and one of Grandpa's brothers was a deacon for a time.

In case you didn't know, Pentecostal folk are also called "Holy Rollers" because they literally writhe and roll in the church aisles when the Holy Spirit of God comes upon them. They dance, shake, "speak in tongues," and get fueled up by an equally wild and emotional music. (Those are descriptions provided by Google.) Although I've never writhed, rolled, or spoken in tongues, I must confess I love powerful, emotional church music. I can feel God in that "wild and emotional" music; the early church must be where that seed was planted within me, and why I love the Spirit-filled Black church and I love to dance.

Aunt C, Sister J, and Sister A would faithfully get the Spirit of the Lord upon them and be rolling and twisting on the floor, sometimes for an hour. Occasionally Gran and her sis would too. Once the rollin' started, Brother and Sister W would lead the church in singing again. Church wasn't over until God left the building, which meant as long as those sisters were holy rollin' everybody stayed. Sunday church could last three to four hours which was hard on the youngsters.

As is typical for large families, the older siblings took care of the younger while the parents worked. When Mom's oldest sister was a young teen, she was often responsible for watching her little brothers. If you've ever watched a younger sibling or been watched by an older sibling, you know how challenging that can be. "You're not the boss of me!" "Oh yes, I am! Mama said!" The older sibling often thinks of unconventional ways to best manage the siblings and the situation. Aunt Sue was no different.

When putting the little boys (three and four years old) down for a nap, she told them to rest so they'd be good. She said if they were bad, the devil would come and stick a pitchfork in their butt, take them to Hell, and toss them into the lake of fire! She even showed them a picture of the devil with a pitchfork. Unconventional, but it worked. Big sister felt like she scored a win.

The following Sunday, the Power of God was coming on their Preacher. The more Spirit he felt, the louder his voice and gestures. Before anyone could move, the four-year-old brother was at the pulpit yanking on the Pastor's sleeve.

"Ssshhh, Brother H, be quiet. You're talking too loud in church, and that's not nice. The devil's going to come and stick that pitchfork in your butt, throw you over his shoulder, take you to Hell, and toss you in the lake of fire!"

Yeowza! That was a mic-drop moment before it was ever invented!

The church was shocked into silence. Pastor's face turned red as a beet; then he asked where the lad had heard such a thing; the little one said it was his big sister who'd told him ... you know there was trouble when they got big sister home. It was laughed about for decades.

During the time Gran and fam were meeting the trains to receive her brother's remains, (years after the above), Mom's oldest sister was pregnant with her first child. Auntie's husband was away, so she was staying with her folks, and therefore bound to go along with the family. One Sunday, the thought of sitting in church an extra hour and then going to meet another train proved too much for her. She decided she would slip out the back door and go home. Sister J had finished at the piano and was headed to her seat; everyone knew the holy rollin' would be happening shortly. Susie knew she had to make her move now or be stuck for at least two more hours with the holy rollin' and the trip to the train depot. She quickly and quietly opened the back door and stepped out into the darkness. She was so intent on escaping that she'd forgotten about the construction project underway and fell into a huge hole, broke her leg, and couldn't get out of the hole. She was successful in missing the holy rollers but still had to wait for church to end because her cries for help couldn't be heard inside due to those big ole church sisters being slain by the Spirit of the Lord, their holy rollin', and the church singing their praises unto the Lord.

That church house often rocked with the Power of the Lord. And, of course, on any given Sunday, some felt it more than others. One particular day the Power of the Lord came upon the Preacher, Brother H. He was shouting and moving about something fierce, which caused the Spirit of the Lord to come upon the holy rollin' sisters, and they commenced to writhing, twisting, and rolling in the aisles. The walls were rocking with the shouting and singing praises unto God. It was obvious this would be a very, very long church service.

Grandpa's brother was a church deacon then and was preparing the Lord's wine for communion. They'd all been holy rollin' around for a long time, and he decided enough was enough. The fact was, deacon or not, my great uncle was churched out. I imagine everyone who's ever been to church has had a day like that. He was churched out, and it was going to be a minimum of another hour of service.

Welp, the deacon sighed, shrugged his shoulders, and decided to sample just a little of the Lord's wine to take the edge off. The church sisters kept holy rollin', and Uncle kept a sampling the Lord's wine. Finally, the deacon of the church got so pie-eyed (drunk) he passed out and pooped his pants!

As you might imagine, that didn't go over well at all. Brother W told him he didn't get to be deacon anymore. Uncle's wife told him what an ass he'd made of himself, IN CHURCH, and never let him live it down. Uncle's "undeaconing" also caused a church split. They started a new church at Brother H's house, which grew into the solid church I attended as a child.

CHAPTER 10

A Night School Lesson

Toward the end of the 1940s, Gran enrolled in night school (aka adult school) to advance her education because she left school in Oklahoma at a young age to support her younger brother. Gran was wise enough to know there is always more to learn, so she was a lifetime learner. When she later became an income tax practitioner, there initially wasn't a legal requirement for continuing education; nevertheless, she studied the new laws yearly to best serve her clients. She instructed each of us to do the same.

Throughout her business career, she bought the latest models of typewriters, calculators, and copy machines and taught herself to use them. Truthfully, she taught the rest of her employees and us to use them. Gran learned to use a computer when she was eighty because they offered tax programs for practitioners. Granted, she had to mark the keys with Wite-out and fingernail polish to remember a few things; however, I was forty-two years younger and was computer illiterate. I wasn't a fan of the computer concept; I thought they'd weaken our minds, so I abstained from learning. Ah, but I was mortified to learn that my eighty-year-old grandmother knew how to use a computer, while I feared them.

Not knowing how to do something was never an excuse for not doing whatever it was; Gran would toss her, "Well, you'll never learn any younger" at you, which cut you down and built you up at the same time. There is no arguing that statement . . . so I quickly taught myself computer basics and the tax program. I started helping Gran prepare taxes and did so for the last few years she prepared them.

I hope you realize all these little back or side stories aren't because my mind wanders. I want you to understand my people as best you can, so I provide examples and insight into their character.

Okay, back to night school. Gran tended to her children before work, worked in the packing shed during the day, tended to children after work, and then went on to night school. Gramps stayed home with their children while she was in school.

According to my mother, her father was a chippy chaser (aka cheater) up until his death at fifty-eight. When Mom caught him amidst some inappropriate action, he'd tell her, "Now don't you tell your mammy."

Mom would reply, "Tell her what, Dad? I didn't see anything."

Oh, but she did see things, and while she had a deep love and fierce loyalty to her daddy and didn't snitch on him, his chippy chasing affected her all her days.

She was somewhat complicit in his extramarital carrying on by not telling her mother. I won't judge Mom for keeping the secrets her daddy instructed her to hold, but I will say it wasn't right of Grandpa to ask that of her. That's too heavy for a child to carry, for a child to know. No parent should put a child in that position. We never discussed it; however, it makes sense that Mom's distrust of men began with the first man she loved.

Her father's chippy chasing was probably why she had a zero-tolerance policy with her men. I don't mean to say one shouldn't have a zero-tolerance policy for unfaithfulness; just saying Mom was a bit extreme with her actions upon discovering such facts about her man.

But this chapter isn't about Mom, so let's circle back to Gran and her night school lesson. The story I was told didn't include recent details as to why Grandpa's chippy chasing was on Grandma's mind when she should have been thinking about schoolwork.

Nevertheless, she decided to teach her husband a lesson one evening after class. This was not a classroom assignment but an "I'm tired of being done wrong, so you can have a little taste of what you've been doing to me, and we'll see how you like it" lesson. Night school ended at 10 pm; instead of going directly home as she'd always done, Gran rode the city bus to "Harold's Club," the one cowboy bar on Market Street in

Salinas.

She stepped off the bus, took a deep breath, pulled her 4'10" self up to full height, and walked into the bar alone. That was a first for her; she was a nondrinker and didn't go to bars. Her next first was to order her nondrinking self a beer. She couldn't stand the smell of it, and it was far too disgusting for her to drink, so she poured it on her clothes. Her goal was to stink of beer and barroom. If you're old enough, you may recall the stench of a cigarette smoke-filled room. You don't have to smoke to smell like cigarette smoke; that stuff permeates the air and everything in the room very quickly. Just thinking about it grosses me out today!

Gran was sitting alone, lost in thought about how well her lesson would be received when a man approached her. Nice enough looking fellow, however, he startled her, and she was already uncomfortable being in the bar. Gran was no chippy chaser and had no intent to become one; she was just going to give her man a dose of what was ailing her. She didn't want to be annoyed by strange bar men. The man said he'd like to dedicate a song to Gran and asked what she liked. Oh my, she hadn't planned on talking to any men! She hadn't planned on talking with anyone; she just wanted to get stinky, kill some time, and go home to shock her husband.

Gran did love music, and she liked to dance, but that was not going to happen with this stranger.

So, she lied to him, "I don't like music. I hate music!!"

She said this emphatically as the jukebox played a favorite country song. The man was not to be deterred by this dainty black-haired, blue-eyed stranger that he wanted to get to know, or best scenario yet, have some sexy time with.

"Well, I AM going to dedicate a song for you anyway. What do you like?"

"I don't like anything!"

"Well, I guess I'll play anything for you."

It turns out there was a song named "Anything" because that cowboy played it for her. And that was when she decided she was stinky enough to leave. She told me that she smelled like a sot, a drunkard. She said she didn't guess the sots poured that old beer or whiskey on themselves, but that was the only way she could be sure her husband would smell it on her.

Safe from her want to be suitor, Gran caught the bus again. She didn't think she'd been gone long enough for the full effect of her lesson, so she rode the city bus all over Salinas to kill time.

When she finally arrived home, she found her husband wide awake and anxious. Mom said Grandpa was insanely jealous of his baby doll bride, and she came rolling in smelling like she'd been partying it up. Grandpa did not think what was good for the goose was good for the gander.

Anyway, he demanded to know where she'd been. Always quick of wit, she coyly replied, "I guess I've been where you've been going all this time."

Grandpa came back at her with, "Where is it? Where have you been?"

You know the old boy had to be beside himself. She was out late, smelled like a barroom, and carousing; you know, the things he often did. But this was the other side of that coin, and he did not like it one bit!

He was about a foot taller than her, but she looked him square in his eye, shrugged her shoulders, smiled, and said, "I guess you better figure out where you've been."

Ay caramba! He was not a happy man! His little woman was turning his world upside down. He was quite irate and had much to say, which didn't do him any good. Although he quit going to school after the fourth grade, it turns out he was an excellent student after all!

I asked Gran if he'd forbidden her from going out like that again. Her sparkly blue eyes turned a bit steely as she looked me dead in the eye and replied, "He knew better than to tell me what I was and wasn't going to do ever again."

Gran said he got the lesson and behaved well for a long time.

Not long after, he'd decided to be the perfect husband. He greeted her as she came home from the packing shed one day, saying, "Look Dutch, don't it look beautiful?" as he waved his hand to show her the intense yard work he'd done that day. He'd cleared the yard of every bush and every shrub, including her cherished rose bushes. He'd raked the clippings into a pile and burned them.

I asked if she'd thanked him for his efforts. She gave me the stink eye and said, "You talk like someone who fell out of a well!"

Friend don't be telling your child to keep secrets from the other parent/guardian unless it's for a delightful surprise. How can a child learn to trust, or be trustworthy, if the parent teaches them to be deceitful to cover their own actions or inactions? While you may be intent on saving your own hide from discovery, you're hurting future generations. Your future generations. It'll break your heart when you watch your child's relationship dissolve and the subsequent lifetime damage that does to their child(ren) and your grandchildren. You'll be cursing yourself.

Most people grow up to behave somewhat like their parent/guardian because that was the modeled behavior during their most formative yes. If you're going to behave badly, don't wrap your kids up in it. Be willing to suffer the consequences of your actions, don't put it off on an innocent child. Even if it was done to you. You remember the pain you felt. You truly know better. Your soul knows it's not right.

Someone must break the generational curse. Why not you? You're truly capable; it just takes determination. It took persistence and determination for you to learn to walk, talk, feed, and toilet yourself. You failed countless times at each of those tasks and look at you today! You do all those things without even thinking!

It might sound ridiculous; however, we can truly change the world, creating peace among us if we refuse the negative lessons unintentionally taught in our homes. Home is where children first learn their worth, where they learn to judge others based on external criteria, and where they learn how to treat others. Just because your people spoke rudely or harshly of others who looked or sounded differently doesn't mean you should. Please make your decisions about others based on their character and your experience with them, not their family or those who look like them. You want to be judged on your own merit, so serve that dish to others.

Chapter 11

17 Mile Drive Is the Place You Ought to Be . . .

Like the Joads in *The Grapes of Wrath*, Mom and family packed everything they had room for and headed west to the Golden State in 1941. Grandma's sister and her husband had moved to California a year or so before and urged them to come west. Gran's sister and family were living in Contra Costa County. For my industrious grandmother, the opportunities California offered were too great to resist.

Mom's parents didn't have savings, so they followed the Dust Bowl migrant's path, which had them working produce and orchards along the way. They even lived in a government tent camp for a year. Every time I think of that, I flash to *The Grapes of Wrath* and shudder, considering what it must have been like for them to live in such conditions. My people living in such poverty and squalor and then treated poorly because they wanted a better life. It hurts my heart for them and all those still experiencing such hardship and cruelty to this very day.

My people accepted that hard life without complaint because they were proud people. Besides, there's just no value in complaining. Life in Oklahoma had gotten even harder before they left. Gran told me they lived in a three-walled potato shed with snow blowing in under the tarp (the fourth wall) when the youngest daughter was born in the fall of 1940. Gran said they found the tarp on the side of the road; it had holes so big she could fit her face through them. That's some grit. Two adults and four children aged three to eleven lived in a potato shed as baby five entered the world. They lived like that because their home had burned, and

Grandma was too proud to accept help.

They'd talked about going west for a while; it was the hydrophobic dogs that caused them to pack up and go when they did. Grandpa always had a pack of hounds for coon hunting, often eight to ten of them. They'd heard stories of hydrophobic dogs (dogs with rabies) foaming at the mouth, acting crazy there in the community. It spread from dog to dog; as the disease progressed and ultimately overtook them, the dogs would search for something like a cave or a den. A dark safe place where they'd eventually die. So, when one of Grandpa's hounds got it, Gran got worried and didn't want them digging under the shed or coming through the holes in the tarp; they packed up and headed west.

Although Grandma and her sister were joyful to be reunited, their move to Concord and Grandpa's work in the Oakland shipyards wasn't satisfactory. On his first day at work, someone asked Grandpa if he could weld. He said he'd never done it but knew he could learn. The men didn't give him welding goggles, which nearly blinded him. Those men then laughed at the stupid Okie for not wearing goggles. That hurts my heart and infuriates me at the same time, especially since humans are still doing that to other humans to this very day. I don't understand mean. I never will. There is no excuse for mean. As a matter of fact, it's downright shameful behavior. Don't be mean. To anyone! Ever!

Mary Ruth, their sixth child, was born there in Concord but died two days after birth. I don't know how long after that they moved south to Salinas, where Gran found the temperate climate perfect and the work environment less hostile. She took a job in the packing house and grandpa in the field. Neither of them minded the hard work; they enjoyed working alongside folks like themselves. They became "produce tramps" for a season or two, following the harvest up and down the Valley and on into Arizona. Their third son was born in Salinas, and their last child was born fourteen months later in Holtville. Gran couldn't take the heat, so they determined they'd make Salinas their yearlong home, whatever it took to do so.

With a fourth-grade education, Grandpa couldn't really read or write, but Grandma could. And Grandma had an insatiable mind for learning and growing. Her mother had been a single parent and business owner in the 1920s; therefore, Gran was not content to go to work and then come home and just live. She wanted and needed more for her family and was determined to have it. One of her "Grannyisms" was, "Where there's a will, there's a way", which was often paired with, "You'll never learn any younger."

Soon as they could, they bought a little shack on the east side of Salinas (Alisal) where most Okies lived. It was single wall construction with gaps between the boards and had fruit crates for cabinets. Grandma and Grandpa learned how to fix up houses quickly. They'd had some experience in Oklahoma, but this was different.

As soon as they saved enough, they bought a second shack, fixed it up, and sold it. It was obvious that flipping houses made more money, much faster, than working produce. Grandpa switched to construction work to enhance his skill set.

Flipping one house at a time improved their quality of life, and they wanted more, better, for their family. As we know, it takes money to make money. Money wasn't coming in fast enough for Gran's entrepreneurial mindset.

Grandma decided to apply for a loan to buy and flip four homes. Another of her "Grannyisms" was, "Nothing beats a trial but a failure." So off to the bank she went. The young male loan officer asked if she had assets. She didn't know what an asset was, so she quipped, "No, but I do have seven offsets." He asked about her "offsets"; she smiled and told him of her children. He asked when she could repay the loan, and she replied, "I don't know for sure, but I'll definitely pay it back when we sell the homes."

The loan officer said, "So, let me be sure I understand you. You want to borrow money, you have no collateral, no assets, and you don't know when you'll pay it back."

"That's right. I'm not going to commit to a promise of repaying you on a specific date when I don't know that I can keep that promise. I'll pay it back as soon as we sell the houses. We'll sell the houses as soon as we get them fixed up. I'd never cheat you out of your money, and I'm not going to lie to you."

He shook his head and said he was sorry, but he could not lend under such circumstances.

Unbeknownst to Gran, the bank president had overheard the entire exchange.

As she turned to leave, the bank president spoke to the loan officer, "Give the girl a loan; I know an honest face when I see one."

That began a lifelong business relationship with Gran and the president of her local Bank of America. She obtained "signature loans" from that bank president whenever needed for the rest of his banking career.

After a couple rounds of four-at-a-time flips, she and Grandpa decided to build some new homes, in fact, a subdivision there in Alisal, and so they did. They also bought old barracks from Fort Ord. They converted them into houses, as well as bought Quonset huts and converted those into commercial buildings. It didn't take them long to be able to carry the note, aka self-finance their sales.

In addition, they built themselves a lovely home, owned new vehicles, bought their driving-age children new vehicles, bought quality furniture, and arranged for charge accounts at clothing stores for their older children. They kept reinvesting but also enjoyed the fruits of their labor after many years of hardship and deprivation. (I still recall playing dress up with Grandma's mink coats when I was a little girl.)

As happens with many, so it went with them; the desire to "move on up" came along with their financial success. They heard 17 Mile Drive was THE place to live. Gran thought the climate in Salinas was near perfect. Yet the allure of Pebble Beach, its weather, and affluent living convinced my grandparents to move on up.

17 Mile Drive is the place you ought to be . . . so they loaded up the truck, their five kids still at home, their horses, moved to Pebble Beach, and joined the Monterey Peninsula Country Club. It was magnificent country, positively breathtaking. My industrious grandparents, who had struggled, done without, picked produce under the blazing Arizona and Central Valley sun, slept on roadsides, lived in a shack, lived in a migrant tent camp, now owned a home on property that was fast becoming the most desired location in the world for the rich and famous!

They hadn't lived there long when their teenage son got in trouble for chasing a deer (while riding his horse Apache) across the fairway. My family hunted deer for food, and the Del Monte Forest, filled with an abundance of wildlife, was pretty much the backyard of their home. Rather than chastise the teen, they should have been grateful he wasn't carrying a rifle and was just chasing the deer for sport! Uncle was an avid and prolific hunter all his life! Imagine being a golfer; you're on the world-renowned

Pebble Beach golf course, ready to swing, when a teenager races by on a horse while chasing a deer! Ay Caramba!

As I said, they were lucky he was chasing and not hunting. In all fairness, my grandparents should have been informed about the no horseback riding rules on the golf course. How were they supposed to know? On the other hand, whoever sold them the property surely didn't think they'd need to tell a buyer that horseback riding wasn't allowed on the golf course; that was common knowledge. But you don't know what you don't know. (One of Uncle's junior high school friends said he was the only person to ever ride a horse to school. What can you say? He loved horses!)

Then there was the issue of the two little brothers sneaking into the pool and tormenting the groundskeeper while he had sexy time in a tool shed with a woman who also worked on the grounds. The youngest still laughs about repeatedly spying on that guy and his gal while they were doing the deed and how it infuriated the man.

Oh, how I loved to get Mom's youngest sister telling the story of her learning to drive; she'd get tickled and laugh so hard you'd start laughing with her without even knowing the story! My telling is just my memory of her memory, so don't be disappointed if you don't laugh out loud.

One day, as Grandpa and his friend drove off in Grandpa's truck to go hunting, Auntie told her daddy she wanted to drive. Her daddy's friend said she could drive his truck; the keys were in the ignition. Mind you, she was ten years old, which some folks might consider too young to be driving. While in my family, ten years old is on the older side of learning. Most of us had some driving experience when we were eight or nine, and were mostly self-taught!

In the early 1900s, the LA Times referred to 17 Mile Drive as the "eighth wonder of the world." With its pristine golf course, Pebble Beach was a tourist destination for the wealthy and elite. Have you seen photos or experienced it yourself? All that said to open your mind's eye and help you visualize Auntie learning to drive.

She's ripe and rearing to go, and her ten-year-old bestie is just as excited. The momentary downside to this great adventure is that Auntie was stuck watching her five-and six-year-old brothers that day. No problem: put them in the truck with her and bestie, problem solved! They all hopped in the truck, Auntie behind the wheel, bestie riding shotgun. Little brothers between them on the seat. Auntie surveys the dashboard, steering wheel, steering column and sees it's a "three on the tree." It didn't matter that she didn't know the gears; she'd watched her daddy shift, so she knew she could figure it out. Figuring things out was ingrained in all of us at a very young age. She was set now, hands on the wheel, and she knew where everything was. She moved to the edge of the seat to reach the pedals. Only she couldn't reach the pedals. Her ten-year-old legs were far too short, but she was not about to let that stop this grand adventure. Bestie said it had been fun while it lasted and was about to get out of the truck when Auntie shouted, "I've got it!"

Bestie said, "Got what, friend?"

Auntie replied, "Boys, you get on the floor and push the gas and the clutch pedals when I tell you to. I'll steer. Friend, you sit next to me and help with the shifter if I need it."

Without a moment's hesitation, they all agreed it was brilliant. Best plan ever. There was driving to be done. Driving without adults. And now, they ALL got to be an active part of the experience. This was going to be an epic adventure!

The five-year-old brother was assigned to the clutch and the six-year-old to the gas. Bestie slid over beside her. Everyone was in position and ready to roll. Totally in charge, Auntie commenced with their launch sequence, "Danny, push the clutch in. When I say go, let it out. Tommy, when I say go, you push the gas pedal. Ready, set, GO!", which was followed by several false starts, the truck sputtering and lurching, the engine revving and lots of shouting by Aunt Pat.

"Danny, let the clutch out slower, Tommy, not so much gas. Friend, try another gear; that one's not working. Tommy, more gas! Danny, let it out."

It was cacophony in that cab, gears grinding, engine revving, all four of them shouting. "Stop yelling at me!" "Do your job!" "Faster!" "Slower!" That went on for several minutes until they were all spent.

All that energy raised the temperature in the cab; they were sweating with excitement and frustration. They took a breather for a few minutes and relaxed. Failure was not an option. Auntie was going to drive that truck today, and her crew was going to help. They decided to switch the brothers' positions. Danny was the youngest; he might do better on the gas pedal.

Everyone calmed down, and they went at it again. About the third or fourth try, the truck lurched twenty feet or so. Fueled by this success, they recommitted and doubled down on their efforts. Remember now, a six-year-old is working the clutch, a five-year-old at the gas pedal, a ten-year-old at the wheel, with her ten-year-old best friend on the gear shifter. They're all clueless about which gear they should be in, but you only have to hit reverse twice to learn that's to be avoided. They've got this. My people are not quitters.

At this point, their fearless energy is worked up to a near frenzy, and their little voices are squealing with anticipation and the conquering of this grand quest that's about to happen. All that was palpable in that cab! My goodness, I can hear and feel it from eighty-five miles away and seventy-two years later!!!

Auntie rallies her crew, "We were close; we're going to do it this time. Everybody ready? Tommy, push the clutch in. When I say go, let it out. Danny, when I say go, press the gas pedal. Be smooth. Friend, you know what to do. Everybody ready? GO!" The heavens didn't open, but those four kids somehow harmonized their efforts and got that truck moving! They all squealed and shouted as it drove forward. Auntie realized she was still sitting on her bottom and couldn't see over the dash. In one hop she was on her knees, able to somewhat see through the windshield.

A super thrilling moment for all! The boys jumped up on the seat to see; the truck started slowing and mini lurching because Dan was now on the seat instead of the gas pedal. Aunt Pat shouted, "Danny, get back on the floor and push the gas pedal." He quickly obeyed, and the truck continued along. The shouts and squeals of excitement continued; this unlikely crew actually got that pickup truck in motion!

Remember, this happened in 1950ish. Vehicles didn't have power steering, and pickup trucks drove like trucks. It took strength to actually control a truck. Ten-year-old Patsy was working that wheel like a two-year-old on the car ride at Disneyland, turning the steering wheel with ninety-degree motions. It was about that time she realized they were now going downhill and picking up a bit of speed. Did you notice that no one had been assigned to the brake pedal? She noticed it about then too. Remember when I asked if you'd experienced 17 Mile Drive? It's curvy and slopy. Dun dun dun.

So, ten-year-old Aunt Pat at the wheel, on her knees . . . still barely able to see over the dash and losing a bit of control as their speed increases. Truck full of squealing little kids being tossed about the cab as she steered to the left, then to the right, driving all over one of the most famous and exclusive golf courses in this world in an old pickup truck. Their "drunk monkey" driving adventure came to a halt when the truck stalled in "some sand." They tried to get it out of the sand several times but couldn't. They left the truck in the sand trap on that world-famous golf course and walked back home, reliving the epic adventure each from their own perspective. It was a fabulous day!

As you might guess that grand adventure caused more problems for her parents. Little kids driving on the golf course, and parking in a sand trap, was akin to chasing deer while horseback riding on the course! It was a BIG no-no!

As I mentioned, Pebble Beach is adjacent to the Del Monte Forest; to this day the wildlife is abundant and not fearful of humans. The whole family enjoyed watching all that wildlife come up around their home. The raccoons were the cutest. My people would put treats out on the patio for them so they could watch them. Grandpa talked about catching a baby coon and raising it as a pet.

Remember, my family hunted for food. It was necessary for survival in Oklahoma. Eating "game" is an acquired taste; it has a much stronger flavor than domestic animals. I suppose that's no different than eating ethnic food; your norm is your norm, and you hunger for those "home" tastes. I've heard that raccoon tastes like dark-meat chicken or turkey, though it's said to be greasier and more tender than either.

Grandpa hadn't gotten around to catching a coon for a pet but decided to trap one for dinner. He was successful in the trapping but nearly lost a finger in the process. Those cute little creatures are vicious and mean when captured. If you think about it, their face does look like a bandit's mask, so behaving ornery upon capture makes perfect sense. That adorable little trapped creature got Banty rooster mad and chomped down on Grandpa's finger, right down to the bone, as he removed it from the trap. Grandpa started rethinking ever keeping one for a pet and decided raccoon for dinner was a much better idea. He cleaned and cooked it right there on their patio on 17 Mile Drive for all the world to see. Somehow that became the deciding factor that they just didn't belong in Pebble Beach and the Monterey Peninsula Country Club. They lived there one summer before moving back to the unincorporated area of East Salinas, also known as Alisal and Little Oklahoma.

My grandparents gave my mom and her first husband two lots on 17 Mile Drive as a wedding gift in 1951. That marriage didn't last, and the lots were sold. But these grand stories keep on living!

My Gran loved watching The Dukes of Hazzard; she once knew a sheriff like Boss Hogg back in Oklahoma. She enjoyed The Beverly Hillbillies for the same reason; she saw herself and her family. Uncle Jed and family (The Beverly Hillbillies) had no idea they didn't fit in with their neighbors; they just lived as they'd always done. I guess my people did the same thing, except my grandmother carried a feeling of being unwanted and unwelcome since her earliest days. She didn't like to be around strangers; she liked to be in her own environment where the people she interacted with accepted her for exactly who she was. That's probably why they moved back to Alisal.

What about you? Are you concerned about what other people think about you? Do you feel the need to fit in yet ultimately feel like an outsider? Just remember you are as unique as your fingerprint, and you bring something unique to the world.

You weren't made to fit in; you were made to stand out. If Noah had fit in, he'd have died in the flood with the rest of humanity, and we wouldn't meet here on these pages! Jesus didn't fit in; he chartered his own path.

We were created in God's image, not in the image of man. It's God we should seek to be like, not everyone else. Fitting in means compromising, giving up parts of yourself, and not being your authentic self. Fooey on that!

You don't need to fit in! No one can be you but you! Do it well, my friend. Be your best self, it'll set you free, and you will soar!

GENEVA MARIE BRETT

Chapter 12

Do You Think It Would Be Rude of Me to Sing a Song?

On August 29, 1955, not quite a month before my first birthday, my mother's older sister made me a yellow dress with white ruffles. She then enjoyed an impromptu evening at home with her parents, siblings, and two of her three sons. They laughed and reminisced about all that had gone on in their lives. It was a delightful evening, one of those pure and simple times that stay with you for the rest of your days.

The following evening Aunt Sue went to a "meet and greet" with a friend. Her friend had too much to drink, so she drove him home in his car. She headed south on East Market Street and turned left onto Monterey Street, there by the train underpass. The light turned yellow as Aunt Sue completed the turn; simultaneously, a big heavy truck (that tows freight trailers) came through the intersection and hit her. The impact caused her door to open and flung her outside onto the ground (no seatbelts back then). The truck's wheel rolled up on her body and smashed her insides. The driver jumped out to check the damage; Auntie was alert and pleaded with him to get the truck off her; she said, "Please get this thing off me; it's crushing me to death!"

As you can imagine, the driver was beside himself and ran back to his truck. He put it in gear . . . Unfortunately, due to his nervousness, he went forward instead of backward and crushed her even more. He later said he'd never forget the look in that little girl's eyes.

Having heard this story many times in my youth, I had a somewhat irrational fear of heavy trucks by the time I was driving. (Maybe it wasn't irrational after all, perhaps it was a healthy respect.) Many, many times, I sat at that same intersection, waiting for the light to change, visualizing the scene I've just shared and thinking of how it'd permanently wounded my family. Decades later, when I'd traverse Pacheco Pass and have to pass a heavy truck, cement guard on my left, heavy truck on my right, I'd think of Auntie's accident and get nervous until I'd cleared the heavy. Fascinating how impactful family history can be.

Well, back to Auntie's accident. Gran said it took law enforcement hours to find out who my aunt was and then find and inform her family. Auntie's youngest sister had dozed off and awakened in the wee hours of the morning.

She woke her daddy and said, "Daddy, something's happened to Susie. She asked me to wait up for her, and she's not home. Something's wrong. I just know it."

Grandpa told his baby girl he was sure her sister was fine, he wanted her to go back to sleep, and he was sure sister would be there when she awoke. Baby sister wouldn't go back to sleep; she continued to wait for her big sissy. Instead of sister coming home, there was a knock on the door around 5 am. They were informed Susie had been in an accident. Gran told them she'd get to the hospital soon; they said now, so she didn't even take the time to get dressed.

Gran and her youngest daughter went to the hospital while Grandpa stayed home with us kids. When they got to the emergency room, they heard her before they saw her. Aunt Sue was asking for her mother. The staff assured her that her mother was on the way and that she'd be fine; she wasn't to worry.

Gran and baby sister heard her response, "No, I know I'm going to die, and I want to talk to my mom."

Auntie lived for nine days, with her abdominal cavity basically an open hole. Her organs were mush. They pumped blood into her continuously; however, it was flowing out nearly as fast as it went in. They packed her abdomen with gauze to soak the blood, but it did little to slow the flow.

She remained conscious and alert from the time of her accident until her last breath. She spoke of her childhood experiences, friends, her beloved sons and told her mother how much she appreciated her and all she'd done for her. Due to their ages and her condition, her boys weren't allowed to see her, but family came in and out, as did her church family. Day after day, they visited. Although they knew she couldn't live without her intestines, they prayed for a miracle. Remember, it was 1955, and there weren't a lot of options for someone in her condition.

During those nine days, baby sister mostly stayed home and cared for her two younger siblings and three nephews. They fetched my mother from her apartment across town to care for my brother and me because her baby sister was overwhelmed. Baby sister was only fifteen years old, which was a lot on her plate and, more importantly, on her young heart. Auntie did get to go back and visit her sister a few times when her daddy stayed home with the younger kids.

Auntie told me there seemed to be a mist about her oldest sister's face and that her face actually glowed. It was evident she was completely at peace, which was somewhat confusing because it was obvious to everyone that she was going to die, soon.

On the ninth day, Aunt Susie's last day of life, her mother, oldest sister-in-law, her youngest sister, their Pastor, and his wife were with her. Gran told her she'd bought her a beautiful new nightgown and she'd be going home soon.

Auntie said, "I'm going home shortly, but not to our house on Garner Street. I'm going home to the Lord."

She began praying, and the Holy Spirit got a hold of her; she began shaking, and then the whole bed shook as well.

When she finished praying, she said, "Mama, I know I've got so much to be proud of. I love you so much; you've been such a good mother. My friends (whom she named) didn't have the chance Louise and I did. I can always look back and say we had a good life and a good mother. My friends didn't have that, and I thank God for you. You were always there when we needed you. I have to leave, but I know you'll take care of my boys and yourself."

She made her baby sister promise to look after her boys, no matter what, and to remember their secret. (Her secret was that she had been gifted a treasured watch by someone she deeply loved. She'd fallen on hard times and had pawned it. No one knew this but the two of them. Baby sister used her babysitting money to buy back the watch, which she wore for many, many years.)

Auntie then turned to look at her Pastor and asked, "Do you think it would be rude of me to sing a song? I just want to sing because I'm so happy."

Pastor and his wife both said, "No, you have a beautiful voice. We love to hear you sing."

Then my twenty-three-year-old aunt began to sing a beautiful gospel song. She took her final breath seconds after she finished her song of love to God.

Grandma took Susie's sons to visit her at the funeral chapel and then to her open-casket funeral. They were five, seven, and eight years old. Being so wrapped up in their grief, my grandparents didn't realize they were burying their oldest daughter on her middle son's seventh birthday. As you might think, the funeral impacted her sons for the rest of their days. In addition to the flowers, the scent of her favorite perfume, "White Shoulders," mysteriously lingered about the funeral chapel. Forty years later, her oldest son said he could see her in that casket as though it was earlier that morning, and her baby sister said the same thing. Neither of them could ever smell White Shoulders again without being taken back to that day.

What do you say to that? I don't believe it was a coincidence that she relived her life with her family the night before she was injured. I choose to believe that was a final gift from God for each of them. With all my being, I believe that God has a plan and a purpose for each one of us. I pray you turn within, and to him and find that plan and purpose. Live your best life, the most extraordinary life the Creator of All designed for you because he loves you as no human ever could. Each of us has a day when we, too, must die. I pray that your, and my, passing be as peaceful, beautiful, and happy as my Aunt Susie's, whether or not we sing a song. Should we choose to sing, God won't care if we can't carry a tune. While he loves a beautiful voice, he cares most about a beautiful song of love from the heart.

CHAPTER 13

Income Tax 101

Gran had an absolutely amazing mathematical mind. I recall going to the grocery store with her when I was twelve. She was a single woman in her fifties with a houseful of us kids. She'd overfill two grocery carts with food, which I noticed was not the norm among shoppers. At my age, norm and fitting in seemed very important. I was already out of sorts for living with my grandmother and cousins, so shopping with my "ancient" grandmother, who didn't dress up to shop, wounded my adolescent ego further when I saw fashionably dressed young mothers with daughters my age. Today I see how shallow my thinking and behavior were. Still, at twelve, it was a lot about me, and fitting in or disappearing into the landscape.

Adding to my horror was that after having the groceries bagged and paid for, she didn't move on along. She stood there, right beside the checkout counter, and tallied the grocery receipt in her mind! She ran her thumb down the list, mouthing the price and sub totaling as she calculated item by item. There were two carts of food; without exaggeration, the list was easily 12" long! Shoppers behind us were waiting for us to move on along, the clerk was waiting for us to move on along, and Gran was double-checking the cash register and the clerk. This was no show folks; this was the real deal; she calculated that vast amount of data within a minute or two. It was devastatingly humiliating, even more so when she found the occasional error. I was never a big person, but I felt ginormous and like I was on a world stage in those moments; all I wanted was to melt into the floor and drizzle unseen out the door.

Today I recognize and admire the amazing mental skill it took for her to add all those numbers in her mind, as well as the determination that she would not be cheated by man or machine and that she did not care what anyone thought about her actions. She alone was financially responsible for the four of us grands who lived with her. She also made sure there was ample food for her other ten grandchildren who often visited, as well as her adult children and their spouses who might drop by. She always had plenty of food and would start cooking as soon as she saw the whites of your eyes:-) Family, friend, or friend of family or friend of a friend did not leave her house hungry!

My 4'10" grandmother has long since become a giant of a woman to me, but I digress from the actual topic of this chapter. This back story was to supply a slice of her mental ability. Let's travel back to when Gran worked in the produce sheds in Salinas in the early1950s.

Someone got wind of her math skills, so coworkers would toss out math questions, and she'd pause, look up for a moment, then provide a correct answer. It didn't take long before coworkers started asking her for help preparing their income tax returns.

Gran was a kind and generous soul, so of course, she helped. Helping one or two friends grew into helping friends of friends. They came to her home, and she went to theirs. I remember meeting one of my neighbors when I lived in Hollister. I was in my early thirties and couldn't place the memory, yet I knew I knew the guy. When we'd talk, I found myself searching his eyes, trying to catch the memory. He was familiar, he was comfortable, and he was a stranger at the same time. I told Gran about the oddity of my feelings concerning my neighbor/stranger. When I told her his name, she said, "Honey, he's no stranger. His parents brought him with them to have their taxes done. We'd put the two of you in the playpen together. You'd play together for hours while I did their taxes and we visited."

I was awed at my recollection of familiarity. We were two tiny little children, pre-conversational age. Yet, I knew him and was comfortable with him thirty years later because of that childhood experience. Humans fascinate me!

Gran's income tax business grew and grew and grew and grew. She taught her daughters, daughters-in-law, a son, and several of us grandchildren how to prepare income tax returns. At this writing, two of her daughters-in-law and one granddaughter are still active income tax practitioners, some working with fourth-generation clients. It's a beautiful and honorable family tradition in which we all took great pride.

I'm still trying to get you to the point of this chapter, but there are so many sub-chapters or lateral chapters that it's a real challenge. Just keep swimming, we'll get there!

Us grands grew up in that home-based tax business. Grandma loved, honored, and respected "her people." Her business prospered and grew almost exclusively by referral. Salinas was a melting pot of ethnicities, not far from the Fort Ord military base and Monterey Peninsula. Gran's tax clients were very diverse, and multicultural.

My elementary school didn't have the diversity I saw in my home. Television shows didn't have the diversity I saw in my house. People of all skin shades, eye shapes, accents, employment, immigration status, and sexual identities were welcomed and treated the same as those who looked like us. I started to say they were treated like family when in truth, they were treated better than family.

In the early years, Gran's desk was in the living room, as were the television and her people. She wouldn't make appointments, so folks would show up and wait, sometimes all day into the evening. She didn't turn people away; she wouldn't even take time away from them to eat. She'd often be exhausted and famished by the end of her workday.

No TVs in bedrooms back then meant you could read or listen to records in your room, but that was about it. We lived in the country, so we didn't hang out in the neighborhood; there were no streetlights. You stayed in your room during tax season or sat in the living room with strangers.

Sitting in the living room meant interacting with Gran's people; I did a lot of that. They loved her, and she loved them. They shared their lives and their children's lives, both the highs and the lows. Listening to Gran and her diverse clientele from a tender age, I learned that people want the same things in life no matter what we look like or where we come from. Food in their bellies, clothes on their backs, love in their families, and a roof over their heads. All people hurt, all people cry, and all live, love, laugh, and die. People are complicated; there's no explaining family, life, and love, are messy.

Gran's people brought her/us ethnic foods, and she loved the gifts and the adventure of trying new foods. I wasn't as adventurous with my food as she; frankly, none of us kids were. Us kids were all trying hard to be "normal" and fit into a world where we felt like outsiders.

After us grands were grown, Gran's tax clients/friends convinced her to travel with them to Mexico, Central America, and the Philippines. She was treated as a very honored guest, and she always referred to them as her dear, dear friends.

That was all well and good, but we often felt her clients were more important than us. Today I understand that within four months (tax season), she needed to make an annual living to support at least five of us. I understood it was her job. However, she spent an inordinate amount of time with each person because she shared their lives. She was a tax professional and counselor; they served as her counselor as well. We felt like she didn't have time for us, or more succinctly, that she wouldn't make time for us. She never came to any of our school functions. Decades later, she told me she did attend her own children's functions, but as she began raising grandchildren, she couldn't physically attend the functions for all of us, so she opted not to attend any functions so as not to show favoritism. It makes sense; however, she didn't explain that to us then. A child interprets such noninvolvement to mean the child is unimportant, which caused a variety of complications in most of our lives, as it does in the lives of most children with uninvolved parents/guardians. Can you relate? If so, don't take it personally. It wasn't you. If you're the parent/guardian, please explain your reason(s) for noninvolvement to the children. They've noticed, and they need answers; they need reassurance it's not them, it's you.

As time went on, Gran expanded her income tax preparation business to include bookkeeping, immigration, and notary services. Although her primary source of income came from the four-month tax season, she worked year-round.

There were many times Gran didn't show up to pick us up at the appointed time from the roller rink, school, or wherever because she was with a client. Although I continued to try out, I couldn't participate in after-school activities because I didn't have reliable transportation.

Other kids were picked up by their parents. We'd wait, and wait, and call, and call (from a pay phone) . . . and a taxi would show up. Either a taxi or an unknown tax client of any ethnicity would roll up to the curb and say, "Mrs. Kennedy sent me to pick you up while she's working on my income tax." For a kid or an adolescent, that was horrifying! We felt so very inconsequential. We didn't really know "stranger danger" because our home was filled with strangers at least four months out of the year! We did know other kids looked at us and judged us for our nonconforming lifestyles.

Gran's funeral service confirmed the life she lived. A couple hundred people were present, there were many, many flowers, and hardly a dry eye among her friends, family, clients, and business associates. Anglo, Latino, Filipino, African American, Asian, Indigenous, Arab, and other ethnicities traveled near and far to pay their last respects. Old, young, male, female, wealthy, and poor. Pentecostal, Methodist, Catholic, Muslim, Jehovah's Witnesses, Mormon, and Baptist. Some illiterates, some Ph.D.'s, murderers to ministers, and field workers to multi-millionaires.

I had never been so impressed in my life. The common thread among us was my dear little Gran. She tried her lifelong to love unconditionally, as did her Savior, Jesus Christ. Her funeral evidenced her success. It wasn't so much the vast number of people, it was the fact that she touched each and every one of those diverse people's lives. There were multitudes of stories of how she helped many people far beyond preparing their tax returns.

Gran taught me to see human beings as they are, how to treat the public, and how to help and serve others. She did so through her actions. She walked the walk. And that's the walk I walk as best I can, every single day.

◇◇◇

It took me over four decades to totally be grateful Mom left me with Gran. My desire for "normalcy" got in my way, and our life at Gran's was anything but the conventional "normal." Thankfully I eventually realized how blessed I was to have had such a young and continuous exposure to so many colors and cultures. It supplied the opportunities for me to recognize and accept all God's children (humans) are the same.

GENEVA MARIE BRETT

CHAPTER 14

A Final Promise, x2

Mom (age nineteen) met Dad (twenty-five) when he was stationed at Fort Lewis, Washington. I don't remember why Mom and Ronnie (my older brother) had moved to the area; freedom and adventure, I'd imagine. I recall a story about Mom's naivety; she was working in a diner near the base when a soldier with a New York accent sat down at the counter. He asked for a pizza.

Mom asked, "A piece of what?"

"A pizza pie."

"Sure thing; what kind of pie."

"A pizza pie."

Mom had never heard of pizza; she thought the soldier was a wise guy, and she had no time to play a fool's game. "Look, pal, I can't give you a piece of pie if I don't know what kind of pie you want. Stop being a wise ass and just tell me what kind of pie you want." The exasperated soldier got up and walked out.

Mom and Dad were in the process of divorce from their first spouses when they met. Dad had no children, and Mom had my older brother, who was a yearling or thereabouts. They married; Mom got pregnant with me within three weeks. She loved Dad but was not happy about having a second child. She married the first time to get out of the house and tending to her younger siblings. She fell pregnant two weeks after her first wedding and was a single parent before her firstborn was six months old. She did not want a second kid.

On the other hand, my father was thrilled the moment she told him. He wanted children with his first wife; he adored my brother and would now have his "own" child. He was having things! He just knew I would be a girl and almost instantly named me Geneva Marie, after Mom's mother and his beloved deceased mother. Dad quickly went shopping for his precious baby girl; I still have one of the socks he bought me as part of an outfit!

Not only did Mom not want a second kid, but she also did not like the name he chose for me. At all. Nevertheless, she promised to name me as he'd chosen.

Mom said Dad was very protective of her "condition" and restricted her activities to ensure my safety. Undoubtedly, she kept her three attempts to abort me secret from him. (My very existence proves I've been a determined soul since I was a so-called "clump of cells"!) Admittedly, it was hurtful to know how genuinely unwanted I was, both before and after my birth. I've rationalized that it wasn't the fabulous me that I am today that she didn't want; I mean, it was nothing against me personally. She didn't want any child. (Spoiler alert, she ended up liking and loving me!)

Her first attempt to keep me from my destiny was early in our pregnancy when she drank copious amounts of quinine water to self-induce abortion. (I've since read that two out of three of us embryos have survived this tactic.) Her second attempt to off me was when she jumped off the roof of their house, hoping to dislodge me when I was at the age science termed me a fetus. (My husband has claimed that once I get a hold of something, I latch on like a pit bull, it sounds like I learned that VERY early on!) Our battle of wills, our battle over my life, continued with one final attempt, this time involving others. After Dad shipped out to Korea, Mom went roller skating at Fort Ord and made sure she was on the end of the "crack the whip" in hopes she'd get injured, and I wouldn't survive. This was in the seventh month of our pregnancy. She underestimated me and God's plan for me, again.

How do I know of these attempted murders? Mom told me. She didn't call them attempted murders; she called them attempted abortions. Same thing, but I never corrected her or argued with her . . . nor will I argue with you. That's how I see it. I'm as entitled to my opinion as you are yours. I don't/won't hate on you because our views are different. I hope you're as accepting of our differences. I believe abortion is murder, abortion's just a seemingly more palatable term for the same action. I never hated or condemned my mother for her attempts to kill me.

I don't mean disrespect or hurt to any woman who has ended her embryo's or fetus's life. There are many women whom I deeply love, respect, and admire who have done so. I don't judge or condemn them or any other woman for such a choice. I have no standing to do so; I know God forgives them when they ask, and so do their babies. Their story is their story. This is my story, don't get tripped up . . . let's move on along here.

Now, you might wonder why my mother would tell me such a thing. For some people, knowing they weren't lovingly planned caused them great heartache and even a need for counseling. Well, Mom was Mom, and she was a straight shooter. She was a lousy shot but a straight shooter. She didn't sugarcoat things; she said them how she saw them, which could be construed as a bit harsh. I accepted that, all of our family did. She was the most outspoken, matter-of-fact person among her siblings and parents.

Let's get back to the final promise x2. Although Dad was in the Army when he met Mom, he was also a Marine during WWII. During the Korean War he was drafted into the Army, which led him to Fort Lewis and Mom. Mom learned she was pregnant with me the day before Dad was discharged after completing his drafted service obligation. He re-upped the next day. I don't know when he told Mom he'd re-enlisted without discussing it with her AND was most likely being sent overseas. Woo doggies, she was mad, mad, mad! Imma bet she was Banty Rooster mad! Mom's anger didn't change anything, except probably the climate inside their home.

Speaking of their home, they lived on base (Quarters 775) at Fort Lewis, Washington. Interestingly enough, my brother's father (#1) was stationed at the same base. Somehow Mom learned that fact and left a message for her former husband to call. When he called, she invited him over for a home-cooked meal and a visit with their young son. Both Mom and brother's dad (#1) told me they all got along well and enjoyed their time together. He was invited back a second time.

Dad got some leave before shipping out, so he took Mom, brother (me, the fetus, too) to her parents in Salinas, where we were to stay until he came home. I don't know if he said it to Mom; however, Dad told my grandparents and some of Mom's siblings that he felt he wouldn't return from Korea and would never get to see me. They all told him he was talking nonsense. Nevertheless, he made each one of them promise to always look after Mom, Ronnie, and his Geneva Marie. That was in July of 1954.

Fast forward to September 19, 1954, in Korea's Chorwon Valley near the 19th Parallel, where my father was serving as a Sergeant in the Military Police Investigation Section. At 1:15 am, Dad and two MPs were coming from/headed to, I don't know where.

Dad was driving; he rounded a curve, and they plunged down an embankment . . . All three soldiers were taken to the 44th Surgical Hospital.

According to the investigation report . . . wait. I'm not going to get into that right here. You'll have to wait for the second book. I've just learned a lot of new/old information I'll share later. You, dear reader, keep getting me off point with all these backstories to the main stories!

So, in that same valley, on that same day, my brother's dad, Lee, (#1) was in a field hospital. The 44th Surgical Hospital to be exact. He was recovering from a double hernia surgery the day before. A Lieutenant nurse walked by his bed, talking about some MPs that were brought in because they'd been in a wreck.

Lee asked, "Will you do me a favor and find out if one of those MPs is named Sergeant Bob Brett?"

The nurse instructed him to go to the front desk and ask himself. Lee hobbled his way up to the desk to repeat his question. As he leaned on the desk for support, he noticed a billfold lying open on the desk. It was open to a photo of a woman and a child; Mom, and Ronnie! Lee asked if he could go in to see the MP, but the Desk Sarg wouldn't let him in. Lee was a bit insistent, and then Sarg asked how he knew him.

Lee pointed to the photo in the billfold and said, "He's married to my ex-wife; that's her and my son."

Lee was allowed to see my father. He had no idea if my father was conscious or even alive for sure. Nevertheless, he stood at his bedside and promised my father he'd look after me for the rest of his life.

Is the hair on the back of your neck standing up like mine did when I first heard this story? What are the odds that these two husbands of my mother were in the same army field hospital some 6,000 miles from home?

That they'd met and broken bread together back in the states? This, along with surviving Mom's multiple attempts to off me, add to my certainty that God has always had a plan and purpose for my life!

Three days later, in Salinas, California, Mom was sitting in the living room of her parent's home with her sister when the doorbell rang. Mom answered the door, not to a couple soldiers in uniform holding a telegram as we've seen in film, but instead to a young man who read the telegram announcing my father's death in somewhat of a sing-song voice. There was no respect, no decorum . . . just seventy-three words. Seventy-three words, read by a teenage boy not much younger than Mom. With that reading, a twenty-year-old woman's life, hopes, and dreams were shattered to bits. (The telegram's at the back of the book.)

The child of the dead soldier was stretching and straining her body until it felt like she would break from the inside out.

Fetuses feel their mother's every emotion. I tried to be quiet and gentle within; I could feel her pain, anguish, and anxiety. I tried to be good, but I just couldn't stay inside her any longer. With the news of Dad's death, she didn't want me times 10,000, but there was no holding me back now. Two days later, I rushed out of my mother's womb as fast as I could, so fast that Mom said I was nearly born in the toilet! She later told me I was the ugliest baby she'd ever seen. Oh yeah, that hurt. But how must she have hurt? Two kids she didn't want, a divorce, and now a dead husband at the age of twenty years and three months. What might that do to a tender heart and a spirit?

Can you imagine being twenty years old, going through childbirth while still being in shock from the news of your husband's death in a war? Husband is dead, and so are all the plans and dreams of the future; that can surely scar a heart for life.

Military wives are still experiencing that same trauma and pain to this very day. The families waiting at home are the silent heroes of our military. They didn't sign up for the anguish many encountered. (God Bless you one and all!)

So, Mom was again stuck at her parents, from which she'd tried to escape twice already, only to have life toss her back like an undertow of the ocean. Then she had to officially name this child she never wanted. She'd been very angry with Dad for re-enlisting, and she did not like the name Geneva Marie, so she'd decided to name me Pamela Kay. He'd be mad, but so was she. By the time he'd receive her letter telling him of my birth and my name, it'd be too late for him to do anything about it, just like she couldn't do anything about him re-enlisting when he'd done so.

Then, he had the audacity to up and die on her. Woof. She couldn't get even with him, with him being dead, so, to honor my father, I am named Geneva Marie. That's final promise #1.

Lee returned to Salinas after he was discharged and found Mom waitressing in a cafe. He told her he needed to talk to her and asked if she'd sit in the car with him during her break. She agreed and joined him as requested.

He said, "I've done a lot of thinking Lou, and I think we should get married again and raise Ronnie and Little Neva. Now, don't respond right now, I'm going down south to visit my brother for a couple weeks. Give me your answer when I get back."

He looked her up when he got back in town, and asked, "Have you thought about my idea of getting married and raising these two kids? What do you say?"

"I don't want no damn part of it."

Once Mom was done, she was DONE.

They both moved on. Lee married his beloved Marylin two years later. They had a son, two daughters, and built a successful construction business. They were married fifty-nine years when she passed. Mom remarried and remarried and remarried, always seeking but never finding. To this day, Lee blames himself for Mom's discontent. He said she was just a child (sixteen) when he took her from her parents' home and that she became a bitter woman when he left her a little over two years later.

When I was sixteen or seventeen, Lee told me about asking Mom to remarry and create a home for the four of us. I'd never heard that story before, so I questioned my mother, who confirmed it as fact. (Sorry, Lee, nothing personal, I've always been a fact-checker.)

I must confess I was seven ways of angry with Mom for a very long time over that. She had the opportunity to give my brother and me a "normal" life instead of the chaos, confusion, and hurt we endured, I endured. I couldn't understand how she could be so selfish. It took me a very long time to get over that hurt and to forgive her for that transgression against me. It took so long because I was focused on my wants and needs, not hers, just as she had focused on hers, not ours. I later realized that when

I pointed my finger at her, three pointed back at me. I don't like that so much! But I've learned to face it.

Not so much in those younger years, but since I was a mobile teenager, Lee has been a part of my life. I visited him, his wife, and his other three children in their home. They all knew the story of him and my father in Korea and of Lee's promise. When his beloved Marylin passed, I was included as a daughter at her service and in her memorial program. He just told me today that he always had his eye on me, whether I was aware, specifically mentioning some of my high school days and friends. That is final promise #2.

There's more to tell of Mom and Lee; I'll get to it before I'm through.

Besides the extraordinary meeting of Mom's two husbands in Korea, what's also significant to me is the integrity in keeping their promises. My father was dead; he wouldn't know or presumably care if the promises made to him were kept. Only they would know they honored their word and kept their promise. The soul who makes the promise knows and lives with their action or inaction. We've all heard of near-death experiences wherein the person's life "passes before their eyes". You want that history, your life review, to be as good and gentle as possible when it's your turn.

A few days ago, I visited my beloved Lee while he was in the hospital recovering from a very scary emergency surgery. Today I'll admit I had concerns about his survival. He was asleep when I entered the room. When he awoke and saw me his face lit up with joy and his eyes filled with love. His look reminded me of my aunt's when her children visited her in the hospital in the days preceding her death. My eyes almost overflowed as I acknowledged that look of love was just for me because I was the only other person in the room. Lee has introduced me as his adopted daughter and has long told me he loves me as his own; in that moment I felt that blood love.

When the lump in my throat subsided, I told him how much his look meant to me, and was again heart-struck, this time by his response. "Honey, when I look at you, I see your dad in that Army field hospital, and that promise I made to him. You look a lot like your dad. I see you, and I've kept that promise."

So, every time Lee sees me, he is reminded that he has been an oath keeper for over sixty-eight years; that he's never let my father down. He has kept watch as promised.

Like the rest of us, he's lived an imperfect life with many regrets over things he did and didn't do. Yet, he's been perfect in this one thing, which causes joy for him, and me. Ours is truly a perfect love.

People make and keep the life oath of marriage; however, every married person in the history of humans has, at some point, disappointed or hurt their spouse. Every parent has disappointed or hurt their child. But Lee and I are different. Seeing me is a gift to his soul, proof that he kept his promise to a dying/dead man. He's never disappointed or hurt me because I've never had expectations; I've just been grateful for his affection. His affection spilled over to his wife and their children, who also love me without obligation. All the love coming from his dad's family towards me warms my bio brother's heart and soul.

Mom didn't understand the relationship between Lee and me. On more than one occasion, she questioned why I loved him. He and I once walked into her hospital room, arm in arm.

Mom looked up, her eyes traveled from him to me, and she said, "What the hell do you see in him?"

"Well Mom, he loves me, and I love him. That's all that counts."

He'd hurt and disappointed her, but never me. Mom didn't let go of pain, so her lifelong friendship with #1 did speak to her underlying feelings. She told my brother, "Sometimes I love you, sometimes I hate you . . . because you look so damn much like your daddy!"

All that said to show you the power of a promise kept.

A few months before Mom died, she was so physically depleted she lost her mind; she didn't know who she was, who I was, when, or where she was. Her doc recommended I place her in a facility; I said I'd promised her I'd never do that to her. He said she wouldn't know.

I said, "But I'd know, and I have to live with me for the rest of my life."

Thankfully her mind came back.

Beloved, don't make a promise you don't intend to keep, and if you do make a promise, let nothing stop you from fulfilling your word. It will matter most to YOU. To thine own self be true.

Speaking of being true to thine own self . . . of the dozens of women I know who've had abortions, there's only one that didn't ever feel some guilt for doing so. Each of the women had reasons why it was their best choice at that time in their life. Nevertheless, it wounded their souls; they've wept, grieved, and guilted over that decision.

The post-abortive fathers I know have the same feelings of loss and regret. They've wondered who their child might have become, who they might have been as a father. Some of the men had no say in the matter, and some agreed with the decision. My beloved Pastor was writing a book about being a post-abortive father when he died. PB (my nickname for my Pastor) was a coveted National Right for Life speaker. He marched, protested, prayed, wept, stood in the gap, and helped provide alternatives for women in crisis. Pastor Bruce Rivers told me that abortive mothers and fathers are still parents; it's just that they're parents of a deceased child.

Thankfully his wife has found his notes, video interviews, and speeches in which he shared his thoughts and feelings to help other men heal and to help the world understand the heavy burden abortion places on a soul. His bride is finishing his work, and I look forward to watching it heal deep wounds and transform lives. There's no doubt God has worked through both him and Emily to share the sad truth of post abortive parents.

Beloved unknown sister, beloved unknown brother, if you've made such a decision in your life and followed through with it, you need some healing. When the thought, the memory, comes upon you, know that forgiveness is yours for the asking. You don't have to speak to another human about your choice.

Write it out, ask God and your baby(s) for forgiveness, and then burn the paper. Forgiveness is yours for the asking. No emotional beating, no berating, no shaming. Period. Full Stop. Once you do that, step into the most challenging part. Truly forgive yourself and be free of it. We all do things we later regret, things that want to haunt us. God doesn't want that for you. He sent his only flesh and blood son to stand in the gap for us. Jesus died for our sins. Yours, and mine. Mine are no less or more than yours.

CHAPTER 15

My Baby Brother Died, and Nobody Cried

Growing up, we didn't have the tender Lucas McCain (the dad on *The Rifleman*) moments wherein a parent explained life, choices, and consequences to us. Instead, we overheard adult conversations and dealt with life on our own, each of us as individuals. We children didn't bond and share our challenges like Wally and the Beaver (*Leave it to Beaver*). We were all on our own figuring out life. It was, and is, still that way for millions and millions of people to this very day.

I don't remember the last time I saw my little brother alive. I remember Mom kept him and not me. Sometimes she'd keep my older brother, too, but rarely me. I later learned it was because my grandmother was adamant that I stay with her. She thought her home safer for a girl. I don't know that it was.

Mom was young; she ran wild and free. Eighteen when my older brother was born, twenty when I was born, and twenty-three when my younger brother was born. Two decades later, I asked what it was about me that she couldn't love. That I was a girl, or wasn't pretty enough (my brothers won baby beauty contests, but I was never entered in one). Just what was it? I was always grateful for Mom's candor; even if I didn't like what she said, she would always shoot it straight.

Her response to my question was, "Oh honey, it wasn't you. It was me. I was young and selfish. I felt like I raised Mama's kids, so she could raise mine while I had fun."

I must admit her truth made me mad. I appreciated the truth, yet I judged her for it and condemned her. I held a grudge and avoided her for several years, but more on that later.

My grandparents wouldn't keep my little brother like they did Ronnie and me. Grandma thought it might make my mother behave more responsibly if she had to take care of her youngest. Mom was off on a fun time when we got word my three-year-old brother was in the hospital three hundred miles away, in Orange County. He'd been badly burned in a house fire; eighty-five percent of his body had third-degree burns. He lived eighteen days like that.

No one directly told my older brother or me; we overheard adults talking. Today I can't remember if it was Grandma and Grandpa or Grandma and Auntie we overheard; perhaps it was both. I remember being scared and feeling sick to my stomach.

About a week after hearing the news, we were packed in the car for the trip to see my little brother and overheard that he probably wouldn't survive. Grandma, Auntie, her husband, and their four children. Three adults and five children, long before seat belts. I was six years old; my cousins were four, three, two, and two months. We were all lean kids, but five squirming bodies in the crowded back seat, especially for kids unused to long-distance car travel, was uncomfortable. I don't remember why my older brother didn't go with us. He might have stayed home with Grandpa, my cousins, and uncles still living at home, or he might have gone to his father's.

Back to the point of overhearing that my baby brother was suffering in a hospital and my mother couldn't be found. (Don't back up, I didn't make that point before, but here it is. This is heavy emotional stuff, it gets, well, I get, a little sideways.) I recall hearing Gran tell many people over the years that "all points bulletins" were issued for my mother, even broadcast over the radio, and Mom didn't respond. I'd always believed that story and wondered how my mother could ignore those pleas over the airwaves for her to be present with her dying child. Now I wonder if that was true. All points bulletins and radio broadcasts looking for the mother of a wounded child in 1960? I'm thinking that might not really have happened. But then, maybe? Truth is, I never wanted to believe that to be true; perhaps I still don't.

Mom lived with a gal friend in the Los Angeles area in 1960. I have vague memories of visiting her for a couple of weeks and a teenage male babysitter who shouldn't have been left alone with little girls. But that's a different story that may or not get told.

My strongest recollections of the trip to see my little brother are of the discomfort and racket in the back seat, the shame and guilt I felt for my mother being my mother, and the repetitive negative adult comments about my mother, mostly coming from her own mother. As crowded and noisy as it was, I was alone with my thoughts that my brother would probably die, and our mother seemingly didn't care. That's a lot of heavy thinking for a six-year-old.

The story I repeatedly heard over the years was that mom left my brother with her roommate in a bar as she was leaving for a weekend with a man. (As horrifying as it may seem to you that a three-year-old was in a bar, it wasn't that uncommon for Mom to take us to a bar throughout our pre-adult lives. We went to the bar with some of her siblings as well. That's just how they rolled. I may tell kids in bar stories in book two.) The story goes that the roommate took my brother home and fell asleep while smoking a cigarette. The house caught fire, and so did my brother.

My grandmother always questioned how the roommate with waist-length hair got out of the house unsinged. The house was locked, Mom's roommate was outside, so the firefighters had to break down the door to get to my brother. The firefighters questioned the woman about her story, but nothing came of it. Gran believed the woman put my brother down for a nap, locked him in the house, and returned to the bar. No one will ever know.

I wasn't allowed in the hospital to see my brother; us kids stayed in the car with my uncle. Today I'm grateful I didn't see him and wasn't allowed in the hospital to hear his cries or the cries of other ill and wounded children. My imagination was terrible enough.

We stayed down there for two or three days; I can't recall a motel room, but then I remember little other than being in the car and my uncle giving us ice cream. I hauntingly recall my grandmother saying that in his delirium, my three-year-old brother kept repeating, "No-no, Nonna." "Nonna" was Mom's friend with whom he was left.

Grandma also said my mother arrived at the hospital while she was there. In retelling the event, Gran criticized my mother for being inconsolable and crying out, "My baby, my baby!" Mom was condemned for not being there and then condemned for being emotional.

My people did not make a display of emotion; you were to suck it up. (We did not get the addition of "buttercup.") My mother didn't come to see me while we were there; I was stuck in the back seat with my cousins feeling out of place, alone, confused, and heart hurt. I imagine Mom was too.

My baby brother died after we returned home. No one sat my older brother or me down to inform or comfort us. Again, we overheard the adults talking. Just as I can recall where I was when JFK was assassinated and when the Twin Towers imploded, I can feel and see six-year-old me standing in the hallway looking out the window to the backyard as I was trying to process the information that my brother was dead.

I understood death was permanent and that I'd never see him again. I didn't understand Mom. I didn't understand my life or my aloneness. I didn't cry. I didn't see anyone cry. I didn't share my thoughts or feelings, and no one asked me about them.

And as for being comforted, we just got along with life. I'm not criticizing my people here; just stating facts as best I can recall them. Death is part of life, and the living get on with living. I always knew my father died before I was born, my mom's older sister died when I was a year old, and two uncles had babies die shortly after birth. There was a lot of talk about death in our home, but no tears. I'm just now realizing that I'd learned not to cry by the age of six.

I remember Mom being at Gran's (my home) after my brother died and before his funeral. She and Gran argued about Ronnie and me attending our brother's funeral. Mom was adamant we did not attend, and I do mean adamant. Grandma and Grandpa had taken my cousins to their mother's funeral five years before. Both Mom and Gran used that scenario as to why we should/shouldn't go.

Mom was all kinds of mad when she saw Ronnie and me at the funeral with Gran. She didn't take our cousins; they must have stayed with Grandpa.

What I can remember of my brother's funeral was feeling very sad. No tears, but great sadness. It was sad! A funeral for a three-year-old who died a tragic death. Even as a six-year-old, I could feel the weight of the grief in the room. I can't remember if Auntie went with us; it might have just been Grandma, Ronnie, and me. We didn't sit with family, meaning Mom or my brother's father (#4). My little brother's body was so severely burned his tiny little casket was closed. I don't remember seeing or hearing any of my people cry. Not saying they didn't; I didn't see it.

I didn't know the word then, but now I understand that I felt validated by attending his funeral. Again, today's understanding was that my mother was somewhat dismissive of me. She was never an affectionate person with any child. Four decades later, Mom complained that my youngest was too affectionate. She was so affectionate that Mom wondered if she might be "retarded" because she should have grown out of wanting to sit on your lap long before she was eight. Oh, mama, the things you didn't know.

Anyway, he was my brother. Attending his funeral was an acknowledgment of MY relationship and MY loss of MY brother. I never wanted to displease my mother, but I was very grateful Grandma chose to honor mine and Ronnie's feelings and let us say farewell.

I'm not sure if we went to the cemetery. I have a glimpse of the cemetery in my mind; however, I also kind of recall Gran compromising and taking us home after the service. My brother doesn't remember any of it.

I never did hear Mom's version of how my brother died directly from her; it wasn't something she talked about. I never asked because Auntie told me Mom couldn't talk about it.

Forty-one years later, my oldest daughter's face was burned at a bonfire. My car was in the shop, and my daughter needed wound treatment an hour from our home. My daughter's father couldn't take us, so I phoned my mother. She drove thirty minutes to my house to pick us up, and then took us another hour to the burn unit for treatment. My daughter knew the story of my baby brother's death, so she sat behind my mom in the car; she didn't want her beloved grandmother to see her face. Mom sat in the car and cried for the hour we were in treatment. My daughter later said, "Mom, everything happens for a reason. Maybe I was burned to help Grandma Lou finally deal with her pain." (My children are beautiful souls!)

In her last few years, Mom promised she'd write the book of her life, so I bought her a blank book. She never wrote a word; she ran out of time. I really wish I'd known her story.

When I think about it today . . . it hit me for the first time ever. I've felt shame and guilt for my mother's behavior all these years. And I've just now realized how awful my grandmother must have felt about her

105

daughter's behavior. I felt shame for Mom and me; Gran probably did as well.

◇◇◇

After the divorce from my former husband, I read several books on how to best deal with my children in the aftermath of divorce. The primary thing I learned was not to badmouth a child's parent directly to them or within their earshot, no matter what you think, believe, or feel. To do so wounds that precious child and causes them to be defensive of that person. Children inherently love their parents, flaws, and all.

Beloved reader, you also make mistakes and occasionally get your priorities mixed up. Don't burden a precious child to make yourself look better or to dispense your wounds from the breakup. Let the children grow to know their parents and see for themselves who each parent is, flaws, warts, wrinkles, and all. Indeed, you must recognize that you too are flawed and imperfect. Time always tells the truth. Be honorable to your children and to the other parent you believed in enough to create a human being with.

As for me, from where I am today, I've freed myself of the judgment of my mother. I'm positive she suffered with guilt nearly every day of her life after her baby died. I don't say that to say she "got what she deserved." I don't think like that. We all deserve the magnificent life God planned for us. There is no human beyond his mercy or grace, no matter what they've done. His is unconditional love; he traded his son's life so that we might have life everlasting.

Mom's child's death was a tragic accident. I'm grateful, very grateful I've not had to deal with the death of one of my children. I also appreciate that Ronnie and I weren't with Mom; we might be with our little brother today. That, or maybe Ronnie would have saved us all. There's no use in going down that road because there's no changing yesterday.

"God grant me the serenity to accept the things I can't change.
The courage to change the things I can.
And the wisdom to know the difference!"

(The Serenity Prayer, Reinhold Niebuhr)

CHAPTER 16

When Grandpa Said No Dating

Grandpa liked alcohol, and early on in their marriage, it got to where he'd get liquored up and hit Gran. When sober the next day, he'd apologize and say he didn't know what he was doing or remember what happened. Liquored up, he'd occasionally demand she dance for him. She'd refuse, so he'd threaten to shoot at her shoe heels to make her dance. Decades later, she said she thought he'd heard somebody else say that and decided to give it a try. She'd dare him to go ahead and try. She didn't dance, and thankfully he didn't shoot at her shoe heels. It's a wonder she didn't get hurt worse than she did. Frankly, it's a wonder they survived one another!

Gran would goad Grandpa to do whatever it was he was threatening. My mom did the same thing with her men. Perhaps it was their way of saying "I'm not afraid" to their men and themselves. My people didn't show weakness even when they were scared. We were all raised with the mindset to defy fear.

Gran told me she thought Grandpa used being drunk as a crutch to beat her up. When they lived in Oklahoma, if she made him mad or wouldn't do what he wanted her to say or do, he'd hit her, even when he was sober.

One time a couple of his friends had stopped by for a visit. Gran cooked for all of them. As they sat at the kitchen table afterward, Grandpa started boasting about his coon dogs. He was telling his friends about how many coons they'd killed and was "flavoring" the story to make his dogs sound better than they were. He turned to his bride to back his story, "Didn't I, Geneva?" She wouldn't answer because she didn't want to lie. He asked for her corroboration again, and again she refused, so he hit her in the face and bloodied her nose, right there in front of his friends.

Sidebar: I don't understand how any person, especially a man, could sit there, watch that happen and not do anything. That's disgraceful! Don't you ever stand by and let anyone bully a weaker one! You'll hate yourself for it later if you do. Stand up for what's right!

When we were recording for this book, I asked Grandma if she was afraid of Grandpa. She replied, "Well, to tell you the truth, I was. But I'd never let him know that."

Gran never drank and didn't believe it when Grandpa said he couldn't remember what had happened the night before. Grandma remembered everything.

After too many beatings, she decided she would get drunk, and God help her man if she remembered what she'd said and done. She accomplished her mission; had a horrid hangover but recalled what she'd said and done. (She had no idea that heavy drinkers get blackout drunk.) She was fed up with his cheating, drinking, and beating. She devised a plan to cure him once and for all.

While he was out carousing one night, she locked all the doors and windows except the front door. When she heard him stumbling to the door, she quickly stood on a chair behind the door. He walked in, and she whacked him on the top of the head with a six-pound flat iron (for ironing clothes), which knocked him out. She then dragged him onto the bed, tied him to it . . . and commenced to wailing on him.

He somewhat came to and started yelling, "You're killing me! Stop! You're killing me!"

Grandma hit him again and again and said, "If I don't, it won't be because I didn't try! You dirty bastard, if I don't kill you, you're going to wish I would have!"

She continued to beat him until she thought she'd killed him. She packed up the kids and left him for dead.

He recovered and set out after her, pleading and crying not to leave him. She took him back, and they moved to California not long after. Although he never hit her again, he continued drinking and cheating on her; that's just how he rolled.

Life was on the upswing in California; they were both working jobs and flipping houses. But Grandpa was Grandpa, a serial cheater. Gran said she got to where she didn't even say anything to him about it. Gran said her husband was, and probably always would be, a whoremonger.

Mom told me about the day she and her younger sister had deep cleaned the house all day, washing walls, mopping and waxing floors. She didn't say what Grandma was doing, except she couldn't find her husband at some point.

Grandpa walked into the dining room to eat and said, "Neva, do you know where I was when you were looking for me?"

Gran said nothing.

"I was up under that floor at so and so's house and fixing the foundation."

She knew where he'd really been. He'd been chippy chasing again. She'd decided not to say anything about it, but then he tossed the lie at her. He had a guilty conscience. It was bad enough that he did the bad deeds, but then to lie to cover the deed was just too much for her.

Gran went Banty rooster mad again. As she threw words, "Ray, you lying bastard! You was in that bedroom with (woman's name)!" she threw a huge pot of soup at him, which busted the wall behind him, and then she dumped the table upside down.

Grandpa did what any intelligent person should do when confronted by a Banty rooster . . . he split.

Those stories took place long before my time, but I heard them many a time. There was never any laughter included in the retelling of Gran beating Grandpa and leaving him for dead. That was serious business. Her shooting off the corner of the house was always accompanied by laughter. As I think about it now, I'm not sure why anyone found that funny, but they did. Maybe they laughed at her being a lousy shot or the seemingly commonplace absurdity of the ordeal.

We lived in Prunedale for a time when I was a toddler; six or so of us kids were in the household. Grandma and Grandpa got into an argument, which rapidly escalated. Grandpa was the one who went Banty rooster mad that time.

He fetched his rifle and cocked it, literally aiming to permanently end arguing with his wife.

As one of the older kids started yelling and pleading with him not to shoot her, she said, "He's not going to shoot. He's too much of a coward to shoot."

Ay Caramba Grandma.

How they survived one another is a mystery or just the Grace of God. Us kids were two to twelve years old . . . very formative years. Even though we younger ones might not remember the details later, the damage and terror from witnessing such violence are buried deep within, imprinted upon our souls.

When I was seven years old, Gran decided she was done with Grandpa and kicked him out. That was a sad time for me; Grandpa was easygoing, easy to laugh, and I thought he was great fun. I adored Grandpa and loved going everywhere with him.

He moved in with their oldest son and his family for a time. He still came to our house consistently, she'd do his laundry, feed him, and talk to him, but he could not stay. He did not like that arrangement at all.

Although I didn't know what had transpired between my grandparents to cause their split, I later learned Gran had filed for divorce two years before, and it had become final. (The stated grounds for divorce were extreme cruelty; I think we can agree she didn't exaggerate.) With the final decree in hand, Grandma had the standing to make him leave.

One day after Grandpa moved out, Grandma informed him she was going on a date. Grandpa told her she would do no such thing.

She was in her late forties, he in his late fifties; she told him, "I'm twenty-one years old (a favorite saying) and will do as I please. There's nothing you can do about it. My business is my business."

Grandpa responded, "I can and will do something about it. I'll shoot any man that tries to date my wife!"

Gran scoffed at him and said, "You didn't have any problem going out or carrying on with other women while we were married, so turnabout is fair play."

"I'm giving you fair warning. If you care a thing about the man, you better keep him away."

"Oh Ray, you're nothing but a blowhard."

Then she turned and walked away.

I remember the day, Grandma's date day, very well. Grandpa had been at our house for part of the day. Grandma told him to leave, and he begrudgingly complied. He knew it was Grandma's date day. He left, but his truck remained parked by the cornfield across the road from our house. Grandpa was nowhere to be seen.

I might have only been seven, but I sensed an energy in the house that day, which continued to build as the day drew closer to early evening. It was a palpable energy like I imagine there is before a tornado. Something was about to happen, and it didn't feel like whatever was going to happen would be a good thing.

Grandma got dressed to go out. Up to that day, I'd only seen my Gran dress up for church. She did her hair, donned a nice dress, and added lipstick and mascara.

For some reason, my aunt and her family were staying with us for a bit; Auntie was trying to talk Grandma out of going on the date. "Mama, you know how much Daddy loves you; it'd hurt him bad if you went out with another man. You know you love Daddy. You don't really want to date someone; you're just doing it out of spite. Please don't do this to Daddy!"

Grandma pulled her 4'10" self up as tall as she could and replied, "I'm not going to be told what I can and can't do by anyone! I'm a grown woman, twenty-one years old, and I'll do as I please. I'm going on a dinner date."

Auntie made me go with her and the other kids to the bedroom at the far end of the hall, the bedroom farthest away from the front door. Now that I think about it in my adult mind, she probably didn't want us near the front door in case Grandpa actually shot Grandma's date.

The average person tosses words and threats around like they toss a green salad. For most folks, such talk is an idle threat. Not so idle in my family.

We weren't allowed to stand by the window in the bedroom facing the road; however, we could get on our knees and peek out the big picture window. We were told not to stand up, we were to crawl around the room if we wanted to move about. So that's what us older kids did. Auntie's kids were four and under, pretty much clueless and uncaring about what was happening. Their daddy kept them together and away from the window.

We saw an unfamiliar car in front of the house, then watched Grandma and an unknown man walk away from our front door, down the walkway, to the car. The man opened the passenger door for Gran, seated her, closed her door, and walked around the back of the vehicle towards the driver's side.

He was at the left back tire when we heard the crack of the rifle. I stood up and was yanked down to the floor. The man quickly got in the car, and they sped away. We heard a few more rounds fired at the car as they left.

In case you haven't figured it out, Grandpa was hiding across the road in the cornfield, shooting at Grandma's date.

My adult mind wonders what that dinner date conversation was like. Do you think they discussed the gunfire?

If so, I'd imagine Gran said, "Oh, he wasn't shooting to kill you; he just wanted to scare you. He's just a big blowhard. There's nothing to be afraid of."

Yikes! Poor fella had no idea what drama he was getting himself into when he asked Gran out on a date.

Auntie kept us in the room for a while, a long while. Grandpa's truck didn't move, nor did we see him the rest of the evening. Grandma came home after dark; by then, Grandpa's truck was gone. Grandma never went on another date that I'm aware of. I imagine her gentleman friend didn't think her quite as attractive after getting shot at. When Grandpa said no dating, he meant no dating!

That sounds kind of traumatic, doesn't it? Frankly, it didn't feel traumatic in the moment. But then, I didn't know the word trauma or its meaning. It was just my life, my "normal" life. I didn't cry, I didn't shout, I didn't hide; none of us did. We saw and kept going; there was no discussion of the event in real-time. Actually, there was never any explanation or comfort offered to us children about what we'd witnessed. Some years later, laughter was involved in remembering "When Daddy shot at Mama's date."

◇◇◇

It's sixty-one years later, so I suppose it's okay to admit it now. I was a little scared. Realistically, I was probably very scared. Grandpa, a hunter, shooting at Grandma's date. Not shooting at Grandma; he loved her; he "just" shot at her date. In all probability (hopefully), he didn't intend to hit him. He just wanted to scare the guy off. He couldn't control Gran, but maybe he could keep men away from her by scaring them. He wasn't a very good husband, but he loved her. Obsessively.

As I write this memory, I live this memory, feeling it for the first time. Seeing myself as a child, all of us children crouched down on the floor, my aunt doing her best to protect us. I recognize our fear had nowhere to go except within. And that's where it's rested, layering one unresolved emotional trauma on top of another for decades upon decades.

Harboring such stuff isn't good for the mind, body, or soul. If you've got some of that built up or building up in you . . . find a place and/or a space to set yourself free. No one can do the work for you. I encourage you to write it out. Write it with your bad spelling, crummy handwriting, and incomplete or run-on sentences. Just let it out. You don't have to share it with a single human, although dogs and horses are excellent listeners. Cats, not so much.

Burn it when you're through; you'll be safe. It's time for you to take care of little you. The people around you couldn't give you what you needed because they didn't know what you needed, or they didn't have the skill. But you know. Love on little you. Forgive yourself for being a victim.

OMG! During one of my children's high school years, one stayed out all night. At about five am, I found out where my kid was and had a police officer go with me to the house on a "civil standby." I knew the cop couldn't do anything. I just wanted to scare that kid and the kid's family. I told the cop, "If I can't control my kid, I want other kids not to want to hang around them because my kid has a crazy cop calling mother."

Thanks, Grandpa. You gave me the idea ~ it didn't work as well for me as it did for you, though. That kid still gave me some fits!

GENEVA MARIE BRETT

CHAPTER 17

Winner, Winner, Chicken Dinner

For most of my youth, we had livestock of some sort. Pleasure horses were a must; we all rode; it just varied with how much we liked it and kept at it. We had beeves, I don't remember how many head, but enough for Grandpa to have built a catch pen and loading chute with a ramp. It surprises me that I don't recall how many cows or hogs we had; I'm a counter!

Grandpa had a big red International truck we used to go to the packing sheds to get culls for the cattle. I don't know how the truck was categorized; they loaded the culls from the top, it could dump the culls, and it had a gate for hauling livestock. It was a grand adventure to ride in that BIG noisy truck to the packing shed, where we'd wait our turn to park under a chute. A machine operator would trip a lever and fill the truck with the "culled" vegetables that weren't fit for humans. We'd take that free food home to our beeves. Horses ate hay, and hogs ate slop.

We got a lot of slop from the farm labor camp down the road; they'd give us garbage cans full of their leftovers, which the hogs loved. I went to the labor camp with Grandpa several times to get the slop; it was dis-gus-ting! The flies, the stench, yuck! The labor camp men would fill metal garbage cans with whatever they didn't eat, including bags of tortillas, plastic and all. It all went in the cans together, then was dumped into the hog troughs at home. I didn't care much for the hogs; they made a lot of noise that eerily resembled humans, lived in dirty-stinky pens, and were always rudely (in my opinion) bumping into one another. Cows and horses gave one another space. Anyway, the hogs just creeped me out a bit. I'd sit on the fence and watch as the stinky slop was dumped over the fence. They'd squeal, grunt, and eat like they were starving, much different from the cows or horses. I wondered if they'd eat me if I fell in the pen; I've since learned they would eat me and not leave a trace! (People have gotten away with murder by feeding the remains to hogs.)

I've heard a story dozens of times, about my "city slicker" father going with my grandpa to feed the hogs. (Grandma and Grandpa had bought a hog ranch in Prunedale while still living in Alisal.) Instead of offering to help Grandpa, Dad grabbed a big stick and jumped up on the fence.

Grandpa, probably a little irritated that Dad wasn't helping, looked at him and said, "Hoss, what are you doing up there? And what the hell are you doing with that, boy?" pointing at the big stick.

Dad said, "I was going to use it to fight off the hogs if they chaaarged you."

I don't know that Grandpa laughed at Dad at that moment, but Grandpa's telling of the story has survived over six decades. My Aunt recounted it again not long before she passed, and my cousins still tell it to this day. No matter which family member told the story, they'd belly laugh at my city-slicker father and his New Jersey accent. It was nowhere near as funny to me as it was to them, but my heart always appreciated how they tried to make my father real for me. He was only around my family for a short time before he shipped out to Korea, but he made a lasting impact on them, and they did their best to gift him to me.

We had horses, beef cows, milk cows, hogs, and the despicable chickens. Those chickens were mean, dirty, and dis-gus-ting. Chickens pee and poo simultaneously, leaving a gross, stinky puddle everywhere they walk. We had to gather their eggs, which meant climbing around the barn because they'd hide their nests from us!

Then when it was time for winner, winner, chicken dinner, we had to catch, kill, and pluck the nasty creatures. I remember Gran once sending three of us out to kill and clean some chickens for dinner. I was eight, my brother ten, cousin eleven. We all complained we didn't know how to do it; she tossed her typical, "Well, you'll never learn any younger." at us and shooed us out the door. It's an appropriate statement, but incredibly frustrating and irritating to a kid trying to get out of doing something.

She mimicked the motion with her hands as she said, "You just wring the chicken's neck like this. It's easy. Once they're dead, you just yank the feathers out." Yeah, right! If only it were that simple!

First, you must chase the chicken around the yard until you catch it. That was a chore in and of itself! I don't remember any youthful cursing, but I do recall a great deal of frustration and yelling between the chickens and us. We decided it best to work together to catch each rooster. Have you seen the movie, *Rocky*? Chickens are fast, agile, tricky, and MEAN!

Once you catch a chicken, they want to peck you to death and/or spur you with their nasty chicken feet. After much work, we captured the first rooster and went ahead with our youthful attempt to wring its neck. The result was a mad, and I do mean Banty rooster mad, squawking, fighting for its life, pecking, evil creature who wanted to exact revenge on us, presumably by killing us.

Since the neck wringing didn't work so well for us, my cousin devised a brilliant plan to hang the chickens by the neck until dead. (Fans of western movies will get the reference; it worked very well in the movies. I should say it worked well on humans sitting on a horse under the tree. Often a tall oak tree, but I digress.)

Back to dinner prep . . . we had to hold on to our captured nemesis while cousin (the oldest and presumed wisest) went after some rope, deciding on twine from a hay bale. I held the wicked beast while brother and cousin tried to tie a noose around its neck. The result didn't look like the coiled rope deal they hang people with, but they believed it'd work. They got the rope wrapped around that vicious creature's neck and then had to tie the other end to something.

The clothesline pole seemed the obvious choice. It was metal, sturdy, and much higher than us. So much higher than us that cousin had to find something to stand on to wrap the other end of our chicken killing line to. Again, not so easy because the evil one was struggling, trying to escape from my scrawny arms by flailing, flapping, and pecking. It was horrid; no one wants to get beat up by a chicken!

Finally, one end of the rope was around the rooster's neck, and the other end around the pole. Cousin figured he'd toss it up in the air as high as he could, it'd fall, and that would break its neck. I don't know if you've thought about the physics of that plan; I know we hadn't.

Cousin stood on the wobbly crates, tossed the rooster in the air and towards its impending doom. That dirty bird refused to fall and break its neck! Instead, it flapped its wings, tried to fly away, and spur us with its gross chicken feet. Rooster squawking, kids yelling = Grandma running out to see what the commotion was about. She'd given us, the three of us, a simple task. She chastised us for our foolish attempt at hanging the creature instead of doing as instructed.

We tried to explain the neck wringing didn't work. She shook her head with disgust and told us to chop its head off then. (At the time, we didn't understand she initially told us to wring its neck to minimize our trauma.)

Removing the twine line from the pole took some work, partly because of that incredibly angry and violent rooster on the other end of the line, but the boys managed.

It was decided I would hold the rooster/rope while brother and cousin set up the killing station. They had to find a big block of wood and an axe and get it all set up as I tried to keep the murderous beast away from me. People who say, "Don't be afraid of that little animal, it's more afraid of you than you are it, have never dealt with a chicken, especially a rooster who'd survived a hanging and a neck wringing. They are bloody warriors, or better said, warriors out for blood!

The rooster never stopped squawking through this ordeal, which made the other chickens squawk as well, so we had to yell to be heard. The yard was full of squawking chickens and yelling kids. I thought all that blood-curdling chicken screaming probably sounded like the horror of war. Little did I know, our horror story was about to worsen.

Even as a child, I was amazed that when Abraham took Isaac to the mountaintop to sacrifice him, Isaac obediently climbed up on the altar to await his father killing him. I doubt it was because we didn't tell the rooster he was to be sacrificed for our meal that he refused to simply lay down on the killing block.

The beast continued to fight as we wrangled it onto the block. My job was to hold its head down on the block by pulling down on the rope around its neck. There was no way any of us would hold its head with our hands while another of us swung an axe at it. We'd all seen Uncle Stub with his missing hand and missing fingers. Nope, nope, nope.

Brother was older and stronger, so he held the rooster's back end, which he figured was far enough away from the axe to be safe. Cousin, being the oldest, was the executioner. Whack! Missed. Whack. Missed.

Whack . . . and cousin whacked its head off!

Success! I had the rope with the rooster head in my hand, which I dropped as soon as I realized I was holding a dead chicken's head on a rope. No head, chicken dead, brother let go . . . then that headless, supposed to be dead, chicken flopped off the wood and commenced to running around the yard without a head!!!

If you think it's bad to be chased by a live chicken, let me tell you about the horror, the abject terror, of being a kid chased by a headless chicken with blood coming out of its neck hole, splattering that blood around the yard, and seemingly coming at you to do God only knows what to you!

OMG! We all began screaming in terror, which again caused Gran to investigate. Again, with her disdain and telling us there was nothing to be afraid of, it was a dead chicken. We didn't know to say "F" that, but I'm telling you now, we thought that f'n rooster was possessed! It had no head and ran around the yard for several minutes. As did we. We were exhausted and spent by the time the creature had the decency to lay down and die.

Then we had to kill two more. Dis-gus-ting! We went straight for the axe method for the other two. It was still very creepy when they also ran around without their heads, but it was nowhere near as traumatic as the first one.

Although it was punishing, we weren't being punished. Those were farm chores we'd avoided as long as we could. Our next task, the most disgusting job I've ever had in my life, was to remove the feathers from the dead chickens. Gran told us to just yank them out. Turns out it's not that simple.

Dead chickens still maintain incredible power in keeping their feathers attached to their body. Pulling out the big ones on top wasn't too difficult, but then there were the under layers, the little pin feathers that seemed cemented into the skin. Semi-naked chickens are gross.

Gran told us if we heated up some water and dipped the chickens in the boiling water, their feathers would come out easier. We tried that; it made me want to puke. Not vomit, but puke, which is grosser and more violent than vomiting. What a stench! If that wasn't gross enough, the stinky, wet, chicken feathers stuck to you like something you'd see in an, *I Love Lucy* episode.

It was not funny; I gagged and gagged and whined and complained but wasn't allowed to quit. My cousin decided it'd be easier to burn the feathers off for the second chicken. Trust me here, you don't want to find out for yourself that burnt chicken feathers stink much worse than wet chicken feathers. DIS-GUS-TING! That was also the first time I saw a naked bird; they are G-R-O-S-S! Too gross for me to go into descriptive detail; if you really want to know what they look like, search the internet.

It took us hours to kill and pluck those chickens; we did not have chicken for dinner that night. We took no pride in our work, just disgust. Gran had to clean up our work to cook them the next day. She wasn't happy about it, but we really didn't care that much. We were over it.

Wait, I just had an aha moment ~ perhaps I'm grossed out by naked birds today because of this traumatic experience!! Doesn't really matter; I'm moving on. I don't want to think about that chicken-killing business anymore; I don't want to bring either of those smells back to life or visualize naked birds.

CHAPTER 18

Hauling Livestock

I loved spending the day with Grandpa at the livestock auction yard. It was terrific to run free all day; Gran didn't allow me to roam as he did. There were many adults, some kids, cows, horses, dogs, action, and noise. I didn't mind the cow or horse poop on my boots too much, nor its smell. It was all part of the adventure. It was especially fun when my girl cousin, two years younger, went with us. We got to buy food and beverage, which was a treat because we rarely ate out.

Grandpa's death in '62 didn't change the need for livestock; it just made it a little more challenging. Grandma sold off most of the stock; she'd kept a few horses, one or two beef and milk cows, and the despicable chickens. Grandpa's truck was sold after his passing, so transporting livestock had to be revisited. Another "Grannyism" is "Where there's a will, there's a way."

We still needed to go to the livestock auction, but it was nowhere near as fun. It was hard for me to get loose from Gran's side; we didn't get to stay all day or eat that non-home-cooked food. She was all business.

Hmm, as I consider it now, it was probably uncomfortable for her. A single woman, a dress-wearing woman, with kids, in a man's livestock world. She'd buy one drop calf per trip. A drop calf is a nursing calf that's taken from its mother to be sold for fattening to slaughter. Having sold Grandpa's truck, that long-legged bawling critter was placed in our car's trunk for transportation to our home. Yeah, she'd put a calf in the trunk of the car.

We'd take it home and feed it milk from a bucket that had a big nipple attached to it. We'd feed it that way until it was old enough to eat on its own. It was fun when they were little; they depended on us and quickly became friendly. They were our big pets. It was tough for me as they got bigger because I was tiny, and they'd push me around while trying to get the last of the milk out of the bucket. We named them, petted them, talked to them, and the boys rode them sometimes. The calves/steers didn't like that as much as the boys did. My brother still has a scar on his arm from his collision with a barbed wire fence while riding one of the steers.

Financially, it was often feast or famine due to Gran being a single-income provider with a seasonal business. It was a great treat when we got to go to the movies. It took me three movie trips to realize we got sent to the movies because she'd hired someone to slaughter our pet steer and didn't want us around. We'd be heartsick, especially me, because I was a little more tender-hearted. It didn't seem right or fair, which stopped nothing. I might refuse to eat the meat from our pet critter for a few days, but then I'd return to my regular eating habits.

Every living thing has its day to die.

I don't remember where the lamb came from because we didn't raise any, but one time Gran bought one and then hired some of her Filipino friends to slaughter it. We weren't sent to the movies that day. Not having any attachment to sheep in general, or this one doomed for death specifically, curiosity got the best of the boys.

They decided to watch and taunted me that I was too chicken to watch the slaughtering business. I was the only girl around, so being tough was important, very important. I did not want to watch the slaughter; I'd been a part of that horrific chicken-killing business and did not like it. However, I was not the puny girl they claimed I was. If they could watch, so could I! I was no pansy.

We went to watch the slaughter and the butchering. I was eight, and that was a whole lot to witness. The sheep had been penned but escaped as the men took it out for slaughter. They had to chase it around the half-acre corral before they caught it.

Sheep are noisy, especially sheep with people in hot pursuit. I don't know if it felt their intentions or just didn't want to be caught. It was bleating up a storm, especially once they'd captured it. That was when I started feeling for the critter, whose bleating started sounding like, "Mama,

mama" to my tender little girl ears. They wrangled the ewe to the five-board high fence and tied her to it, not far from where we perched. A couple of the men got on each side of her back end. My tummy didn't feel so good.

She was frantic; bucking, kicking, and bleating for mama with every ounce of her strength. I could feel my heartbeat race and my breathing quicken. My tummy continued to roll around, and I thought about running away from the soon-to-be killing scene. But I couldn't. The boys were there, and the boys were watching this imminent slaughter as well. I could not, would not, show weakness. My people don't show weakness. I repeat, I was no pansy!

Quick as an eye blink, they slit her throat, and I heard her last bleat. I could hear the blood curdling in her throat, drowning her. Then, silence. She was dead. I wanted to puke. There'd been many deaths in my eight years of living; this was the first I'd witnessed. Except for the chicken killing, but this was very different. The slitting of the throat, the blood. Yuck, yuck, yuck. It was violent and not something I ever wanted to see again.

The moment between life and death is cavernous.

The men quickly hung her upside down by her back feet to drain the blood. Instead of letting the blood flow into the dirt, they placed a bucket beneath her. I thought the boys were lying when they told me the men had done so because they planned to make blood sausage with the sheep's blood.

On second thought, I knew they were lying, trying to gross me out and make me look a fool for believing their wild, concocted tale. Civilized people did not do such things! Only heathens or cannibals would do something so vile!

Besides, the men who slaughtered the ewe were good men; they were Grandma's tax clients and had been Grandpa's friends. They'd been in our home many times. I'd been to the cockfights with them and Grandpa. (I might tell you more about the cockfights later, I'm already way off-topic here.)

Although I denied it, the boys could see my distress (I might have turned a sickly shade of green) and kept at me with the blood sausage business. This, while watching that critter's lifeblood drain from its body into a bucket, was getting a bit much for me. I called them liars and said I would go ask Grandma for the truth. They goaded me on to do so, knowing what she had to say would gross me out more. (They were keeping some of the organs to eat as well.) They didn't realize it was also an excuse for me to leave the slaughtering, soon-to-be butchering, scene.

I ran into the house and hammered Gran with questions about the men's intentions with the ewe's blood and organs. She confirmed what the boys told me. My queasy tummy had no desire to go back outside to watch more blood flow or the actual butchering. I found other things that needed my attention inside the house! By the time the boys came in, I was okay; I admitted they hadn't lied, and who cared anyway.

This chapter is supposed to be about livestock hauling, and I've taken you to livestock slaughtering instead. Let's get back to it, shall we?

Remember, Grandma hauled calves in the car trunk from the auction yard to our home, probably ten miles away. She did that because "Where there's a will, there's a way." Which she often coupled with. "Nothing beats a trial but a failure." That was her motto about everything, and that motto was cemented into our brains at very young ages and continually reinforced throughout our lives.

The Salinas Rodeo, "Big Week," was/is a big deal in Salinas, CA. The city goes cowboy-crazy Thursday - Sunday, the third week of July. There's a huge horse parade through the downtown, followed by a grand entry into the arena for the four days of the rodeo. It's just the coolest to ride your horse in the parade, to be part of the hundred horses in the grand entry, and to hang out on your horse all day. It's not quite the old west, but it is a great good time.

One year when my aunt was living in Prunedale, some of her kids decided to ride their horses in the parade, which meant riding their horses from their house to the rodeo grounds. The only time any of my people trailered a horse into town for the grand entry was if they had a little kid who was going to ride. Us big kids were allowed to ride our horses, by ourselves, to the rodeo grounds and stay the day. At the time of this adventure, I'm about to share, my aunt's youngest was about twelve years old. She didn't have a horse; she had a very pokey pony named Sue.

Four of Auntie's five kids saddled up, the youngest on her pokey pony. The three teens said they wouldn't wait on the youngest and her pokey pony. It was a ten-mile horse ride down Highway 101 to the rodeo grounds. Horses walk about four miles per hour, so that's a two-and-a-half-hour ride on a regular horse. Ole pokey Sue would slow them down by at least another hour, so the teens left little sister and her pokey pony at home. Little sister decided all she could do was cry because that was far too long of a ride for her and her pokey pony to make alone, alongside a busy state highway.

The big kids had been gone a short time when one of her mom's brothers stopped by and saw her crying. "What's the matter, honey?"

"The big kids left me. They said Sue is too pokey; they wouldn't wait on us, so now I don't get to ride in the parade."

Uncle said, "You stop your crying, honey. Uncle's going to take you and your pony to the parade. Come on now, everything's going to be just fine."

With that, Uncle wrangled the pony and his niece into his passenger van along with the rest of his family and drove them into town to be in the parade. Yes, Uncle put a pony in his van and transported it ten miles to a parade. (A parade, not a circus, people. My people aren't clowns! They were MacGyvering long before he was created.)

When the big kids got to town, they were shocked little sister had beaten them to town. Truth is, none of us were totally shocked that uncle put the pony in his van. We were all raised on, "Where there's a will, there's a way!"

Around that same time, another of Mom's brothers had bought a pony for his children. Uncle had also recently bought an "irrigator car." An irrigator is a field hand who puts dirty muddy irrigation pipes, shovels, and such in the vehicle's back seat, which puts that ride pretty much in the hooptie car category.

If you don't know, it's a hassle to connect the horse trailer to the truck; well, maybe not a hassle, but it is time-consuming. So, Uncle would occasionally tote the pony around in his irrigator car.

Due to my trauma of having my pet beeves slaughtered for dinner when I was a youngster, when my oldest daughter couldn't take her market hog to the Junior Grand National at the Cow Palace, I decided to keep it as a pet. I'd overcome my fear of hogs because I'd watched my daughter work with her hog. I got to know them as the intelligent, funny, affectionate, and clean creatures they truly are.

And this time I had some say about whether "this little piggy went to market." I said this not-so-little piggy was going to stay home. (FYI -

white pigs sunburn; pigs don't sweat, so they wallow in mud to keep cool. Unlike sheep, a pig will designate one area of its pen for toileting, one for eating, and the rest for hanging out. Sheep, those fluffy, not-so-bright critters, walk and poop, and poop while eating. Pigs have an undeserved bad rep. But again, I digress.)

At the same time I decided to keep the hog, my youngest decided to buy the ag barn's bummer lamb that was headed for slaughter. (Bummer lambs are those rejected by their mother at birth or couldn't be fed by their mother for one reason or another. Unable to be paired with adoptive ewes, bummer lambs are bottle-fed and raised by humans from birth. This particular bummer lamb, Squirt, was one of four lambs the ewe birthed.

Squirt was the smallest, weakest, and least likely to survive. The ewe instinctively knew she wouldn't produce enough milk for all four, this one would probably die anyway, so she kicked Squirt to the curb to minimize her loss.) My youngest had bottle-fed Squirt a few times at the ag barn and has an even more tender heart than me. She couldn't stand the idea of a slaughter, so she bought the bummer with the money she'd been saving for a Disneyland trip.

During our move from Hollister to Los Banos, husband put the hundred fifty-pound lamb in a crate in the back of his truck for transportation to Los Banos. He'd attempted to borrow a trailer to transport the four-hundred-pound hog to LB; sadly, the trailer was broken. We had no idea how we'd get the hog to Los Banos.

No disrespect intended; however, my husband had no farm experience. He was a city slicker and not as devoted to saving these two farm animals from their destiny as were youngest and I. His only experience with anything other than a dog was caring for his Grandpa Sandy's duck that froze to death with its feet in a coffee can while in husband's care.

Not blaming the duck's death on him; just saying it was freezing there in Iowa when he left the duck outside with a coffee can of water to drink and no shelter. Cutting him a little slack, I'll tell you he was only a boy of eight, without experience. Anyway, I just knew I would have to figure out this hog transportation on my own. If it was to be, it was up to me! And, where there's a will, guaranteed there's a way!!!

Husband and daughter left Hollister with the lamb in a crate in the back of the truck. I'd just washed my car and given the hog, Petunia, her weekly bath when a flash of brilliance came upon me. The hardest part of hauling livestock was the loading of said livestock. Once they were loaded up, they simply rode the ride. My car was bathed, my hog was washed, and she'd just peed and pooped, so when she saw the bread on the back seat of my car, she hopped in for a taste. Whoop! Whoop!

I slammed those back doors of my huge, four-door Oldsmobile (a grandpa car) and hopped in the front seat, not thinking about my attire or anything else but getting to Los Banos. These were pre-cell phones, so no one knew my plans or whereabouts. Petunia, who, snout to tail, filled up the entire back seat of my boat of a car, door to door, seemed okay. We headed out on the highway, not so much looking for adventure as we were destination bound. She was managing well. Truthfully, I was pleased with myself.

Typical for hogs, she was talkative. I didn't understand her Pig Latin (ha-ha) or whatever pig language she spoke, but I did understand it was a different experience for her. To soothe her, I kept up a conversation and sang to her. FYI - I did not recite "This Little Piggy Went to Market"!

Our destination was fifty-one miles away and would take roughly an hour due to the climb over Pacheco Pass. Pacheco Pass is a low mountain pass in California's Diablo Mountain Range in southeastern Santa Clara County. It's the main route through the hills separating the Central Coast/Silicon Valley and the Great Central Valley. Although it's been dramatically improved since the 1960s (when it was known as "Blood Alley") and the building of San Luis Reservoir, it remains a tricky traverse over the mountain range.

There are two lanes in each direction with considerable heavy truck traffic. From the base of the Pass on the west side, one climbs over a thousand feet via twisty, winding roads and an area known as the wind tunnel. Those heavy trucks can cause you to slow down to thirty mph while other travelers are zooming along at eighty-five mph. Although the cement dividers between oncoming traffic are there to protect, they seem to call your vehicle to meet them.

Once you reach the summit, you drop twelve hundred feet as you enter Los Banos. From the west side, it's twelve miles to reach the summit, then eleven miles to drop to the Los Banos elevation of 115'. There aren't many options to pull off the highway over the Pass, so one must be in the moment for this drive.

Petunia and I were doing well on our trek; we were talking. I was singing to her, and people were staring. I opted to drive in the slow lane unless I needed to pass. I can't count the people who passed me and then slowed down to look and point. It was as though they thought, "Wait. Did I just see a huge hog in the back seat of that car?"

We managed the Pass just fine, then as I slowed to approach the four-way stop at "9 Mile Station" (nine miles west of Los Banos), Petunia became unsettled. She placed her front hoof on the console. "Ruh-roh, this is not good!" rolled through my mind. One hundred and fifteen pound me tried to push four-hundred-pound Petunia back into her designated traveling space. She became increasingly restless, so I pulled off the highway to get her under control. Or so I planned. I pulled over to a stop . . . and she transferred to the front seat! YIKES!!! No bueno!

When she hopped into the front seat, her front end faced the passenger side. I was pinned in the seat behind the steering wheel. It was then, and just then, that I realized this might not have been such a great MacGyver move after all. I was pinned behind the steering wheel of my car with a four-hundred-pound hog on my lap!

Crikey! What was I to do? I was on a side road between two cities, trapped behind the wheel by a four-hundred-pound hog, and no one knew my whereabouts. I couldn't phone a friend, and couldn't stay in that space forever, so I had to come up with a solution! On that day, I was thankful I wasn't tall. I moved the seat back as far as possible and managed to squeeze in front of Petunia, who sat her butt down on the seat behind me when I did so. Even though the seat was all the way back, I remained pressed up against the steering wheel because there was a ginormous, unmoving hog sitting on the seat behind me.

What did I do? What could I do but press on to our destination? With my chest pressed against the wheel, my arms out at forty-five-degree angles, I got back on the highway. We had fourteen miles to go, so onward I drove. We'd driven about nine miles when we came upon the outskirts of Los Banos, where I needed to slow down for traffic. Petunia seemed fine while we were moving; she became restless when we slowed down. I knew there to be a bevy of traffic lights from the west side of town to the east side, so I decided to take a side road to circumnavigate the city traffic.

I slowed and turned onto Ortigalita, and Petunia remained restless behind me. I thought it best to pull over to settle her, so I edged to the side of the road. As I did, I failed to notice how close I was to the dry irrigation ditch. My car slid down the ditch, rolled onto its side, almost upside down, and came to rest in said ditch on the passenger side with the driver-side wheels up in the air! Oh no, oh no, oh no! This was my worst idea EVER!!!!!

I was in the front seat of a car, on its side, with a four-hundred-pound hog smooshed against the passenger side, pretty much on her snout. (In the game of "Pass the Pigs," that's called a "leaning jowler.") I thought, "OMG! Petunia could panic and hoof me to death!" I was also very concerned she would have a heart attack and die. Pigs, like people, can literally be frightened to death. Our hearts are so similar that pig heart valves have been used in humans for decades.

This was a time for action, so I climbed into the back seat and opened the rear passenger door that faced the sky. That was no easy task because I drove a big boat of a car with very heavy doors! Once I'd opened the door, I climbed up, out, and jumped onto the ground; I was thankful I was safe and on solid ground!

Before I even had time to think, I heard, "Are you all right, ma'am? Don't worry. The paramedics are on the way!"

"Um, I'm fine; I don't need paramedics. I'm just worried about my pig."

"Your pig? Do you have a pig in that car?"

So right about then is when I totally evaluated the consequences of my actions; how ridiculous I looked and sounded. I was wearing my very long blonde hair in a "Pebbles" (*The Pebbles and Bamm-Bamm Show*) ponytail on top of my head because I needed it out of my way for hog washing. Also, due to hog washing, I was wearing a crop top, bike shorts with an overskirt (I like to dress fashionably no matter the task), and mud boots. I realized I looked the epitome of a ditzy blonde!

A big pickup with a gnarly winch pulled up. The driver offered to pull my car out of the ditch. I accepted the offer, and he winched the vehicle back onto its four wheels. I surveyed the car and was thankful there was no evident damage. Still concerned about my hog, I tried to open the car door. Petunia remained smooshed against the passenger door; she refused to return my gaze. She would not speak to me. I was concerned about what people thought of me, but much more concerned about my hog's wellbeing.

About that time, the paramedics rolled up. "Are you okay? Do you need help?"

"Thanks, I'm fine. I'm just worried about my hog in the car."

"Wait. What? Did you say you have a hog in that car?"

"Um, yeah." That was when they started to laugh.

"I've been doing this eighteen years, and I've never seen a hog in a car. I need to see this."

I'm 5'2", but I was shrinking with every comment. I thought it might be best to let Petunia out of the car so she'd feel grounded; she'd just experienced the unwanted ride of her life! Couldn't do it because she had her hoof on the door lock, which was a good thing because I might not have been able to catch her once she was freed from the car.

We were on the outskirts of town (meaning city police didn't respond to calls), so that's when the California Highway Patrol showed up, followed by Fish and Wildlife, Fish and Game, and a County Deputy Sheriff. Those rascals were calling one another to come to see the show! I repeated my story to the CHP and Deputy, now fearful I'd be ticketed for hauling livestock in my car. I didn't know if it was legal; I'd just realized it was a bit dangerous.

Now I was horrified and humiliated. I was moving into a new city, and this was my grand intro! Yikes, I prayed the media didn't show up and dreaded a blonde joke.

About that time, the tow truck driver showed up. (I don't know who called a tow truck.) Mr. Tow Truck Driver got out of his truck, surveyed the scene, put his hands on his hips, and before he spoke, I could tell this was the guy who'd make the blonde joke.

He said, "Well, that's about a Portagee move." I loved him instantly, and we've been dear friends for the twenty-seven years since my grand arrival in town. I didn't know then that the tow truck driver also owned a local newspaper! By God's grace, he didn't have a camera with him on that hog-haulin day!

Moments later, my husband rolled up in his truck and parked across the road. Someone had phoned him at the new house, said his wife had been in an accident, was okay, and supplied the location. As he walked across the road towards me, a rubbernecker (the road was lined with them now) said, "You must be the husband."

"How can you tell?"

"By the look on your face."

"It looks like my wife is okay. Do you know what happened?"

"No one knows what happened. They're still trying to get the hog out of the car."

"What? She's got that hog in the car?"

"Yeah, you mean she doesn't drive around with it all the time?"

My city-slicker husband was so embarrassed he wanted little to do with me. He saw I was fine, and he kept his distance. My new best friend, the tow truck driver, put my car on his flatbed and drove us to our new home, where I had a much harder time getting my hog out of the car than I had getting her into it. Thankfully, she was fine. She did take a little hog chomp out of the dash when it rolled and had pooped, but other than that, she was fine, as was my car.

About a week later, I was rolling into town and hadn't realized the speed limit had dropped from sixty-five to fifty-five. I was doing about seventy-two and got pulled over by law enforcement. I don't try to talk my way out of a ticket; I own my mistakes. The officer wrote me up, and as he handed me my ticket, he said, "Excuse me, Ma'am, I don't want to be rude . . . but isn't this the pig car?" Insert mic drop.

My hog-hauling story has literally traveled the world. One of my C21 colleagues laughs so hard that she cries nearly every time she hears the tale. She's promised to tell it at my celebration of life many, many years from now.

◇◇◇

Thanks, Gran, for teaching me, "Where there's a will, there's a way." That way might only sometimes be the best!!

P.S. If you were a *MacGyver* fan, you've got no room to be dissing folks like my people, who were also inventive when problem-solving. For those who don't know, *MacGyver* was a TV series from 1985-1992. Angus MacGyver was a secret agent; he became educated as a scientist and served as a bomb technician in the Special Forces in the Army during Vietnam.

The guy used whatever was available to solve any problem when he was secret agenting out in the field. He carried a Swiss Army knife, seemed to always have duct tape and matches, and kept his calm when he found himself in life-threatening situations . . . which was just about every episode.

My people carried pocketknives and used baling wire and duct tape to solve many a problem. By the way, duct tape was invented by a worried mother! Vesta Stoudt had two sons serving in the Navy in 1940 and was working at a factory when she got to thinking that there had to be a better way to package cartridges. The cartridge boxes were sealed with wax and then taped to keep the moisture out. The boxes didn't always open properly, which was dangerous in the heat of battle.

That her son's and other mothers' sons' lives were endangered because they couldn't get a box opened quickly enough really ticked Vesta off. She had an idea to fabricate a tape made from strong, water-resistant cloth to wrap the cartridge boxes in. Using her concept, the cartridge boxes could be opened in a split second; however, her company wasn't interested.

Mama was still worried about all those boys. So, she wrote a letter to President Franklin Roosevelt. Her letter detailed her proposal and included a hand-drawn diagram of her product and her plea to his conscience, "Please, Mr. President, do something about this at once; not tomorrow or soon, but now."

Surprisingly, the President passed Vesta's idea to military officials, who quickly reviewed it and approved it! Johnson and Johnson got credit for the invention; however, now you know the truth, a worried mama created one of the most versatile products used today.

Yes, that's more information than you needed . . . no, it's not a useless fact. I bet you find an opportunity to use that in a conversation. You are welcome!

CHAPTER 19

You Know What Memory Really Stands Out from My Childhood?

Most of my cousins lived with their moms and dads, but my brother and I lived with our mother's parents. Living with Grandma, Grandpa, my aunt, uncles, and a couple cousins was my normal. I knew my father died before I was born, knew I had a mother who came around occasionally and accepted I lived where I did. As I said, that was normal to me.

I don't remember longing for my mother before second grade; I felt my grandparents' love. Having not lived with Mom for any length of time since I was five days old, I didn't know her well enough to miss her. My longing for Mom originated in my classroom.

Gran told me that I'd once handed her a paper I'd written on which I'd earned an "A." She praised me for the grade; I scoffed and said I didn't deserve the "A" because my writing was a lie. Upon questioning me, I told her I'd made up a story about my parents, brother, and me because the kids in class repeatedly asked why I spoke of grands and cousins instead of parents and siblings.

That was in the early 1960s when nuclear families were the norm; I didn't have a nuclear family, and therefore I was a misfit. As is typical for an eight-year-old, I wanted to be like everyone else, to fit in.

My home life was unconventional and chaotic. Fighting, shooting, the law showing up; oh, how I began to yearn to live in a "mother, father, sister, brother" home! I longed for the home life I saw on television, for gentle parents who explained life. I undoubtedly imagined such a life, especially after spending the summer with my grandparents in New Jersey when I was eight. An entire summer in a traditional home! Granted, Grandpa and Grandma were old parents to my aunt and uncle, who were two and three years older than me.

Nevertheless, they were a nuclear family, and I was already used to old grandparents. There was no chaos in the Brett household! They lived in a neighborhood, we played with kids, went to Vacation Bible School, visited family, went to the shore, New York City, Washington, D.C., Arlington, and I don't recall wanting to go home. That summer, I learned that life didn't have to be as it was in my California home. It could be free of chaos and stable … and I wanted such a life!

At the age of eight, I didn't know a thing about gambling, but I knew I'd hit the mother lode of jackpots the following year when Mom married #5, a friend of one of her brothers.

Number five lived three doors down and across the road from that uncle, his wife, and their son. Mom's sister, her husband, and their five kids lived next door to #5. Just up the hill from #5 was another brother, his wife, and their two kids. No wonder the road was named Paradise Canyon Road!!!

Mom asked if my brother and I wanted to live with her and #5. I don't recall the moment, but I'm positive my resounding yes was out of my mouth before she finished the question.

I didn't realize Mom and Grandma had to discuss a potential move. (Grandpa had passed by then.) Mom was my mother; I knew kids truly belonged to, and with, their mother, ergo, bye-bye Grandma's house. I also thought Grandma would be happy for me to go. I recalled the bitter sting of overhearing a conversation between Gran and one of her tax clients.

The client noticed my grandmother and I shared the same name, and asked if I was Grandma's little girl. My interpretation of her response wounded me to my core for decades. She responded, "Well, Louise had her, but she just dropped her off like a cat dropping a litter of kittens. I raised her, so she is my little girl."

Meouch. Gran thought of me as a stray kitten dropped at her door? I was obviously unwanted by Mom, but now I learned I wasn't wanted by Gran. I was taken in out of pity! That was a Sunday gut punch that affected my behavior for years. Decades later, I learned some of my cousins resented my "goody two shoes" attitude, but as I explained, I was unwanted by all and had nowhere else to go. In my mind, I needed to behave well so I'd be kept. I didn't want to be "Little Orphan Geneva Marie"!

Today, as I think this through, Gran's words make sense, they weren't as harsh as they impacted me, and frankly, they're true. I don't want to raise any of my grandchildren, it would be a burden, but I would stand in the gap if needed.

I also know my grandmother adored me; I was her golden girl child. However, the words she never meant for me to hear or knew I heard cut my spirit like rusty, jagged knives. Dear reader, words have enormous power. Power that can devastate or elevate a life, please be careful with the words you choose to speak. Even when you think the one you're speaking of can't hear.

Okay, back to Paradise and my dream come true. Glory Hallelujah, those were the best years of my childhood, bar none! Mother, father, sister, brother became reality, MY reality!! Number five was a good man and a great stepfather. He didn't have children and embraced us as his own. I even called him Dad, which was HUGE for me; my deceased father was my hero. This was my fictional "A" paper assignment come true. I lived in a chaos free nuclear family; I was surrounded by my cousins, who had served as friends in place of friends when I lived with Gran. Life wasn't perfect, but I was joyful and happy.

I didn't appreciate that no adult accompanied me to my first day at my new school; I was told where the bus stop was and rode the bus alone. I didn't like it, but up to that point, a lot of my life had been, "You'll never learn any younger; figure it out yourself," so I did. Our new life with Mom had more structure and order, which I adapted to quickly.

We ran up and down the canyon, in the woods, in and out of one another's homes, and traveled to rodeos. I made neighborhood friends and had more freedom to wander than I'd ever had at Gran's. (There weren't many kids near Gran's home, and she always kept me close.)

I was so busy loving the life I'd longed for that I didn't miss Gran or the cousins I left behind. Those cousins and I weren't that close even though we lived together. We were living parallel lives at Gran's, each doing their own life. I didn't want to go back to visit, but Mom made me do so occasionally. I felt more out of place than ever in my life! Additionally, I carried the guilt of knowing how deeply I'd wounded Gran, so my visits were indeed awkward.

Can you imagine? Gran truly believed the best place for me was with her. Yet I denied her and her love, saying no matter what she'd sacrificed for me, I wanted to live with the woman who'd abandoned me shortly after birth. A woman who'd changed few diapers and never comforted me in my time of need. Yeah, it was awkward, to say the least.

At the time, I didn't know that Gran had agreed to let me leave because she thought I'd get homesick and would come back quickly. My two-week New Jersey trip that turned into a summer-long stay wasn't a fluke; I didn't want to live in her household. Nothing personal, I just wanted my dream, and I wanted peace, but I never said that to Gran in that specific way.

Christmas, that first year on Paradise, Auntie bought all her kids' bicycles, and she bought one for me! Now I had the type of freedom my brother and boy cousins had. This girl was on fire! I loved having nearby friends and the freedom to run the road. As I said, life wasn't perfect, but it was spectacularly different and better for me. My life was almost TV show quality! There was an order to things. Dinner conversation included "How was school today?" Mom didn't wear heels and pearls, but I didn't mind one bit. This life was my dream come true! Paradise indeed!

I continued to get good grades in school but never gave it my best. Frankly, I don't know that I ever gave school my best effort. I was bright, I am bright, and I could get away with giving "some" effort, which resulted in A's and B's pretty much by showing up. No since wishing I'd have done differently because I didn't.

Let's fast forward to my 40th high school reunion for a minute or two to get to the meat of this story. (The meat? Am I saying what we just went through was hors d'oeuvres? Yeowza!)

One of my elementary school friends from my dream come true life on Paradise Canyon Road and I stood alongside one another, looking at the room full of our classmates, when she said, "Neva, do you know what memory really stands out from my childhood?" I said, "No. What memory is that?"

"Do you remember that day your dad was running down the road, and your mom was chasing him, shooting at him?"

Dear reader, although I too vividly, and I do mean vividly, remember that day, her comment was so unexpected I felt like a fly getting sucked out the car window at 89 miles an hour! I literally felt like I was spinning on the inside. There was no way I could have expected her comment. We hadn't stayed in touch over the years, and that's not exactly the kind of thing one just tosses out there . . . except it was, and she did.

One of my kids thought it rude of her to toss it out like that and churn my world. As I explained, it was a very traumatic experience for her as well, and very outside her life experience. I was seasoned at witnessing family shooting at family. I was one of the few people on the planet that she could discuss that impactful day with. Hmm, I wonder if she ever told her parents what she'd witnessed. Don't be judging my childhood friend for her normalcy.

Anyway, I quipped back, "Yeah, that memory really stands out from my childhood too." I didn't have a mirror, but I felt my face flush through just about every imaginable shade of red before I excused myself and walked away to regain my composure. My head was spinning, my heart was racing, my stomach was flipping, and you know me well enough by now to know my eyes were dry.

I found a place where I could stand alone for a few moments to pull myself together without risking speaking to someone while I was so spinny. I stood there and relived the scene as I had done countless times before. Oddly enough, after the mental run-through, I felt validated.

That day, those moments, dramatically changed my life and had always seemed very otherworldly. My friend's recollection brought it back as truth and fact. I appreciated that, not so much that I sought her out and relived it again, but enough that it seemed to finally settle. Fifty years later, it found its resting place within.

For a time, I was hopeful my friend would be at our 50th reunion so I could get more details about what we said to one another and who else was with us. After giving it more thought, nah, I don't want to do that after all. Well, maybe. I just might ask her the next time I see her. I do want to know. (Update - she wasn't at our 50th, so time will tell if I ever ask those questions.)

Right now, you're probably thinking, "WHAT??? Details, woman! I want DETAILS about this memory!"

Sooooo, about two years into my dream come true life on Paradise Canyon, friends and I were riding our bikes up and down the canyon one afternoon. We parked at our school bus stop to plan where to go next. We lived in Prunedale, an area of gentle rolling hills where many homes are situated 10 to 20 feet above the road with driveways sloping down to the road. Our bus stop was on the west side of Auntie's house, who lived west of us, and at the bottom of the long uphill driveway to Uncle's.

Three or four of us were sitting on our bikes when we saw beloved #5 running down the middle of the road toward us. He was moving at a fairly rapidly pace. Seeing a grown man running down the road was quite unusual, but we didn't have time to process the scene. Milliseconds after we saw him, we heard the "pew, pew, pew" of bullets being fired, then we saw my mother walking down the road towards us, shooting at #5.

"Pew, pew, pew." No words, just Mom doing a *Dirty Harry* intentional walk towards the perp, the "pew, pew, pew," and its echoing in the canyon.

We were all so transfixed by the movie scene playing out in front of us that we didn't even take a moment to look at one another to see if we were all experiencing the same thing. About this time, #5 realized he'd best change direction because his pew, pew, pewing wife was hot on his heels. He veered left to scramble up the hill, attempting to get behind the house directly across from the bus stop.

As he was grabbing dirt and ice plant on his way up, we could see the bullets hitting the ground behind him. "Pew, pew, pew." We heard him shout, "Ow!" and grab his ear. We never thought of moving. We were transfixed. Mom kept coming at him, "pew pewing," until she ran out of bullets. When she ran out of ammunition, she turned and ran back to the house. She walked while shooting at him, but ran home when her gun was empty. Number five was presumably still hiding behind the house across from the bus stop.

As Mom pew, pew, pewed, I realized my dream come true life, this nuclear family I'd longed for, had come to its end. Shattered to pieces, in fact. I knew their marriage, our life, would not recover from today's drama.

I don't recall how my friends and I parted or what, if anything, was said among us. I have a very hazy recollection of Mom, my brother, and me in the house that night and my great sadness that my best childhood had ended. Undoubtedly, it'd be back to Grandma's:-(

Many years passed before I learned what had transpired before that life-altering event. Mom said #5 came home from a rodeo and confessed he was leaving her because he was in love with another woman. Neither of them noticed my brother in the kitchen as #5 spoke the words that shattered our life beyond redemption. Mom listened to his confession and stood stone-cold still and silent for an uncomfortable amount of time.

He broke the silence, "Louise, you haven't said anything. What do you think about what I told you?"

She slowly turned to him, her beautiful blue eyes hardened to steel, and said, "I think you better run, mother fucker, because I'm going to fucking kill you."

Number five knew Mom was a scrapper with a penchant for fighting. We'd been at the Coarsegold Rodeo the year before when one of #5's former girlfriends made a comment to Mom that she took offense to. It didn't matter that we were in a family restaurant; Mom went at her and kicked her ass before the fight was broken up.

Some people will say they're going to kill you figuratively, and others mean what they say. Number five was in the midst of a deciphering moment as to whether his wife's comment was meant figuratively or literally. No matter how she meant it, she was definitely mad enough for him to recognize he should leave her alone, so he went outside.

Mom calmly located her .22 pistol and ammunition and then turned to my brother, "Ronnie Lee, load this gun like you were taught. Right now. Load this gun for me."

My brother's heart was broken. He knew Mom and knew she intended to kill this man we loved so dearly. He remembered she'd already attempted to "de-penis" #4 by gunshot.

Now, my brother's faced with being an accomplice to Mom killing this wonderful man who had provided us with the home we'd always longed for with our mother. He knew that life was over. So, my brother put the bullets in backward. Then he ran out of the house and shouted, "Run #5, run! Mom's got a gun, and she's going to kill you!" (Brother called him by name, however, it's easier for you to identify Mom's husbands by number.)

Mom walked outside and tried to fire the gun. She realized what her son, her 13-year-old son, had done. She yelled, "You little asshole!" as she emptied the gun and reloaded it.

Mom raised the gun and fired. Number five now understood that Mom was indeed serious, and did, in fact, literally intend to kill him. He spun around and ran down our driveway to the road. He ran, but she didn't. She walked. She walked with purpose and intent. Intent on killing this cheating husband who'd just broken her heart, their marriage, and her beautiful life with her children. She was devastated, and he was about to pay for his cheating ways with his life.

As you know, Mom fired at him until she emptied the gun, then ran back to the house and demanded my thirteen-year-old brother reload the weapon. He refused. He, too, loved #5; besides that, we all know shooting people is not okay.

So, um. What memory really stands out from your childhood or your high school reunion? Am I still winning in the doozy of unique experiences?

◇◇◇

I read this chapter to my forty-four-year-old son, the father of three daughters. He didn't make any sounds or have any comments like his older sister did when I read it to her. Not even a "Wow," a chuckle, or his typical, "That's funny."

He remained silent for a few moments after I said, "End of chapter." Frankly, I felt slightly uncomfortable; he's very smart, quick-witted, and a wordsmith. I wondered if he thought me a poor writer . . . and then he spoke.

"That's so sad. Mom, I'm sorry you had such a hard childhood. I wish I could have raised you."

Woof.

Friend, his reaction, his beautiful heartfelt words, were as unanticipated as my childhood friend's retelling of the memory. I was again sucked out the window at 89 mph, gut-punched, and heart-stabbed. I was lightheaded and spinny all over again, perhaps even worse this time. That my own child who knew ME, pitied me, was intolerable. That his reaction to what his no quitter, no pansy, get it done, get through it, gotta keep on smiling, positive, where there's a will there's a way, overcomer mother, wrote elicited his pity . . . was nearly too much to bear. What will strangers think?

His reaction caused me to pause and reconsider sharing my story. I can't be having people feel sorry for me. I'm not. It's my story, my people's story, and I am who I am because of it. It's all happened FOR me, not TO me. His words crushed me because I didn't write from sadness; I didn't write to elicit pity. I can't tolerate pity on me. I can't be telling my story if people are going to pity me. Nope. Nope. Nope!

In the milliseconds after he spoke his loving words, my book publishing dream was in a death spiral, heading to the ground to crash and burn. Sorry Gran, sorry Auntie, I was gonna honor that promise to tell our people's story, but this might be too much for sensitive Geneva Marie.

In the next moment, I realized that I can't control what people think and must honor my word to Gran, Auntie, and me. I can't not tell the story that I've already written, which can help countless others heal and grow, simply because I'm afraid of what people will think about me. That they might feel sorry for or pity me. No matter the public's thoughts, I'M NO PANSY!!!

And then, my heart was in my throat; I was as overwhelmed with love for my son as the first time I held him, perhaps even more so. That first moment we met was filled with wonder and visions of the man I hoped he'd become, and at this moment, he was all that and then some. Such a beautiful human, man, father, and son.

My son's hurt for me was even worse than my own hurt in real-time. Just this moment, I realized that my reaction to his response was because he saw behind the curtain. He saw behind the curtain that even I haven't always seen behind. No matter how entertainingly I told the story, my son saw the sad and wounded little girl who often felt helpless and alone amid family. Yeah, I hid her behind that curtain, even from me.

Thank you, son, for seeing us and for freeing us. You, who've had your own heart hurts.

I love you forever.

(Hmm, I might get that tattoo yet! Oops, you don't know that story yet. Let's see if you remember reading about the tattoo later in the book. I bet you didn't anticipate I'd toss a quiz at you:-)

GENEVA MARIE BRETT

CHAPTER 20

Children, Take This Equalizer

It was probably the mid-1960s; Auntie was a single mother of five and lived about ten miles from us. One afternoon a man my mother had been dating stopped by my aunt's house, asking for Mom's whereabouts. It was apparent he'd been drinking; nah, I'm not going to be polite here; he was obviously drunk. Drunk and obnoxious from the first word out of his mouth. Auntie told him she didn't know where her sister was, and he said she was lying. They went back and forth with that two or three times. He became more belligerent with each question and denial; his language worsened as her children uncomfortably watched the back and forth.

Auntie's little children weren't exposed to the chaos and violence I witnessed in my home; she sheltered them from such behavior. Although they weren't accustomed to chaos, you can sometimes feel a thing is going to happen before it happens. The air carries some kind of energy. You may not know what is going to happen, but you sense something's going to happen.

The last time the man called my aunt an f'n, lying, you know what b word, he also slugged her so hard she flew up against the wall and slid down it like a cartoon character. She didn't have little stars circling her head like the cartoon characters, but she was obviously dazed and defenseless. That didn't bother him one bit. He went at her, continuing to beat her and cuss at her for allegedly lying about my mom's whereabouts.

Her children, aged three to eight, screamed, cried, and attacked him. As he punched my aunt, her kids bit him, kicked him, hit him, jumped on his back, and did everything they could to get him off their mother. He tossed them off him like he was flicking fleas.

As she was somewhat recovering, she began to fight back, but to no avail. He was a foot taller than my aunt, at least seventy pounds heavier, and a man with a physical job. Obviously, my aunt and her kids were no match for him. This brawl went on for several minutes before he got tired of the fight, got up, stumbled out the door, and drove off.

My bloody aunt did her best to calm her little children. Once she got them settled, she packed them up and headed to her mama's house. As soon as she walked through the door Gran knew she'd been beaten. Auntie told her what had happened. Grandma silently went from room to room, picking up what she'd stored behind each door, and then handed those items to each of us kids. She gave us lead pipes, hammers, and tire irons. Equalizers is what she called them.

Gran was a small woman; four foot ten to be exact, she didn't own a gun, was single, and had four minor children living with her. She kept a pitchfork behind her bedroom door, along with a lead pipe and a tire iron. She stored at least three equalizers behind all but the living room door. I never knew why she had so many. That day, I realized it was in case she needed to arm a posse as she was doing.

Wow, I just realized I was a posse member, although Gran didn't make us raise our right hand and take an oath. The blood running through our veins was our oath. Being in a posse might look cool in westerns, but it's not so cool in real life. It's an enormous responsibility to hunt down a wrong doer and mete out justice, especially for a child.

Gran told us to take those equalizers she handed us and get in the car, which we did without question. Once in the car, we asked where we were going; she said we were going to find that cowardly SB (her by word for son of a you know what) and beat him to death. She didn't say beat him half to death; she said beat him to death. She was serious, she meant what she said, and we knew that.

We drove around town to every bar he frequented, his house, his work, and favorite cafes. By God's grace, we didn't find him that day. Had we found him, we would have done as Grandma instructed. Gran was fifty, Auntie twenty-five, I was eleven, and Auntie's children were eight, seven, six, five, and three. We would have literally killed a man had we found him.

Today I shudder at the thought of what we might have done and how it would have impacted us for the rest of our lives. But on that day, we had no choice. We'd have used our equalizers and made sure that man never attacked another woman and that he knew what it felt like to be beaten.

Well, not too long after that day, he did learn what it was like to be beaten, bloody, and bruised; one of my uncles made sure of that. Gran phoned her toughest son, told him what had transpired and instructed him to mete out some justice for his sister. Uncle drove the six-hundred-mile round trip solely for that purpose.

Yeah, so that's a lot to absorb. I'd forgotten about it until a cousin and I were talking on a road trip. You might wonder how someone could forget such an event; perhaps it's what they call post-traumatic stress memory loss. I had an excessive amount of such events in my young life.

This was a challenging memory, and I haven't recalled it to the degree that it's vivid or I feel it again. I don't want to do that; I'm setting it free on these pages. I'm a gentle person, perhaps in part because of the violence around me, and to think of the violent act I might have, we might have, committed on another human being is unsettling. To fight back "in the moment" is one thing; premeditated is a whole other ethical dilemma. I remain grateful to God for saving us from ourselves.

Does it bother me that my uncle beat up the bad guy? Nope. Does it bother me that Gran instructed her son to beat up the bad guy? Nope. Does it bother me that that doesn't bother me? I'm not sure, but I don't think so. The Bible does say, "An eye for an eye." Just sayin'. I can't tolerate a bully. Underneath their meanness, they're actually cowards. Nothing wrong with being afraid, but there's everything wrong with being mean, especially to a lesser one.

Friend, if you've had big events like this in your life, please consider writing about them. You don't have to tell the world as I'm doing. However, you do need to get it out of you. It's not healthy to keep this kind of thing pushed down inside you. I've learned that writing helps you process your fear, shame, conflicting thoughts, and emotions. As you write, long-lost memories and emotions well up and spill out. It's rough in the moment, but the release is well worth it.

Writing is much easier than verbally telling of the experiences because it's a slower pace, which allows more memories and feelings to emerge. It's easy to get distracted if you're talking to someone; they ask a question or make a comment, and the thread can be lost. Writing and burning your past also keeps your secret a secret if that's what you need. Ashes don't talk. People do. Not all people, but most. Do whichever you need to do. Just do it.

Writing this book is helping me move on from things I thought I'd left far, far, in my past, but in truth, lay beneath my surface. We bury what we couldn't get rid of, hoping it would go away. It doesn't go away until you face it and set it, and you, free.

CHAPTER 21

Come Get Your Kids

Working in the produce sheds, fields, and construction was comfortable for many migrants like my people. They worked alongside others who'd made the same journey, understood their life and lifestyle, and maybe even came from near the same area. When their children became old enough to work, they'd take summer jobs in the sheds and fields. Some quit school early and went straight to work or got married.

That's what their life would consist of anyway, work and family. It was hard work, but enjoyable to work and talk with people like you, people you grew up with, people who understood you. Even into her late thirties, my mother loved working in the produce sheds.

As a teen, I thought it embarrassing that she did so. I wanted education and to rise higher; manual labor, common labor, was not for me. I worked a day in the strawberry fields when I was twelve, one single day, and I acknowledged that was no life for me.

Many of the boys I went to high school with worked in the fields and the sheds during summer break. I decided I'd have no such life. However, I did work a summer at a packing house in my early twenties for vacation money. I stood on my feet all day, cutting the butts off carrots as they came down the conveyer belt. It was terrible! I was nauseous at first; I didn't know if I was standing still, and the conveyer was moving or vice versa. I didn't know anyone on the line; most of the other workers spoke a different language, and I did not like the work at all. Definitely not for me.

My mom and her younger sister enjoyed the produce work and working with their friends. Mom's brothers all went into construction like their daddy. After a hard day's work in the shed, the field, or in construction, many wanted "a cold one" before heading home. Several bars near the sheds became popular hangouts for my people. The Five High, 526 Club, Lettuce Inn, and B&E there in Alisal offered drinks, conversation, dancing, and the occasional fight.

Working with your hands, being strong, rough, and tough was commonplace among the migrants. Being the strongest, and the toughest, carried a lot of weight in those days. Country life depended on strong men, and being that man was a source of pride. No matter where you lived, a man might have to defend whatever he had from some ill-intentioned individual.

Mom's generation were children of the exodus from the "Dust Bowl" of the 1930s and 40s. As people and livestock starved to death because of the drought and the winds, survivors were evicted from their lands without a dime throughout the Southern Plains of the USA. Those folks didn't know quit. Most didn't talk about feelings; they just lived past their feelings. There wasn't time to stop and reflect. The patrons of those aforementioned taverns/clubs were like my people.

Many differences were resolved by a fistfight among families and among friends. One of my uncles once told me, "Growing up, I didn't know it wasn't okay to hit my wife; Daddy did it, the neighbors did it. I didn't know it wasn't okay to cheat on my wife; Daddy did it, the neighbors did it. It wasn't until I got out in the world that I learned it wasn't acceptable behavior." That's human nature. Well, I mean it's human nature to see what's going on in your home and neighborhood as normal. You don't know any different.

Remember, these folks were born in the '30s, and 40's; popular movie genres in the '50s and '60s were war, gangsters, and westerns, with a great deal of violence in all of them. Television didn't come into households until the 1950s. In addition to the shootouts in the gangster and westerns, there was a lot of fighting; however, the westerns ranked number one in barroom brawls. You should consider that before you judge my peeps with your set of values today. You don't know what you don't know.

One evening, probably around 1968, Mom's sister, her husband, Mom's brother, his wife, and another sister-in-law decided to go out for a drink. They parked their cars in the shared parking lot behind the B&E and the Five High. The men meandered towards the back entrance of the B&E and the women towards the Five High. It was then one of my aunties heard some loud arguing; she turned her head towards the noise and saw a man standing at the open driver's door of a vehicle. A man was whaling on a woman sitting in the car. I mean prize fighter whaling; he was beating her viscously. Uncle was conversing with his brother-in-law and hadn't seen or heard the ordeal. Auntie turned to him, nudged him in the ribs, and whispered for him to look. Uncle turned his head, saw the beating taking place, didn't pass go, didn't collect two hundred dollars. Instead, he strode quickly to the car, pulled the man off the woman, and stopped the beating. The man backed off, the arguing stopped, and the couple made their way into the bar. It looked as though Uncle had settled the matter, so my people went on into the bar, ordered their drinks, and continued their conversation.

About an hour later, Uncle rose from his bar stool and headed to the bathroom . . . that's when Mr. Parking Lot Wife Beater sucker punched Uncle from the back to the side of his head. Uncle stumbled, recovered, and spun around swinging (who wouldn't). And that's how the fight started.

Mr. Parking Lot Wife Beater's friend jumped up from his bar stool and began throwing punches at Uncle. So, Uncle was fighting both men when the guy's wife, the woman he'd just saved from a beating by her husband, jumped onto Uncle's back.

Three against one isn't okay; it's particularly rude when the third one was the woman who'd just been rescued! Auntie was off her bar stool in a heartbeat and commenced thumping the woman as she dragged her off her brother. Two of my aunts were all in on the fracas, kind of enjoying the brawl; the third just wanted to go home and get away from the mess!

That sucker punch turned into an all-out brawl, with nearly everyone in the bar involved except the bartender. Friends, each taking sides, men fighting men, women kicking downed men, and women fighting women. The only thing missing was people getting thrown through swinging doors/big picture windows and chairs getting busted over people's heads like in the westerns!

As the fists were flying, another of Mom's brothers walked in with a friend and immediately went to fisticuffing it. One guy (whom my mother allegedly married, yet I found no proof) decided to fight the brother who had recently walked in. It was a source of pride to fight a tough guy and win. Another brawler said, "Don't you know who that is? He's a Kennedy, the boxer; he'll beat you to death when he finishes with the man he's fighting now if you swing on him." The alleged husband quickly changed his mind and turned to find someone else to duke it out with.

So, fists were flying, people were getting knocked down, and then someone yelled, "Cops!" because five carloads of the law had pulled up. That barroom was instantly like a rowdy classroom when the teacher steps back in; the fighting stopped, and everyone quickly returned to their seats as though nothing had happened. The cops didn't stay too long because no one was fighting, and no one said anything about anyone having been in a fight.

Just when it seemed "safe to go back in the water," some of the other people decided they wanted to fight a little more, so they went at it again. The brawl made its way out to the back parking lot. Uncle number two found Mr. Parking Lot Wife Beater sucker puncher, and they went at it. Uncle bit the guy's ear off, then chased him down the street about 1/4 mile, trying to give him some more. (Hmm, I wonder if Mike Tyson heard of this story and copied the ear-biting move ...)

My family didn't realize that the bartender had made two phone calls. One call to the law and one to Granny, "Mrs. Kennedy, you better get down here and get your kids; they're in a fracas and will end up killing people if you don't get this stopped." It should be noted the women in my family were also tough and adept at fisticuffs.

As the brawl continued, a family friend said, "Look, there's Mrs. Kennedy." as Gran walked into the bar. My people instantly stopped fighting. Grandma did not frequent bars, so they knew they were in trouble.

"Mama, what are you doing here?"

Gran replied, "I want to know who the bastard is that sucker punched my kid."

No one responded, and that was a good thing. Gran had an equalizer (a lead pipe) concealed under her cape. She turned to her kids and said, "Come on now, it's time for you kids to go home."

Her kids were all in their mid to late twenties. However, they stood up and walked out the door behind their 4'10", one hundred twenty-pound mother as the whole bar laughed because those tough Kennedys got sent home by their mama like school children.

GENEVA MARIE BRETT

CHAPTER 22

Come On Sis, It's Your Birthday!

My mother, speaking to her sister in 1968, "Come on, sis, it's your birthday. Let me and #7 take you to dinner, and then we'll have a few drinks." (I won't, but Mom said his name.)

"No. I don't want to. The last time we went out, we got in a fight. It's my birthday; I don't want to fight."

"Come on, hon, I promise we won't fight this time."

Number seven said, "Sis, I won't let her. I promise, no fights."

Auntie put on her brown corduroy mini dress, and the three hit the town for her birthday celebration. They enjoyed a nice dinner, then started hitting their favorite hangouts all over town. They ran into friends at every stop, and everywhere they went, someone gave Auntie a bottle of alcohol as a birthday gift, which she placed in the big bag she was toting.

Unlike Mom, Auntie wasn't much of a drinker. She said she had a three-drink limit, anything after that, she said she'd be "shit-faced." But you know how it is on your birthday, friends want to buy you a beverage. Besides, she was safe; sister and #7 had promised no fighting; it'd be a fun night.

They split up when they hit Alisal Street; #7 went to the 526 Club, and Mom and Auntie went to the Five High next door. The birthday girl was sitting on the edge of the pool table talking to a friend when Mom walked out of the bathroom and spied #6 at the bar.

Although they'd separated, #6 was one of those husbands Mom hadn't actually divorced. This although she was married to #7. She also had some hold over anger because #6 had slashed her tires at some point, and she hadn't gotten any justice afterward. Sooo, Mom walked over next to her sister and threw an ashtray at #6, which connected. (Mom was a lousy shot; however, she threw ashtrays like a pro ball player!)

Almost instantly, #6 threw a swing at Mom. Mom had anticipated his swing could follow the ashtray hit, so she ducked. Number six's fist connected with Mom's sister, which knocked her off the pool table. He knocked her, and one of her teeth out. Next thing Auntie knows, her friend is holding her leg up, telling her to get up and talk to him. She was still a little fuzzy but recognized another childhood friend was holding her head and telling her he was going to beat that SOB (#6) to death.

This started a free-for-all fight among the bar patrons. Mind you, this wasn't a bunch of strangers; all those folks had known one another for years, decades even, many having gone to school together.

Before the childhood friend could act, someone went next door and fetched #7, who nearly stomped #6 to death. (Are you keeping up with these husband numbers?)

Meanwhile, back at the ranch, the bartender had called the law. The law showed up while Auntie was still on the floor. One of the officers, a small Asian man, picked her up off the floor and twisted her arm behind her back, thinking she was my mother, who started the melee with the ashtray throw.

Still stunned, Auntie said, "What are you doing?"

The officer replied, "I'm taking you to jail, Kennedy, for starting the fight."

He refused to listen to her claim of innocence nor pay attention to the others telling him it wasn't she who'd thrown the ashtray; it was her sister who'd done so. The cop would have none of it; he kept twisting Auntie's arm behind her back, trying to walk her to the door.

Welp, Auntie had enough of all of it at this point; she was innocent, it was her birthday, and she'd been promised no fighting but got knocked out. Nope, she was not going to jail for something she didn't do. Like most of my people, when she got mad, she got mean and would say the meanest, cruelest things she could think of to hurt your feelings, damage your self-esteem, and damage your body however she could. Winner takes all! No holds barred!

Auntie jumped up and around to straddle the officer's waist with her legs. She commenced wailing on him with her free hand. Her friend was also trying to get the cop off Auntie. The whole bar was at one another, so the bartender called for backup to prevent the two cops from getting badly beaten by the "Okies."

Auntie continued to fight the cop she'd wrapped her legs around because he continued to twist her arm behind her back.

She shouted at him, "You son of a bitch, don't forget we already whipped your ass in the war! I'll whip YOUR ass right now! Turn me loose! I didn't do anything!"

By this time, there were cops everywhere. Liquored up, Mom told the officer who was tangled up with her sister, "Listen, just leave my sister alone. Just leave her alone. She didn't do anything."

Her sister was still locked in battle with the officer, who turned to Mom and said, "Look, do YOU want to go to jail?"

"No."

"Well, back off. You can follow us down there because we're taking her to jail."

Auntie told me, "And there's chickenshit Lou in the background, 'Don't worry, sis, I'll get you out of jail!'"

Mom thought the whole thing quite funny; her sister was the only innocent one in the whole deal, and she was the only one who went to jail.

Auntie was arguing with the arresting officer, calling him insulting names and telling him he needed to listen to her story. The officer told her she could tell her story to Judge so and so, he was taking her in.

She said, "Well, fuck you, and fuck Judge so and so."

Contrary to her promise, Mom did not trot down to the jail to fetch her sister on her birthday. The cops had threatened to arrest her and one of Auntie's girlfriends, so they quietly moseyed on out the back door. Mom recognized she was too drunk to drive to the jail, so she walked over to the 526 Club instead and continued drinking.

One of Grandma's tax clients booked Auntie, "Oh my God, Patsy!"

Auntie looked terrible, and then Auntie spent the night in jail. Mom knew better than to call Grandma to bail her sister out of jail. She and her friends spent hours trying to find someone to bail her out.

They finally got a friend's mom to go to the jail very early in the morning, like six am early. It took more than two hours to get her processed out. She was not looking her best. At all. She'd spent the night in jail; her hair was a fright, her tooth missing, her face swollen like a puffer fish and starting to bruise. She asked where her sister was, her sister who had promised to get her out of jail. "Yeah, about that. Well, she was too drunk and fearful of arrest, so she sent me."

Auntie went directly to the District Attorney's office to tell her tale of innocence so they wouldn't prosecute her for something she didn't do. She was able to speak with a Deputy DA (DDA) right away.

She explained, "It was my birthday. We were just going for dinner and drinks. I didn't know my sister's ex-husband would be there."

The DDA asked what happened; Auntie recounted the events. He responded, "But Miss Kennedy, you had all that contraband in your purse."

"What contraband? What are you talking about?"

"Rum, vodka, whiskey, bourbon, and one of those bottles had been opened. We can't drop those charges. You had all that contraband."

"Well, yes. Those were my birthday presents. Can I have them back?"

"No, it's contraband; we're going to confiscate it."

Auntie went before Judge so and so, charged with disturbing the peace. He said, "Miss Kennedy, did you say all those things in this police report?"

"I don't know. How would you feel? I was talking to my friends, and this little cop came up and twisted my arm behind my back."

"Did you lock your legs around the officer and repeatedly hit him?"

"I don't know. It could be, I was awfully upset."

"And did you say fuck Judge so and so?"

"Does it say I said that?"

"Yes."

"Hmm, well, I was pretty mad, so I probably did."

Auntie pointed at Mom, "It was my birthday. It was her and her ex-husband that started the fight, not me. Her ex-husband hit me and knocked me out."

"Miss Kennedy, she's not the one on trial; you are. You're the one who was fighting with the officer."

The DA recommended probation and that Auntie not frequent the Five High, 526, or any cocktail lounges of that caliber. She could go to the

Italian Villa, the Pub, and places like that. The DA also told the Judge that she wanted her birthday presents back, all ten bottles.

"Miss Kennedy, you cannot have your birthday presents, the contraband, back."

Auntie didn't go back to the Five High or 526, but Mom did. And Mom had a few more bar fights.

People seem quick to judge others, often saying what they'd do if they found themselves in such a situation. The truth, the fact, is that every human has a different life experience than every other human, we internalize those experiences differently, and they shape how we view the world and how we respond to life. When you grow up seeing violence as the way to handle a dispute, you're much more likely to manage your conflicts with violence.

You can talk all you want, but the fact is that none of us can accurately predict how we'd handle any situation until we're in the moment because of all the experiences that brought us to that moment.

You do you. I'll do me. Or, as Gran used to say, "Clean up around your own back porch before you start talking about someone else's."

GENEVA MARIE BRETT

CHAPTER 23

Grandma Becomes a Jail Bird

There was a woman who desperately wanted to be part of my family and bear the family name. I don't recall the introduction of her into our lives. Gran could have met her at church, or maybe Gran did her taxes. Well, however, she came to be connected; she wouldn't let go.

At first, she was welcome; she'd show up at tax time and help some. She'd do a bit of cooking on occasion, run errands for Gran, pick up some of us kids, or take us to church. I'm thinking I was ten when I met her; she seemed a bit judgy, controlling, and intrusive. She was always nicely dressed, her hair and makeup done; she wasn't unattractive. I liked her less as time went on. We all liked her less as time went on.

Most of us found it offensive that she called our matriarch "Grandma," not because we didn't like the name; that's what we called her. She had no standing to reference Gran that way; I don't recall even one of Gran's tax clients calling her anything other than Mrs. Kennedy.

As time went on, Gran's daughters tried to keep away from the woman and warned their mom to keep the gal away from them. Gran's sons and grandsons avoided her because they thought she was trying to put the make on them so she could capture one for keeps.

Gran was kind and generous; she not only taught her family how to prepare income tax returns, but she also taught several others who eventually went out on their own. It'd start out that they'd work for her, filling in the names and addresses on the tops of the forms, addressing envelopes, and simple tasks like that. As she saw their ability increase, she'd provide more responsibility. She'd check every return of her trainees until she felt they were ready to capably represent her clients.

The woman I'm talking about never got past the point of heading the forms and addressing envelopes. But the gal was a single mother of three and needed money, and Gran had a soft spot for people in need. She gave her the duties she could manage and paid her for them. Gran paid everyone much more than their job was worth.

Gran made a lot of money during the tax season, much of it cash, which she kept in a cookie jar on her desk (the cookie jar now sits on my kitchen counter, but I keep dog cookies in it). We all knew not to touch that cookie jar, and common sense would tell a reasonable person not to reach into someone else's money holder.

Yeah, well, as time went on, that woman lost more and more of her sensibility. Gran caught her reaching into the cookie jar more than once to "make change" or get some money to pay for whatever Gran was sending her to buy. Gran grabbed her arm and told her to keep her hands off of, and out of, the cookie jar.

The woman would behave responsibly for a time, then go right back at it. Gran had been missing money a time or two but couldn't prove who took it. We all thought the same thing; not a one of us would ever get into Gran's cookie jar; only one person had done that.

Gran devised a plan to break the woman from getting into her cookie jar. She took all her cash out and placed a loaded mouse trap inside! We all anxiously waited for the gal to stop by and get her just reward. Although we didn't take side bets on her reaction, in truth, we all gleefully waited for the day she'd get caught and maybe show some respect. I think that's the only time any of us were looking forward to the woman coming through the door.

At the time, seven or eight of us family were preparing income taxes in different rooms of the house. The trap had been set, and we were all quite excited when you know who walked in the door. We worked as silently as possible, intent on hearing that SNAP! One by one, we'd cruise through Gran's office, hoping to catch the show. We didn't hear the actual SNAP, but my how the gal screamed and cried when it did, and she was literally caught with her hand in the cookie jar!

She was indignant that Gran would play such a terrible trick on her. Gran explained it was no trick at all, it served her right, and she'd

160

better never touch that cookie jar again. She didn't. Meanwhile, there was a great deal of snickering and outright laughter in the other rooms.

Over the years, the woman would borrow Gran's car and return it empty of gas. She'd forget to give Gran the change from a purchase. She'd take food home without asking. She had her nose in everyone's business, gossiped about everyone, and none of us liked being around her. My aunt and my mom would chase her off, warning her she'd best stay away if she didn't want to get her ass whipped. She'd stay gone for months at a time and then show up again when she thought everyone had calmed down. This was a rinse, repeat for at least a decade before the big event.

Rumor was that her Pastor asked her not to return to church because she was divisive and a troublemaker. We all took it as fact. Nevertheless, Gran let her back in repeatedly. Gran even took her and some of her kids on trips with us. As I said, Gran had a soft spot for people in need, especially single mothers.

After tax time in 1970, the woman borrowed Gran's car and got a one-dollar parking ticket, which she didn't pay or tell Gran about. Two or three months later, Gran received a five-dollar ticket in the mail because the one-dollar ticket hadn't been paid. The woman happened to be present when Gran opened her mail. Gran was hot, hot, hot, and told the woman she knew it had been her.

No one else had used Gran's car, and Gran hadn't been on Gabilan Street, where the car was ticketed. The woman made excuses, apologized, and then confessed she didn't have five dollars to pay for the ticket. Gran gave her a five-dollar bill and the ticket and made her promise she'd leave right then and go directly to pay for the ticket. Only she didn't. She kept the five dollars, didn't pay for the ticket, and didn't tell Gran.

A month or three passed when the cops showed up at Gran's to arrest her for not paying the ticket. Woo doggies, she was hot, hot, hot, and humiliated! She'd never been arrested; this was horrible! She told the officers the truth; they said pay up or go to jail. Gran didn't have cash, and they wouldn't take a check, so they handcuffed my 58-year-old grandmother (hands behind her back), stuffed her in the back of a cruiser, and hauled her off to the hoosegow. Gran made her one phone call from the jailhouse. She called my mother, who was living in Gran's rental, situated down a long driveway behind our house (I still lived with Gran).

"Louise."

"Mornin' Mom."

"This is your mother."

"I recognize your voice, Mom; what is it?"

"I'm in jail."

Mom started laughing and laughing hard. She told me it was so funny because her mother had never done anything to get thrown in jail. (I guess her shooting at Grandpa wasn't a jailable offense in Mom's mind.)

"Why do you think you're in jail, Mom?"

"Honey, I'm in jail, and you'll have to come down here and get me."

Mom raced to the jail, still laughing at the absurdity of her mother being jailed, and realized she didn't have cash or her checkbook as she parked the car. Gran wrote a check, Mom took it to the bank, cashed it, returned with the twenty-five-dollar cash bail, then took her mother home. (Mom didn't make her ride in the back seat like the cops did.)

I don't know which of them was madder at the woman, the jailbird, or the jailbird's daughter! My aunt was just as mad when Mom called to tell her. Of course, they both laughed and said the gal was lucky Granny couldn't get her hands on her that day. Gran called the woman and worked her over verbally, telling her she better never show her face around our home again.

So, the gal hid out for about six or seven months and then couldn't stand the distance any longer. She just knew Gran had to have forgiven her by then because Gran always forgave. One day Gran heard a horn honk at the back house (Mom's) and saw the woman's car parked in the drive. The gal had gone to Mom's house, presumably testing the waters with Mom before Gran. As Mom walked out to see what the gal wanted, she saw Gran practically flying down the driveway, her short little legs whirling like a cartoon character, running towards her and the driver's side of the woman's car.

Mom could tell by the look on her face that Gran was Banty rooster mad again. Meanwhile, the gal's back was to Gran. She'd rolled the window down to talk with Mom and didn't see Gran flying down the driveway towards her.

She was taken completely by surprise when Gran "appeared" at her driver's door and shouted, "You witch!", then reached through the window, grabbed the woman by the hair of the head with one hand, and began punching her in the face with the other. Gran was trying her best to drag the woman out the car window because she couldn't get the door opened.

The woman was screaming and crying, "Stop! Stop! Please, you're hurting me! Grandma, stop! Louise, help me! Make her stop! Grandma, please stop!"

Gran said she was trying to get the gal out of the car so she "could get some good licks in." Remember, Gran was fifty-eight then; the woman was in her early thirties. Gran kept telling her to get out of the car, which she was obviously not going to do, and wisely so. She had greatly underestimated Grandma, and she knew it.

She shouted, "I'm a lady; I don't fight!" as she continued to cry out for Mom to help and for Grandma to stop.

Gran shouted, "No, no, you're not. You're not a lady. You're a chickenshit coward and a thief!"

Gran did her best to drag the woman out of the car to get some real satisfaction, but the gal held on to the steering wheel for dear life, which was a wise thing to do.

Mom let Gran whip on her for a little while longer before she dragged her off to keep Gran from really hurting the woman. Gran told her if she knew what was good for her, she'd leave and never come back because she would kick her fat ass for sure; she'd be waiting for the opportunity.

Yeowza! Do you think the woman (a) stayed away forever or (b) came back around again? If you guessed (b), you're right. She came back, and Gran let her back in, to the extreme dissatisfaction of every single one of us.

It might have been about seven or so years later, maybe not quite, when the woman said or did something that pushed one of my tax-preparing cousins over her edge of warning. Cousin kicked her ass without remorse. Rinse, repeat; after a time, the woman came back. The next time she went too far, it was my mom who slapped her. She was lucky Mom just slapped her because Mom was a seasoned and skilled fighter; it's odd that Mom "just" slapped her.

A couple years before Gran's passing, her sister was complaining about that woman again because she'd recently been interfering during Gran's hospitalization.

Gran's sis said, "I don't know why you let the woman keep coming around when she's lied to you, stolen from you, and caused upheaval at every opportunity."

Gran said, "The Bible says you have to forgive and forget."

Her sister stopped that conversation with, "You can't let the devil in and expect him to act like an angel."

I'm with my great-aunt on this one. When this story was told for the audio recording, I shared the story of the boy and the rattlesnake with Gran, Aunt Rita, and Mom. (Snake asks the boy to carry it and promises not to bite. Boy carries snake, snake gives boy a lethal bite, boy asks why. Snake said you knew what I was when you picked me up.)

A cousin and I once talked about how someone we knew could do some heinous act against some other person we knew; I asked why whomever it was would do such a thing.

Cousin responded, "Because they can."

That was a mind-opener for me. I could never understand how a human could be mean or cruel to another, how a human could hurt a child or an elder. I'd always had a near-desperate need to understand others, but at that moment, I realized I will never understand some things.

We teach people how to treat us, and it's our responsibility to be treated well. You, beloved unknown sister, or brother, are as worthy of love and respect as any other human on this planet. No matter how much you care for another, don't let them treat you poorly. You're worth more than that. Your life, your happiness, and your JOY matter, beloved. Jesus gave his life for YOU! Imperfect, flawed, you.

The Bible says that God knew everything we'd ever say or do before we were knitted in our mother's womb. He has a plan and purpose for your life. And unlike people, he will forgive you and not throw it back in your face, ever again.

CHAPTER 24

Go For a Ride with Me

My great-aunt told me she was a "rounder" as a child. She liked to get out and around whenever, wherever, or whatever there was to do. She loved to follow her uncle around the ranch, visit her friends, and of course, go to church. She said my grandmother was the opposite. Gran always preferred to stay in the house near her mother and grandmother. (Gran kept me close like that.)

On one of the audio recordings, I asked Gran if she ever visited girlfriends when she was little. She timidly replied, "A time or two, but I felt unwelcome and unwanted, so I didn't go again."

She was that way all her days. She didn't visit her children, didn't visit friends, and very rarely visited her sister. Do know that she loved people, and all were welcome in her home; however, she felt out of place unless she was in her own space.

Great Auntie told me that when they were little girls, Gran realized she only had a middle initial while her sister had a full middle name. Gran was crushed; it was proof she wasn't loved as equally as her sister. Their mother gave Gran a full middle to satisfy her; she used that middle name all her life. When writing this chapter I checked her birth certificate; middle initial only. Gran never told that story!

That fascinates me because that's who she was as a tiny little child and who she remained all her life. Nature versus nurture. Some people just come the way they will always be.

Contrary to, or maybe because of, their mother's desire to be at home, all her kids, except my mother, loved the road. They enjoyed going just to be going, as do I. Gran's kids all loved to have company on the road, many of my cousins are like that too. I'm good either way.

As adults, Gran's kids often stopped by her home for a cup of coffee, to see who might be around, or to say hi while they were headed elsewhere. The spur-of-the-moment passerby would say, "Come on, go for a ride with me. I'm just going down the road. We'll be right back." Famous last words!

You'd better have at least half a day to spend with that person, especially Mom's youngest brother and sister. You'd be driving down the road towards the alleged destination when they'd say, "Oh, I forgot I need to stop by such and such a place." Or "I promised so and so I'd drop off or pick up . . ."

Auntie's trips usually involved some shopping and/or a quick bite to eat. Uncle's trips often ended the day having a cold one with a friend or two at a tavern. It was always a good time with either of them, but as I said, it was at least a half day. They always had places to go, things to do, and people to see . . . which could really complicate your life in those pre-mobile phone days when you had your own things to do.

Yet we'd climb in with them again, and again, and again . . . always making them promise, trying to hold them to the promise, but deep down knowing what was really going to happen.

Not only was my mother a serial marrier, but she also tried on some glass slippers between the marriages. I don't know if the breaking of a glass slipper or a marriage caused her to be so distraught and depressed one day her sister stopped by to visit.

Mom was heartbroken and inconsolable, so distraught she just wanted to die. Factually, she told her sister she wanted to kill herself. Based on a letter Mom had written my dad's parents some years before, I know there was much more troubling her than just the loss of this one man. In that letter, she mentioned that within a six-year span, her husband, sister, child, and father died. She wondered what she'd done to deserve such tragedy and pain.

By the time of this about-to-be-described event, she'd been married perhaps six times, with three alleged marriages in there as well. She was around thirty years old. Isn't that hard to fathom? My mama was in overdrive in her young life. When you continue to keep the pedal to the medal, something's gotta give. Evidently, on this day, it was Mom and her will to live such a hard luck life.

By now, you know my people aren't pansies; they don't tolerate weakness in themselves or others. You must suck it up and get on with it. Auntie gave Mom a little leeway to whine, then said, "Come on, Lou, go for a ride with me."

Mom didn't want to go anywhere; she wanted to sit and stay in her misery. Baby sister wouldn't allow that.

Mom's sister coaxed and cajoled; she said she needed to do something that couldn't wait and wanted her sis to ride along. Same old line: it was just down the road, they'd be back soon, and she'd feel better. Sitting alone crying wouldn't help anything anyway. Auntie got her into the car, promising she'd stop at the liquor store for a pack of smokes and a six-pack of beer. Did I mention Mom was already three sheets to the wind?

Auntie headed straight for the nearest liquor store and bought her sister a pack of Pall Mall (unfiltered) and a six of Budweiser, carried out in a brown paper bag.

Those who knew Mom, well, those who ever rode with her, can visualize her sitting in the passenger seat with her six of beer in the brown paper bag on the floor. Didn't matter if the beer got warm. For the rest of you, that's how she rolled for a very long time. If she was passengering, that was how she'd be rolling.

Speaking of rolling ... they rolled out on the road and then headed out on the highway, Highway 101, to be exact. Mom wasn't paying attention to where they were going; she was crying and talking nonsense. Drunks like to talk, and they often talk nonsense.

While Mom whined, drank beer, and smoked, her sister drove northbound on the 101. Mom was so into her tale of pity and woe that she paid no attention to the miles behind them and the time that had passed. And then ...

"Patsy, where the hell are we? This looks like San Francisco! Are we in San Francisco? What the hell? I thought we were just going down the road." (It's a two-hour drive from Salinas to San Francisco.)

With that, Auntie gassed it. She started speeding up the hill on that street that's used in great car chases. You know the one I mean. The one where the car races up the steep hill, so steep you can't see the top, and becomes airborne before touching down? Well, that's the street they were on when Mom realized they were in San Francisco and how my aunt started driving!

As my aunt continued to race up the hill, Mom started yelling, "Aaaahhh! What the hell are you doing, you crazy bitch? You're gonna kill us!"

Her sister replied, "I thought you wanted to die, Lou. That's what you said."

"Not today! Slow this fucking car down now, you crazy bitch, and take us home! What the hell is wrong with you?"

"Nothing's wrong with me, sis. I was just helping you out. See, you don't want to die now. I knew you didn't really want to die. I told you you'd feel better. We can go home now."

And so, they did. Every time she told this story, Mom's sister would laugh so hard that she'd lose her breath. The listener always got caught up in it too.

If Mom was around during a retelling, she'd comment, "Damn crazy bitch. She could have killed us!"

This next tale isn't exactly on topic, but it's close enough to include and it's funny. Well, my people think it's funny. With their bar fighting, outlaw ways, athleticism, good looks, and intelligence, my people were well-known in Monterey County; frankly, they were legendary. Known by Johnny Law as legendary too.

Life and leniency of the law were very different in the '60s and '70s than today. Often times if kids or adults got caught drinking, they'd be instructed to go straight home if they lived close enough.

Late one evening, Auntie received a call from a deputy sheriff. He told her she needed to come get her sister right then. Louise was close to home, too drunk to drive, and he didn't want to haul her in.

Auntie dutifully went after her sister. Mom had miscalculated a turn and high-centered on the side of the road. (High-centered is when the bottom of the car is stuck on something higher than the wheels, so the car can't move forward or backward. The wheels just spin when you press the gas pedal. Picture a turtle whose legs don't reach the ground, and the turtle's still paddling.)

Mom was too drunk to realize what had happened, so she kept pressing the accelerator. When she looked out her driver-side window and saw the cop, she floored it, deciding she'd outrun him and get home before he could pull her over. She'd collected enough DUIs; the next would require time in the slammer. The car remained high-centered, not moving. She gave it more gas.

She kept shooting side glances out her driver's window. She was shocked to see the cop still alongside her, no matter how fast she went. (She wasn't moving.) She'd see the cop, look back out the front windshield, and give it more gas. She'd let up on the gas a little when she thought she'd outrun the deputy. Then she'd look out the side window and see him keeping up with her, so she'd hit the gas again.

She couldn't understand how the man could run so fast; he had to be fucking bionic or something. This slapstick comedy continued for several minutes.

When Mom's sister walked up to her door, Mom said, "Hop in, sis. We've got to get out of here. The Law's after me!"

Auntie said, "No, you come ride with me, Lou. My car's faster. I can outrun them for sure!"

It worked. Mom stumbled to Auntie's car and Auntie got her safely home.

My favorite let's go for a ride story is when an uncle was working construction in Ukiah and going home on weekends. Ukiah is a couple hours north of San Francisco and three and a half hours from Uncle's home. One Friday, he stopped at a tavern in Ukiah for a cold one before hitting the road. He got to chatting with a stranger, a good conversationalist, and a pleasant fellow, so Uncle asked if the guy wanted to go for a ride down the road with him. The guy said sure but couldn't be gone too long because his dog was in his truck. After another round or two, they hit the road, and the stranger fell asleep.

He awoke briefly as they crossed the Golden Gate Bridge, then went back to sleep. He slept for the rest of the trip. The next morning, he asked Uncle where they were. Uncle said San Juan Bautista; the man said, "Uh, is that in North or South America?"

Uncle kept him for the weekend; the guy phoned a friend and made sure his pooch was cared for.

I do miss those adventurous go-for-a-ride days. We always complained, but they were always a good time.

Earlier this year, I was planning on visiting an aunt in Oregon. We haven't seen one another in decades; I always loved her and wondered what she might be willing to share for this book. I'd mentioned this to #1, and he wanted to go with me because he felt the same way. While we were working on coordinating our schedule with my aunt's, #1 said it'd be great to bring Uncle along. Uncle said he would be interested in going, depending on the timing. I loved the idea of spending hours in the car with my favorite uncle; oh my, so many stories I'd hear, so much life we'd share. I was all in!

An absolutely brilliant plan was hatched. Once we confirmed the date, I'd drop by Uncle's and ask him to go for a ride down the road with me! Teehee! Then, I'd take him "down the road" to Oregon! HA!

Finally, he'd get a taste of what he'd dished out for decades. His daughter was all in; we wouldn't tell Auntie in case our plan wasn't as well received as we had hoped. We didn't want her to be complicit or him to be angry with her.

Cousin would pack a suitcase for Uncle and slip it out to my car; I wouldn't tell him where we were going until I was out of options. We'd pick up #1 at the airport in Oregon (he lives in Washington) and have a grand visit.

Unfortunately, the timing with my aunt didn't work, and now #1's had some health issues and needs to stay closer to home. It was incredibly fun for a while, though!

CHAPTER 25

Sharing A Toke

I was an excellent "A" student throughout elementary school and junior high. I was never reprimanded in junior high, only once in the fourth grade, which was one too many times. I'm not at all proud of that fourth-grade situation; matter of fact, I'm downright ashamed of it. But I've told my children and the classes of children in which I volunteered so that I might save a child from making the mistake I did or worse. At this point, I might as well tell you.

I didn't have a lot of friends throughout my younger years. We lived in the country with few neighbors, none my age. For most of the time I lived with Gran, and she didn't allow me to wander. I wasn't what you'd call shy however after sharing that I'd visited a relative in prison over the weekend during first grade "Show and Tell" and recognizing the shock on my teacher's face, I realized my home life was "abby, abby, normal" (*Young Frankenstein* fans will get that reference) so I didn't get too close with classmates for fear of spilling more weirdo beans.

Early 1960's, my home life was very uncommon. Kids lived with their parents, which made me a misfit because I didn't. Kids didn't know what a prison was and definitely didn't visit one. Most adults didn't know anyone in prison, nor had they visited one. That kind of life wasn't on television as it is today.

So, recognizing that look on my teacher's face, I became cautious about what I shared. I was already an outsider and didn't want to make it worse. I was a dutiful student during class; at recess and lunch, I played jump rope, 4 square (loved that), swings, monkey bars, jacks, and marbles with whomever. I wasn't much of a tether ball fan after getting thunked in the face with one by a much bigger and stronger kid. I'd have liked to have a close friend besides my cousins.

I was thrilled when Gran sold a house a couple doors down to a family with a girl my age; at last, I'd have a nearby friend! She had a teen brother and a sister, too, I think. Anyway, she was okay. I was used to playing with my brother and boy cousins; lots of football, army, agitating the bees, and Cowboys and Indians. Action play!

Our army play included digging foxholes and tossing soda bottles with a bit of gasoline and a rag you lit on fire. I later learned that it was called a "Molotov cocktail" and was quite dangerous. Lighting and tossing a string of firecrackers sounded like machine guns rapidly firing, which added great authenticity to our war games. Thankfully we didn't have grenades to throw!

One of my cousins was half Indigenous and half white, so you know which side he took when we played Cowboys and Indians. During that game, our primary weapons were bb guns; I don't remember using bows and arrows. One of my cousins still has a bb lodged in his cheek some sixty years later from the day he was a loser cowboy and got shot to pretend death.

Back to the new neighbor girl, she liked to color and play with dolls. I had dolls, so that was okay. It wasn't as exciting as army, but it was a girl my age to play with. Her household was very different than mine. I stopped by during their dinner time once, and her parents had me sit alone in the living room while they consumed their meal in the kitchen. That was utterly foreign to me; Gran had an open-door, welcome table policy. I felt very awkward and tried not to take it personally. It'd have been easier on me if they'd sent me home; I have no idea why they made me sit and wait, nor why I did.

Anyway, one day in fourth grade, Mrs. Medina announced a math test. No big to me, "A" was almost always my grade in everything. I was a bright child for whom learning came easily. We took the test and were instructed to exchange and grade one another's tests. The new neighbor girl wanted to exchange tests, so we did. (I was thinking, "Yay, our friendship is blossoming.")

Then she made a very undignified and ugly request of me. She asked me to cheat on the grading; if I did, she'd be my best friend. She said it was no big deal; she'd done it plenty of times at her old school. To do such a thing was against my core values and beliefs; I was "goody two shoes," believing I needed to be well-behaved so my grandmother would keep me because I had nowhere else to go.

Yet there was the allure of this girl offering to be my best friend if I'd do this one bad deed for her. "Best friend. Two doors down, best friend. Not my cousin best friend." Oh, how my little girl tummy roiled and rolled about, how my heart raced, and my head hurt. I could almost feel the angels on one shoulder and the devil on the other, arguing about what I should do!

Regrettably, the prize of her friendship proved too great for me to resist, so I consented. We were about two-thirds of the way through grading when Mrs. Medina caught me erasing an answer. Having zero experience, I was a lousy cheater. Mrs. Medina called me out in front of my entire classroom of fourth-grade peers!

I wanted to die or vanish, and either was equally desirable at that moment. She asked me if I was cheating, changing answers. She'd already seen me erasing and writing, so she knew the truth. But teachers gotta teach. And teachers teach much more than assigned subjects. I'm surprised the bright red lipstick she wore didn't melt off her face with the heat of the embarrassment emanating from my red and horrified face.

There was no point in lying; I knew I was busted. I confessed with a pathetic "Yes." I did not cry. My yes wasn't enough; she wanted to know why. I was even more ashamed that I thought so little of myself that I'd traded my honor and dignity for the offer of a friendship that I couldn't allow myself to utter the words. Instead, I gave her a shrug of my forlorn little shoulders. The girl spoke not a word, as though she had nothing to do with it.

Mrs. Medina took the test from me and my almost best friend and handed them to nearby students to correct as the girl, and I sat at our empty desks. In that moment, I realized I could no longer be friends with a person who would ask me to risk my pride, dignity, and honor for them and then not step up in my moment of need to say it was by her request that I cheated. That friendship was not worth the price I was paying.

I can see the scene clearly today; however, I'm moving fast enough to not relieve the actual pain and humiliation. When our tests were scored by others, I earned an A and she a C-. This kid was nowhere near being in my league, and I'd given up so much for her. AND it looked like she hadn't cheated for me, that I alone was the dirty cheater. What a revolting development. I was dis-gus-ted with myself, her, and horribly humiliated.

To make matters even worse, my punishment was to walk around at recess and lunch recess holding on to Mrs. Medina's skirt! Gaaaaa, kill me now, please, because all the kids on the playground would know I was being reprimanded. If a playground kid asked what I'd done to be punished, a classmate surely would have told I was a dirty cheater.

As we left the classroom for recess, a classmate asked, "Why'd you do it, Geneva?" My shame was such that I couldn't speak, definitely not the pitiful truth, so I offered up another pathetic shoulder shrug.

This is terrible stuff, and I know you're feeling my little girl pain by now. But wait! There's more! Mrs. Medina was Grandma's tax client!!! Not only was my school life ruined, but I also feared she'd tell Gran. She had her phone number, could easily call her and tattle on me.

Who would I be in Granny's eyes? I could not become my mother! I could not be one of those family members who kept getting in trouble and bringing shame upon the family. It was awful!

Thankfully, Mrs. Medina left my unbecoming conduct and humiliation at school. I didn't. I carried it to this day, and it affected my love of math. Math stopped being so simple and easy for me until a few months ago when I told a friend I was returning to college to finish my degree. He was thrilled and offered help in math if needed, as he's tutored many. I accepted his invitation and shared my horror story and my loss of math being easy. He told me it was nonsense and compared it with a situation of a mutual friend. I instantly saw the ridiculousness of my attitude and freed myself of my loss of math love.

Crikey, the only thing that story has to do with this chapter is, I don't know what. This book is causing me to spill a whole lot of beans! Since I'm serving old stuff, does that make them refried beans?

Back on track ... a good student, and then I started high school and tried to find where I belonged. My own people, but better than my people. I wandered around alone a lot during junior high, feeling lost and alone. That was partly due to the trauma of the custody battle between Mom and Gran, which I'm not getting into in this book. The telling of these stories is a lot for both you and me, sometimes they're overwhelming. I need a rest from all these deep emotions; delving into the custody battles (plural) will have to wait until the next book.

Back on track, I didn't want to do four years of being lost and alone in high school. Initially, I hung out with the smart kids, the going places kids. I even tried out for cheer, not understanding most of those girls already had years of experience and forgetting I didn't have reliable transportation for after-school practice.

I was comfortable with those kids, then went to an after-football game party and saw many kids drinking. Not something I wanted to do. Plus, some of those kids returned to school on Monday and criticized the cowboy and drama kids for drinking. I thought them kind of two-faced and phony. They weren't so comfortable any longer.

I was interested in acting, so I tried hanging out with the drama kids. The first time I ever drank alcohol, I got drunk on cheap wine, and it all came back up. That first time wasn't the last. (My how quickly my attitude changed about what was acceptable behavior for me.)

I got busted my freshman year smoking cigarettes (Marlboros) in the girl's bathroom. Spent a week of detention on the bench outside the Dean's office, which was as horrifying as my fourth-grade debacle. My smart friends, my going places friends, saw me there, so I believed I'd no longer be accepted by them. None of them ever treated me differently or said anything about the detention; I projected my feelings onto them due to my shame, and I pulled away from them.

I smoked pot with a cousin and his neighbor during my freshman year. I was looking to fit in, conform, be cool, and belong, which took me off the path I'd designed for myself. I was struggling within to find my place and my space. I was struggling between where I wanted to go and where I came from. I had my ideals and values, yet high school was real life with real humans, not the motivational quotes I collected.

My sophomore year, I found FFA and the rodeo kids, people like my people. I was at home. Although I didn't want to be my mother, I slowly began partying. Drinking and smoking the pot. I smoked cigarettes on a fairly regular basis. I was still getting good grades, now more B's because I wasn't putting in much effort. At home, I began playing goody two shoes instead of being goody two shoes.

My brother was living with Mom in the house behind ours. One

175

of my cousins was still at home; it was just him, Gran, and me. Cousin was three years older than me. We continued to live parallel lives; rarely did he and I genuinely interact. When we did, it was never about anything of any importance or significance. Cousin mostly kept to himself.

I thought Gran might have suspicions about me drinking, but I wasn't sure if I wanted to face it if she did. ("Spoons in the Drawer," which is a chapter you might or might not read within this book.)

Our house had a pass-through bathroom from the dining room to the two back bedrooms. One day I noticed a nice fat doobie (marijuana cigarette) sitting on the counter in that bathroom and thought, "Score!"

I used to read my aunt's detective magazines, so my next thought was that it was a setup. It might not be pot, or Gran could have had cousin place it there to see if I'd keep it, and then she'd bust me. Nope. Not going to fall for that trick and get in trouble!

What did I do? What could I safely do? I picked it up and took it to Gran. "Look, Grandma, I found a marijuana cigarette in the bathroom." I truthfully said I didn't know where it came from. We went back and forth on its potential origin, finally agreeing it must have been cousin's.

Grandma somewhat surprised me when she suggested that since we were all alone, we should lock the doors and smoke it. Then we'd see if it made us crazy like cousin got crazy. She didn't completely surprise me because I remembered that she'd once locked herself in the house and gotten drunk to see if Grandpa's excuses of not remembering what he did when drunk held water.

I was fifteen years old and all in! Smoking pot with my fifty-seven-year-old granny. Oh yeah, this would be an epic tale! However, I had to be careful; I could not let her know I was a seasoned pot smoker!

We didn't have any matches, but we did have a fire burning, so Gran plucked a twig from the fire and lit the joint I held to my mouth. I was very careful to lightly inhale ... I did not want to inadvertently snitch on myself with my actions. Those detective magazines were paying off!

I got it burning and handed it to Gran; she took a puff but didn't know to inhale. She'd never smoked in her life. As for me, I'd smoked corn silk with the boys when I was eight years old, then at twelve, a cousin and I smoked some of Mom's nonfiltered Pall Malls, and now I was a current smoker and weekend pot smoker.

We both took a couple tokes again; I was not inhaling or holding it like a joint, nor did I instruct Gran on how to smoke. Auntie's detective magazines taught me that the little details catch you up and convict you.

Then Gran said, "Huh, I think he's just crazy. I don't think it's that stuff that makes him crazy. I'm not crazy; did it make you crazy?"

I said, "No, I'm not crazy."

Much to my dismay, she tossed almost all that big fat doobie into the fireplace.

About a year later, my brother, who was living with Mom in the house behind us, was busted when he came home from a rodeo. Mom found his bag of weed and confronted him, "What the hell is this?"

"Just what it looks like, Mom; it's a bag of weed."

"What the hell are you doing with a bag of weed?"

"What do you think I do with it? I smoke it."

About that time, I walked in the door and quickly grasped what was happening. I wondered what would happen next. Might Mom give my recently turned eighteen-year-old brother an ultimatum or put him out? As siblings do, I stepped up to help.

"Hey, Mom, I have an idea. Let's the three of us smoke a joint. It's just us; no one else will know. What do you say?"

Surprised, not surprised, she said yes. We smoked a joint together, mother, brother, and sister. It was great fun. The only repercussion was that brother couldn't keep Mom out of his stash after that!

Beloved reader, if you must "pay" for friendship or love, said friendship or love is worthless. You've seen the movies. Just like with blackmail, that first payment won't be the last; the demands will increase. Any human who would place a price tag on a priceless relationship doesn't understand its value or worth.

When a person makes such a demand or request, they are incapable of giving what they offer in return for your self-sacrifice. In that moment, the requestor is simply too wounded to accept or love their own selves, which makes them incapable of accepting or loving you.

Don't take it personal. It's about them, not you. They don't believe they're worthy, so they can't see the worth in you.

Someone will love and accept you. Let it start with you loving and accepting you, just as you are, exactly where you are. You are as unique as your fingerprint!

The odds of winning the lottery are 1 in 42 million. The odds of a sperm fertilizing an egg at the precise moment needed are 1 in 100 million. With abortion so readily available and acceptable, your existence is nothing short of a miracle!

There is a plan and purpose for your life! Your life might be all messed up right now, but it can change in the blink of an eye, which is one-third of a second.

Like me, you're who you are because of where you're from. We all are. What we do with that is up to us. We can be like our people or not. 100% our individual choice.

P.S. I'd forgotten this pot-smoking memory until I listened to the CDs I'd converted from the audio tapes I recorded twenty-eight years ago. At the age of forty, I confessed to Gran that I was a pot smoker at age fifteen. I appreciate my grandmother and her continued curiosity.

CHAPTER 26

Young Entrepreneur

My mother's younger sister was always very intuitive; somehow, she just "knew" things. This gift increased dramatically when she had children. She was zoned in.

So, one day Auntie noticed her thirteen-year-old daughter didn't come home at the same time as her twelve-year-old daughter, which wasn't uncommon because they each walked home from the same school with their own friends. Auntie asked the younger where the older was; the younger didn't know and said so. Auntie sensed something wasn't right, so she called the thirteen-year-old best friend's house. That girl wasn't home either. Something didn't feel right.

Not one to quit, especially on one of her children, my aunt started driving to homes, school, and church and making phone calls. This is back in the day when you only had a house phone or used a pay phone. She ultimately learned cousin and three same-aged kids from church had taken off together. Two boys and two girls; it wasn't a boyfriend, girlfriend run away from home situation; they were friends from a church group.

I don't recall whose idea it was, but these barely teens had devised a plan to start a business and make some big, really big, bucks. The plan: drive to Mexico, buy some marijuana, bring it home, and sell it. They'd be rich in no time at all!

Yeah, they were thirteen years old with a plan to drive to Mexico, buy pot, drive back to California's Central Coast where we lived, and be drug dealers. Cousin later told me she wasn't interested in being a drug dealer; she was interested in making money, big money!

Although they were all too young to have a driver's license, one of the boys had bought a truck with plans to fix it up sweet. It'd be ready when he was old enough to legally drive. I don't recall how much start-up cash they had, nor where it came from. I'm sure cousin had some money; she often cleaned house and took care of our elderly neighbor's yard; she was always the enterprising sort.

The non-truck-owning boy called his cousin, a sailor stationed in San Diego. The boy asked his cousin if they could spend the night at his place on their way to Mexico. Cousin asked who he was with, and the boy told him their names and their plan. Cousin said sure, you can stay. The sailor knew he wouldn't let the foursome leave his place once they arrived; he'd keep them until he knew the plan to get them safely home to their families.

As soon as the call ended, the sailor called the boy's mother to tell her what was happening, knowing his aunt wouldn't have allowed such a venture or trip.

To make this even more interesting is knowing that the sailor and I dated before he enlisted in the Navy. He knew my family well, instantly recognizing my cousin's unusual name. This was in the '70s; phone numbers were kept in your head, and this was only a year or so after the sailor and I had broken up. I'd lived with Gran, and he still remembered our phone number. He told his aunt to call my house, let us know my cousin was okay, and get her mother's number.

His aunt did so. My aunt was relieved and then furiously mad. Who wouldn't be? Can you imagine your barely teenage daughter is on her way to Mexico with three other kids with plans to become a drug dealer? So very, very scary, and you know how most of us are. Worry, worry, worry, and then when you find out your loved one is okay and put you through such worry, you get MAD!

The boy's mother asked what my aunt planned to do.

My aunt said, "I'm going to go get them, of course! And then I'm going to beat my daughter half to death!"

The boy's mother said she wanted to go with my aunt, which was okay with Auntie.

Somewhere during the fast and furious four-hundred-mile drive, the boy's mother told my aunt she was having a hard time securing a job.

Everywhere she applied, they took exception to the fact that she'd recently been released from prison and was on parole. Once they learned she'd been imprisoned for bank robbery, they doubted her reliability and trustworthiness and quickly ended the interview. (Go figure.)

I don't recall if that worried my aunt more than she already was. The woman was friendly, easy to talk to, and could be funny, but she was a bank robber and a bad one at that! And her teenage daughter was with a bank robber's son on their way to Mexico to become drug dealers.

Yikes! Can you imagine?

Now, if you have difficulty believing this story, you might choke on the following details. I promise you; this is all true. Bizarre but true. Everything in this book is true.

The old truck broke down somewhere along the route, so the kids bought a car from someone. I can't imagine their story about why four teens were buying a car and what type of person would sell it to them. Nevertheless, they ditched the truck and continued on their way to becoming millionaires in their new drug car.

My aunt pulled into a random gas station in San Diego to get gas. She was casually looking around as she pumped gas when she noticed a teenage boy on another island pumping gas into a car. His back was turned to her, and the island and car partially obscured him. She gave him a quick once-over glance. Then her eyes caught his feet.

What was this? The lad was wearing the same "Jesus" sandals one of her daughter's guy friends always wore. The guy friend who was on his way to Mexico with her daughter to buy drugs and become a dealer! OMG!!!

At about the same time, Auntie's mind makes that realization: her daughter saw her.

Cousin said, "OH SHIT!! THERE'S MY MOTHER!!"

Before my cousin could make a move, my aunt was across both islands and had yanked the car door open.

"Get your ass out of the car right now! All of you! RIGHT NOW! Do not say a word, not one *** damn word, or I swear I'll rip your head off right here and shit down the hole!"

Auntie had moved so fast the boy's mother (still sitting in the car) didn't even understand what was happening as Auntie flew across the lot.

Those four kids got out of their car, hung their heads, and silently climbed into the back seat of my aunt's car. I do mean silently.

The gas station wasn't far from the base, so several sailors were standing around. Back in the '70s thumbing a ride was still an acceptable mode of travel for some, especially a sailor, and a gas station was a logical place to hitch.

My aunt pulled the keys out of the ignition of the kid's drug car and called out to a couple nearby sailors, "Hey, do you boys have a car?"

One responded with, "No, ma'am."

Auntie tossed him the keys to the kid's drug car and said, "Well, you do now."

She walked back to her car, looked at the kids, and gave each one of them the evilest eye she could render before she climbed in the front seat. She pointed her finger at her daughter and said, "Not a word. Not one fucking word."

All four complied. They were afraid to even look at one another. Can you imagine how those kids felt? They went from being almost thirteen-year-old brilliant millionaires to little kids knowing they'd been caught in the midst of doing a bad deed and punishment would be extremely hot and heavy.

Somewhere along the silent-in-the-back-seat ride home, they stopped for food. My aunt made all the kids go in with her and the ex-bank robber but would not allow them to eat or speak.

In my mind, this was a direct intervention by God to save those four would-be millionaires from who knows what could have befallen them in Mexico. Most likely, they'd never have been seen or heard from again.

I don't know how long my cousin was grounded, or any of them for that matter. Auntie and the unsuccessful bank robber became very good friends. Gran hired the ex-bank robber to cook and clean the following income tax season.

Uncle Stub thought she was gorgeous and would torment her by following her around, pinching her bottom with his two good fingers whenever he got the chance when he visited during tax time.

After learning the woman taught my cognitively impaired cousin to walk into a room full of tax clients and say things like, "Hey, taco benders, how's it going today?" Granny's compassion dwindled, and she fired the ex-bank robber.

At some point, my cousin dated the ex-bank robber's son. After they broke up and the ex-bank robber again fell on hard times, my aunt and uncle allowed the woman and her two children to live with them for a time.

I don't know what happened to the other three kids; however, in adulthood, my cousin became the number one salesperson for a mobile phone company for several years. She attributed her success to her passionate belief that every woman should be equipped with a cellular phone to call 911 in an emergency. The action she took to help others took her to the top of her industry.

Cousin left corporate America because she needed a lifestyle change. For years, she was in overdrive, primarily fueling herself with coffee and cigarettes to keep the pace she wanted. One day, her body let her know it had had enough, so she made a career and lifestyle change.

Today, she's a certified L.E.A.N. Coach. (Lifestyle, Exercise, Attitude, and Nutrition), Master Gardner and Commercial Farm Representative, Her passionate belief is that every man, woman, and child should be in control of their health so they don't have to call 911 for a health emergency. On the path of rising to the top of her industry by again helping others, she sells vertical gardens. She teaches gardening to nourish and heal the mind, body, spirit, and soul.

Cousin is a successful farmpreneur in the vertical garden sector. Using 21st-century technology (some call it a space-age food growing system), she and her husband are helping to expand the food revolution by offering better nutrition for all. They also grow and distribute seedlings for their vertical farming venture. Ironically enough, my young entrepreneur cousin did become a successful plant distributor after all:-)

She is also one of the people I most admire on this planet. She is married to the love of her life; they have two daughters, five grandchildren, and a new great-grandchild. All their lives are Christ-centered.

GENEVA MARIE BRETT

CHAPTER 27

Two Pivots

My great-grandmother married at the age of fifteen. My grandmother, effectively an orphan, married two months shy of turning fifteen because her beau promised to provide for her and her younger brother. Gran had been doing so on her own for some time. His pledge of undying love didn't do much for her, but the promise of financial security was too much for her to resist for herself and her brother. In truth, the life he promised didn't exist; instead, it was a life of hard work and heartache. Nevertheless, she was all in when she said I do, and she gave her best effort for the duration.

Knowing of the false promises of an older man to a naive girl, Gran was horrified when she learned her oldest daughter (age fifteen) had run away from home with a nineteen-year-old intending to marry in Reno. By the time they caught up to them, they'd already married and bedded. In those days, they thought the damage had been done because she'd lost her "virtue," so they didn't have the marriage annulled. Auntie never returned to school because her new important role was "homemaker." She became a mother ten months later.

Five years after that, my grandparents allowed my sixteen-year-old mother to drop out of high school to marry her nineteen-year-old boyfriend. I understood that getting married and having a family were what was expected of a woman in those days. A couple of years wouldn't change that, particularly among my people who weren't well educated but were doing well financially due to their work ethic and intellect. Mom and her beau didn't have to run away; her parents paid for a wedding with one hundred fifty guests. Decades later, both Mom and her husband (that first one) told me she was too young to marry; however, it was a way out of the house.

Mom said she felt like she didn't get to be a kid because she was too busy taking care of her siblings. Mom was pregnant with my brother within weeks. Number one told me, "We knew how to have sex; we just didn't know how to prevent making babies." So much for the freedom from kids.

Not exactly a rinse-repeat, but kind of. They allowed their youngest daughter to quit school and wed just two months before her 16th birthday. I'm sure Auntie wanted out of the house as well. Like my mother, she had been caring for siblings, nephews, and a niece most of her life. And another one bites the dust . . . She, too, was pregnant within weeks. Those Kennedy daughters were fertile! (So was I!)

There were a lot of changes once the baby daughter left the house, which was about a year after the oldest daughter died. Grandma and Grandpa still had six children they were raising; two sons of their own and four of us grands, not to mention the other grands who'd often stay at our house to play with us. Our range was from me at two years to their oldest son at home, aged twelve. That's five boys from five to twelve; Yeowza, that must have been tough! We ran a bit wild. Gran said she didn't know how she did it all those years. One needed a diaper changed, another fell, two were fighting, and all needed to eat, have their clothes washed, dried on the line, and then starched and ironed. When you look at it from that perspective, you can understand the girls who were forced to do the domestic work, wanting their freedom. Ah, but isn't life ironic; all had babies of their own within the first year of their marriages. So much for the freedom they sought.

Being the youngest of those raised by my grandparents, I didn't have to take care of little children, nor was I required to do much domestic work. Gran was probably too tired to teach and figured it faster and easier to do things herself by then. I helped some when younger cousins would visit, but I didn't have a lot of responsibilities in my young days.

But oh, how I wanted out of that house! The constant chaos and confusion, the law showing up, was all hard on my tender, hidden self. Gran's house was the hub for a family who used more physical expressions of emotion than verbal ones. Meaning they didn't talk through issues; they typically fought through them.

I loved my people, and it grieved me when they hurt one another with words, weapons, or fists. That's not to say I didn't participate myself. You had to if you wanted to survive. You didn't cry, definitely didn't tattle, you stood your ground, and you did NOT show fear. If you got knocked down, you got up and kept on keeping on.

My last fist fight was when I was in eighth grade; it was my first and last fight with nonfamily. (That time I bloodied the lip of my former husband's friend doesn't count as a fight. He started bouncing around, throwing pretend jabs and asked if I wanted to fight. I ignored him for a minute or two, but he kept bouncing and pretend jabbing, "Come on, Nev, let's box." So, I threw one punch and bloodied his lip, shocking and awing both him and my husband! I said, "Sorry, I didn't mean to hurt you. In my family, when someone asks if you want to fight, they mean it, so you'd best put a stop to it quickly." That immediately ended the "boxing" I had no desire to play.) Ah, but again I digress, which seems to be a recurring theme with me.

A girl a year younger than me lived down our road a ways when I was in junior high. I didn't like her very much because she wasn't friendly, and she treated me with what I felt was disdain, like she was better than my people and me. I suppose I was getting too full of such treatment that was based upon my family's actions, and that as I aged, it was the kids themselves (as opposed to their parents) who were doing the talking and judging me for things over which I had zero control.

I didn't appreciate that at all, so when I heard that girl had been bullying one of my younger cousins, that poor ole camel's back was severely weakened. I couldn't and didn't go for that. I didn't have a problem with a fair fight, but picking on someone smaller or weaker infuriated me then and does to this day. In those days, I struggled with anger; there was lots of it around me, but none was expressed appropriately. I'm not proud to say I yelled, hit the walls, and cousins a few times, trying to relieve my anger and frustration.

Welp, the girl and I went at it after getting off the bus one day. The best part was that she agreed to leave my cousin alone. I left that encounter with a mixed bag of emotions. I'd stood up for the weaker one and stood my own ground, yet I felt dirty and disappointed with myself. I was becoming one of them that I tried so hard to be unlike. I wanted a better life, a life chaos and fight free. I wanted more for myself than what I saw at home; what I'd just done would definitely not take me to wherever it was I wanted to go.

I told my cousin she didn't have to worry about that girl ever bothering her again. Cousin must have told her mom because Gran questioned me about the fight. I didn't get chastised; in fact, I was honored for sticking up for the younger one.

Our junior high was a long bus ride across town. After that debacle, I didn't want to ride the bus. I considered my actions morally right; however, I also felt I humiliated myself by sinking into fighting with outsiders. I didn't want to extend my family's reputation by my actions. I knew that what went on in my family wasn't typical, so I tried to keep my home life hidden. By fighting, I'd just proven that I was indeed no better than them.

For quite some time after that, I purposely dragged my feet in the morning to ensure I'd miss the bus and Gran would have to drive me to school. I made excuses to get picked up from school as well. By and large, junior high wasn't a good two years for me. I was self-isolating as I was emotionally recovering from my undesirable behavior, the custody battle between Mom and Gran, and being an adolescent in an uncomfortable, unconventional environment.

Mom said I could live with her, and we'd be moving to Imperial, California. I was all in, thinking my new life in a new location would provide more normalcy and freedom. Gran put the kibosh on that, so that's when the custody battle ensued. Mom lost . . . and I was still stuck at Gran's. Sorry, but that's too much emotion for me right here, so we'll have to catch up with that story in book two.

So, I did what I often did; I got lost in some books. I'd always been an ardent reader; however, during this time, I read more than the fictional works I found at home. I found nonfiction, overcomers, heroes, leaders, and motivational quotes. I started hanging those quotes all over my room, reading them repeatedly and believing that I could become a better me, a best me, no matter where I started or how the deck was stacked. If they could do it, so could I!

I was excited to start high school and step out of Gran's and into my own great life. It was trying to find myself all over again, but it was more challenging because I knew I didn't want to wander around alone. I knew those next four years would propel me into MY life, the life I designed myself. I stumbled and stuttered some and had a crush or two but didn't date my first year. I didn't think a "normal" boy would/could like me. How could I ever explain my people?

Around the time I was fifteen, I dated a boy who was two years older than me. Turns out his parents were best friends with my mother and #8. Oh, joy! The boy loved me for who I was despite my family. Wonderful, wonderful, wonderful. I so desperately wanted love and to get out of the house that I said yes when he proposed.

He sold his car, bought me an engagement ring, and then joined the Navy to stand for our country (Vietnam War) and establish a foundation for our future because he didn't want to do the work his father did. I would obviously stay in school while he sailored. And this was acceptable to our families!!!

I was FIFTEEN and engaged; that's so crazy to me today. There is no way, zero, nada, zip, zilch, that I would have allowed one of my daughters or sons to become engaged at that age. Indeed, it was a tradition for the women of my family to marry that young, but Crikey, times had changed!

My social life blossomed during my boyfriend/fiancée's boot camp because I'd found my homies in the aggies and rodeo kids. I began questioning the commitment I'd made. I hung out with my girlfriends, went to dances, and tried to just be fifteen. Boyfriend and I spoke as often as possible; he wrote me wonderful love letters.

When his graduation from boot camp was approaching, he asked me to go with his parents and sister to his graduation in San Diego. I had a little trepidation about traveling alone with his family. Still, I loved him and wanted to honor and support him, so I thought I could do that. That's when he sprang his plan on me; "You and I will sneak over the border to Mexico and get married!"

Insert the sound of screeching brakes here, smell the burning rubber, and visualize long lines of skid marks! I didn't say the words, but my heart slammed on my internal "Whoa, Nelly, this ride isn't what I had planned at all!". Marriage in three years was one thing but in three weeks at fifteen? Nah, it wasn't for me. I'd already started watching my girlfriends and seeing what I was missing out on. I was beginning to think I didn't want to be engaged right now; I just wanted to be a fifteen-year-old kid. His plan doomed our relationship.

I wanted out of Gran's house, yet I couldn't be like the women in my family, not one of whom had graduated high school. They'd traded an education for a husband and babies; I hadn't seen where that was something I wanted at my tender age. I wanted to break the cycle, graduate high school and college, have a career, and do something with my life more than I wanted out of Gran's house.

I wasn't just a Kennedy; I was also a Brett. My father was elected to his County Democratic Committee when he was twenty-two years old; his father was elected to City Council, then Mayor, and later rejected his party's request that he run for Congress. Dad's brother-in-law had also been elected to City Council. I had things to do and places to go!

I gave some excuse as to why I couldn't attend his graduation and later broke his heart with a "Dear John" letter. Breaking his heart also broke mine because he was a good guy who truly loved me and wanted to spend all his life with me. He nor his family forgave me for many, many years. He is still friends with some of my family, and he has grown to be a rock-solid man.

So that was Pivot #1.

That pivot was good for me, but I was unskilled in ballet, so I stumbled. Although partying and cutting school was standard behavior for my new friends, it wasn't for me. I'd been goody two shoes, good grades, no behavioral problems to deal with. It was a challenging scenario because I still aspired for my great future, but I felt at home with my new friends; I felt like I was accepted for ME. My friends didn't judge me for my family; some of their parents did, but my friends didn't.

Who I wanted to be and where I came from began battling it out within. That feral nature I saw in my people was rising up in me; I was feeling a bit wild and acting it.

I began partying and cutting school. I don't remember the name of the attendance policy they had at school; however, it was ridiculous. We didn't need to bring a note from home to explain an absence; we were on an honor system whereby we wrote our own excuse and signed it. Seriously. How absurd is that? That policy wasn't conducive to attendance for teens who had more fun things to do and could get away with it. Regrettably, I wasn't honorable with the policy. I maintained grades but often cut school with the six-pack of girls I hung out with back then. We smoked weed, drank beer, and drove up and down the Salinas Valley.

Unfortunately, my guidance counselor provided me with little guidance. He asked if I planned on attending college, and I said yes, but he never told me the classes I needed to take for admittance. There were many core classes I should have taken but didn't because there were more fun classes that would provide the credits. Filmmaking sounds much more fun than biology, doesn't it? I did not want to slice up dead frogs; I'd had the trauma of chicken killing and didn't need to see frog guts. There was no guidance at home for this because no one had the experience to be a guide. I accept responsibility for not independently researching what I needed to do, but you don't know what you don't know.

Ag and FFA were my home; we had great teachers who genuinely cared about us. I competed in cattle judging, parliamentary procedure, open and close, and public speaking. When I learned I could take Ag Math instead of a traditional math class, I signed up, again, different from what I needed for college. I partied and cut school a great deal during my junior year. Reasonable grades: my lowest was probably a C due to poor attendance. The school never contacted my grandmother about my many absences. My Gran nor my mom questioned why I was no longer getting A's and B's. I don't remember either of them ever asking if I had homework.

Midway through my junior year, I got to live with my mom again; she was married to #8. Although there was another emotional custody hearing (to be discussed in book two), I was having things!!! He was no #5, but he was a decent man who treated me very well. He and Mom went deep sea fishing together and had dinner parties and barbeques; we water skied and camped on the weekends; it was a decent family life.

Number eight served in the Navy during the Korean War and had issues resulting from his service. Many times when he'd get drunk, he would talk about seeing his best friend getting blown in half right next to him. Then he'd say, "And who the hell cared?" For a long time, I'd offer this one, and that one cared; eventually, I'd decide it was time to exit the scene when I heard the best friend was about to die again. They didn't call it post-traumatic stress back then, but he had it and didn't deal with it well.

Initially, we had no chaos or confusion in our home, but as Mom and #8's drinking progressed, home wasn't so good. They'd be getting along fine when they left the house to go have "a" beer at the "FBI" (Frank's Bavarian Inn), the Shamrock Inn, or the Capitol Motel, all within a few miles of home. They'd be in a heated argument when they returned; I didn't like the disrespectful way #8 talked to Mom when they returned. I began resenting #8. That was until the night they stayed home and got drunk, and I saw their progression.

I don't know what Mom's issue was that particular night, or in general. Perhaps her hard-luck life was an undercurrent in everything. Anyway, all was well; they were having a good time and then disagreed on something. Number eight didn't cuss too much; Mom, as you know, liked, no loved, the "F" word. They went back and forth a bit, then she slung a "Fuck You!" at him.

He replied in a reasonable tone of voice, "Louise, don't say that. You know I don't like that word. Don't use that word."

Mom responded by quickly crossing the room, stopping within two inches of his face, so he could not only clearly hear her words, but he could also feel her breath as she enunciated them and her intent . . .

"FUCK! FUCK! FUCK! MOTHER FUCK! FUCK! FUCK! FUCK! MOTHER FUCK! And FUCK YOU! MOTHER FUCKER!"

"*** dammit Louise!" as he turned and walked away.

Yeowza, my viewpoint immediately changed, and I understood why so many men hit her. I wanted to hit her! Crikey, that woman was a lot!

Mom didn't mind if my friends and I drank, so long as we did it at home. It sounded good then, but it wasn't. Mom had a drinking problem. I was humiliated when she got wasted in front of my friends.

In my junior year, there was a big cowboy dance at Bolado Park in Tres Pinos (near Hollister) that my gal pals and I wanted to attend. Thinking we'd end up drinking, #8 didn't want me driving myself and friends the thirty miles to and from the dance in the fog. He said I could go IF Mom went along. No problem, she was fun, and my friends loved her.

Welp, it was freezing inside, we complained a bit . . . but we were teenage girls at a cowboy dance. We warmed up dancing! Mom stood around the perimeter of the dance floor, miserable, until an adult invited her upstairs into the bar, where it was toasty warm. Mom proceeded to get hammered, not quite stumbling, but ever so close. I didn't drink and ended up driving home, while Mom kept calling one of my girlfriends "Charlie Potatoes" and asking her to keep checking to see if her lighter had sobered up yet.

Mom had dropped her lighter in her beer while trying to light a cigarette. Woo doggies, #8 was Banty rooster mad when he saw Mom weave her way up the sidewalk into the house! Mom was a happy drunk that night, and she knew she'd failed us . . . so she didn't get into his face with her flying F's.

Although, at first, it seemed cool for my parents to let us drink, I came to realize my friends didn't truly respect Mom because she did so and because she got hammered with us. Mom was drunk when I got home from school on more than one occasion. I lost a lot of respect for her as well.

One day, my six-pack of gal pals and I cut school; we didn't drink or smoke weed that day; we just traveled around the valley. (I still love to just get out and drive the back roads.) As I went past my house on my way to drop off my last friend at the end of the day, I saw my Ag Teacher's truck parked in front of my house.

"Uh oh, uh oh, uh oh! The jig is up! I am so busted, and there's no way out of this." My friend and I came up with stories, but ultimately, I knew no lie would work. He knew I wasn't in his class and came to my house to find out why. Because he cared.

That day started turning things for me, it wasn't THE pivot, but it was the beginning. My teacher saw enough value in me to stop me from hurting my future. That he saw a future for me was monumental. I started examining my life; where I was going with what I was doing was not where I ever wanted to be. I slowed my partying and cutting class, and I started doing homework and paying attention in class. I accepted what I'd always known was true. The friends I hung out with didn't really have the same aspirations as me; we weren't equals.

Pivot #2 was not being elected to the FFA office I sought. I learned my peers didn't trust me to do the job because of my reputation as a class cutter and partier. Oh my, that was a stab to my soul! I'd already decided that my behavior would not produce the desired results, so I had to change. I'd earned the rep but was nevertheless horrified and humiliated. That ended my party days and class cutting. As it turns out, the person elected to the position I sought started his partying time and didn't do his job. He resigned from the position, and I was elected to serve.

Which I did and did well. I was selected as a delegate to the State FFA Convention, placed high in speaking and parliamentary procedure competitions, and ended my senior year with awards in Ag for being me and doing what I'd always planned. My best me.

Beloved, you need to associate with people who are, at minimum, your same level. If you want to move forward and grow, you need to associate with people who are at a higher level than you. You need to grow to be inspired by the success of others. To see that you can! It doesn't matter where you came from, who your people are, what you've done, or what your people did. Your future is up to you and you alone. Your future starts with your next breath.

As my Gran said, "As long as there's life in the body, there's hope for the soul." Go get yourself some goodness. You are a human being, and you are as entitled to bliss and success as is every other soul on this planet!

Read Ed Mylett's book, *The Power of One More*, and Eric Thomas's (ET- The Hip Hop Preacher) book, *You Owe You*, to fuel your inner winner. Then read *75 HARD*, by Andy Frisella. Mmm, mmm, mmm; he's in your face about all the excuses we make every single day. About how we quit every single day.

Whether or not you accept the 75 HARD challenge, the book's a must-read. Someone needs to talk to you like that! I completed the 75 HARD challenge in the spring of 2022 and hated it. Swore I'd never do it again because it is indeed HARD! Five daily tasks, zero compromises. If you miss one single task, you must start over. [Two 45-minute workouts (one must be outside, regardless of weather), read 10 pages of nonfiction, self-growth book (no audiobooks), drink one gallon of water, stick to a diet (no cheat meals, no alcohol) and take a progress photo. You choose your workouts and diet.]

I'm almost a third of the way through my second run at it (in 2023). I'm doing it because it is HARD. Because it gives you grit and focus. I don't like it any better this round, but I have a stronger mindset. Quitting is not an option. I'm going to be the victor and love day 76!

CHAPTER 28

Do NOT Arm Wrestle My Mother!

Family and friends gathered at my home after a family member's burial for fellowship, storytelling, and reminiscing. Most of the friends had left, so it was just family. The topic of conversation shifted to my mother. All of my people had stories to tell about Mom. Great stories.

My brother shared that before he took his wife (then girlfriend) to meet Mom, he gave her a warning.

"Look, sweetheart, no matter what my mom says, do NOT arm wrestle her. It will not end well. Don't do it, don't do it, don't do it. If you don't take my advice and you do arm wrestle her, LET HER WIN! I know my mom, and I'm telling you, this is for the best. Trust me on this!"

Brother didn't say if she gave him an eye roll, but I imagine she did in her mind. Who warns someone not to arm wrestle their mother? That's ridiculous!

You should probably know that the first time Ron introduced his beloved to Mom, they met her at a bar, not just any bar, but one of Mom's regular hangouts. Mom had been there a while before they arrived - some fairly heavy drinking was going on. It was all fun and good times, laughing and shooting pool. That was until Ron's advice was ignored.

Ron's lady, a State Champion Horseshoe Player, was competitive and couldn't see the harm in an arm wrestling challenge. She was young, fit, and strong; Ron's mom was twice her age! Sooooo, when Mom's inevitable challenge came, she resisted a few times but ultimately agreed to the match.

I mean, she had her own dignity to uphold, so she not only arm-wrestled Mom, but she also won the match! As forewarned, it did not go over well.

Mom was liquored up and so mad (and I'm sure embarrassed by the loss) that she didn't want a rematch. She wanted to go straight to fisticuffs and lunged across the table at Ron's love to get it started. Knowing Mom and predicting her response to the loss, Ron launched himself into the middle of them, thereby preventing Mom's first blow and a very challenging future relationship between the two women he loved so much.

One of our cousins was amazed at my brother's story, "Who tells their girlfriend not to arm wrestle with their mother the first time they meet? I mean, in what world is that a conversation?"

Not to be left out, my husband told of an evening Mom came to our house during our first year together. She'd been drinking before she arrived and brought along a man-friend we hadn't met. We sat around the table, talking and drinking beer when Mom decided she wanted to arm wrestle my man.

Like my brother's words, I warned him not to do it. Several times. I told him not to do it. (You do understand I warned him not to arm wrestle my mother, right?) Mom was insistent, and eventually, he, too, relented. Husband was in his prime, water skied, and had a physical job. He was buffed, Mom twice his age, male vs. female . . .

Soooo, they engaged in the challenge, and husband (then boyfriend) was easily resisting Mom's pressure to slam his arm to the table. He was a bit cavalier and, well, probably cocky. He continued to chat and took a sip of his beer with the other hand. Mom didn't appreciate such an act of dismissal and disrespect, so she stood up and started applying body weight to push his arm to the table. It didn't work immediately, so she bounced to pressure his arm down with her body weight. Remember I said she'd been drinking? As happens with drunks, her balance was off, and her hands slipped off his, thereby releasing the pressure he was resisting. Without the pressure, his hand returned to the upright position, where it connected with my mother's chin!

Yeowza! No bueno. Nothing good would come of that!

That snapped Mom back into the moment. She responded quickly, "You hit me! You dirty bastard! You hit me! Did you see that? Mother fucker just hit me!"

My man threw his hands up in the air and stammered, "No, no, I didn't hit you! It was an accident. You slipped off my hand, and my hand came up without the pressure I was resisting. I didn't hit you! I wouldn't hit you. It's your fault; you did it to yourself. I didn't hit you. YOU hit you!"

I jumped up out of my seat, knowing my mother would have zero problem hitting a man. Especially one she decided had just hit her. My mind was racing like a Maserati! If Mom started swinging at my man, what might her man friend do? Did he see what happened, or did he believe what Mom said? I was extremely grateful my children were with their father that night!

My eyes were darting back and forth between them like that gif from *The Good, the Bad, and the Ugly*! I moved into position between them, all the while thinking, "Boyfriend, you're in a hole. STOP DIGGING! Shut your pie hole!" as he continued to backpedal.

Mom was coming at him, hand fisted and drawn back. My mother fought like a man, and she was wanting to kick some man ass. So, there's me (5'2, 110 pounds) between Mom (5'5, weighing in at 130) and my man (5'9 and 150), and then there's her man friend (5'11 and maybe 185). I'd probably be the first one to get their ass kicked!

I was talking as fast as I could, trying to bat her fist down and push her back to her seat. This was a dangerous move on my part because she was liquored up, agitated, and could easily shift her focus to me. Mom liked to fight, and now she was amped up for one! Ay Caramba!

I got her calmed down, and she sat back down. We started telling jokes to lighten the mood. I kept my eye on Mom because she could hold on to and nurse a grudge; I knew better than to trust her right then. Mom could be brewing herself up a storm of any size.

As time passed, my man relaxed a bit; me, not so much. Mom kept throwing him the side eye. The hair on the back of my neck got a bit sensitive when I saw her working her jaw from side to side. That was typically the sign that she'd been thinking on whatever and was getting fueled for action. Welp, when my unsuspecting man turned his head to look across the room, Mom fisted up, loaded her punch from below the table, and Sunday punched him.

"There, you rotten son of a bitch. That'll teach you to hit me! You better never hit me again, mother fucker!"

She threw a solid punch that connected to his jaw, which seemed to satisfy her. Mom's ego was now intact, and she was willing to move on. We did.

Ahem. Need I tell you, there was never another arm wrestling match with my brother's woman or my man?

Among all the stories told that day after the family service, it's bizarre that male and female siblings told their significant other not to arm wrestle their mother!

If you're in a relationship and your significant other warns you about a family member, I suggest you trust your beloved. It doesn't matter whether or not you think a person would/could do whatever. Your person probably knows from experience, and that's why you are warned. If you don't trust your significant other, you should move on along.

CHAPTER 29

Folsom Prison Blues

Same prison, different blues. My blues are from relatives doing time, "tours" of California's penal institutions, and the trickledown effect upon other innocent family members and me.

About a decade ago, a cousin asked if I had any pictures of them as a kid. I searched the family pics and found one of us; I was seven, cousin was a few years younger. We were holding hands, had great big smiles . . . visiting a relative in a youth prison.

Do you have a pic like that? If so, you know the jumble of emotions it generates. You, the reader, can't tell the photo was taken in prison by looking at it. However, I remembered the moment I saw it, and so did cousin.

It was the early 1960s when incarceration wasn't commonplace or portrayed on television as it is today. The most jail a kid was exposed to was in a Western, or maybe *The Andy Griffith Show*. Not us, though. We'd visited the California Youth Authority and Preston School of Industry (reform school/penal institution for minors). Yet, we didn't know shame then, because visiting family in lockup was our norm.

Shame found me on Monday morning during first grade "Show and Tell" when the teacher asked what we'd done over the weekend.

Innocently and naively, I shared, "We visited so and so in prison."

I read the teacher's instant reaction and knew what I'd shared was "abby, abby, normal." (Children who live in a violent environment, or one with chaos and confusion, learn to read people. Hypervigilance is a survival technique to help deal with whatever unknown might come next.)

Boom, another moment of innocence lost and the realization that I'd best keep home at home if I didn't want to be a further outcast. Ah, but that was far beyond my control or the control of any of us except the outlaws. Their exploits and incarcerations were well known in the community, and we were known as their family.

People trusted Gran enough to come to her year after year to have her prepare their tax returns. Yet, they gossiped behind her back about her family, and many refused to allow their children to associate with us. By the time I was in sixth grade, Gran had stopped taking us to church because she couldn't tolerate the gossip about her family. Most of it was true.

We undeservedly wore cloaks of shame and embarrassment while, at the same time, we held our heads high in defiance. As I've told you, my people were legendary. Some were truly badass outlaws, feared and admired by outlaws, the law, friends, and enemies. They were also used by one another, by family, friends, and foes alike. We of the younger generation refused to follow their example.

I remember a family member telling one of our outlaws they'd just heard their song on the radio. The song, "I Fought the Law and the Law Won." Even the outlaw had to laugh at that! No matter how hard life gets, there's always humor to make it a little lighter. It might sound strange to you, but we'd occasionally joke that it looked like so and so was on their way to Sing Sing again. Sing Sing is a notoriously harsh maximum-security prison in New York. None of our people ever did time there, but Sing Sing sounds funnier than San Quentin, Folsom, Soledad, or Death Row. Tis better to laugh than cry.

No matter where they actually lived, throughout their entire lives of crime, the outlaws used Gran's address (also mine) when they were arrested, so that's what was published in the newspaper. Gran operated her income business from that well-known address as well. There was no hiding.

The shame was tough to deal with, but we forgot about the shame when the law told our outlaws that they were on the top ten hit list of the "NF." The NF, Nuestra Familia, was a Soledad Prison based gang that split from the Mexican Mafia. Their motto was "blood in, blood out," meaning they had to shed blood to get in; the only way out was by their own death.

Back then, they had to do time to advance in the ranks of the NF;

therefore, many eager to advance were egregious in their acts to get into prison. No one's life had any value to them, including their own, so they were open and flamboyant in carrying out hits. They expected, even wanted, prison time. We literally feared for the lives of our beloved outlaws, and then we realized our own lives were also in danger. The NF was notoriously brutal; harming women and children was simply part of their business model. They didn't even consider it collateral damage. Dude, they killed their own family members. Life had no value to them. (That's super sad.)

One of our outlaws was ambushed and shot five times (in one shooting) as he sat in a truck, allegedly waiting to "talk with someone." Although he categorically denied (to the cops) that narcotics were involved in the incident, he refused to answer questions during the preliminary hearing of the shooters about whether the shooting was related to a purchase of heroin, which resulted in the dismissal of charges against the shooters.

He said he didn't know why he was on the NF hit list. He admitted having been in the AB (Aryan Brotherhood) in prison (which sometimes sided with the Mexican Mafia, the archrival of the NF) but said he quit the AB when he got out of prison. He didn't know why they wanted him dead.

A few weeks after the ambush, he and the other outlaw on the NF hit list were at Gran's. The one recovering from the gunshots was sitting on the couch smoking a cigarette and looking out the window while the other read the newspaper. The one reading the newspaper said to the other, "Hey brother, they found another dead Mexican out in the field." The recovering outlaw said, "What's this world coming to?"

Sidebar: Within months of the ambush, at least twelve gang members were found dead; the law called them "suspected" gang members. Well, it's not like they carried membership cards.

A cousin told me that in his adulthood, he met a couple former DEA agents while playing golf; somehow, our family name came out in the conversation. The former DEA told cousin that they could have sent our outlaws to prison for life several times but chose not to do so. They said our outlaws and the NF were taking care of one another (by killing each other), which saved DEA lives.

The NF hit list business changed life at Gran's; she kept the lights lowered and the drapes drawn. When recently sharing the above with a different cousin, she recalled being about ten years old, visiting Granny one evening and being told to stay low to the floor and very quiet because there was a car full of the NF parked in front of the house, presumably waiting for one of our outlaws to show up. Cousin's family and some of the others avoided Gran's for a time, literally fearful of getting caught in the crossfire. But family is family, and Gran's home was our hub, so little by little, they started visiting her again. Several of us also worked there during tax season, so forever avoidance was off the table.

Preparing income tax returns was our livelihood, and we worked there at Gran's, whose address was always cited as home by the outlaws and always published in the paper. That first tax season after learning about the hit list was unnerving. There was an unstated but felt undercurrent of being terrorized by lawless, vicious, violent criminals. There were unknown, lawless people who were ordered to kill our family. Yet, we had to open the doors to the public every day for four months, never knowing if the next one through the door was a client or a planned gangster attack.

Additionally, one of our outlaws lived in the house between Gran and me, so I was in the line of fire whether I was at her home or mine. As was my husband, and later my children. Nevertheless, my people did what we always did. We held our heads high, showed no fear, and faced whatever might come our way.

Gran had bars installed on all the windows and the doors. Ironically, her home became somewhat of a prison itself. We lived through this trauma and drama as we did every other one. As though it didn't exist. Thankfully, we never endured any invasions or shootouts at Gran's. None of our outlaws were slaughtered, although attempts were made to do so; my people were just tougher or wilier.

A different verse to the prison blues were the times I visited my mother in jail and the halfway house. Those were harder and more hurtful because it was my M-O-T-H-E-R. Mom wasn't a badass criminal; she was "just" a serial fighter and serial drunk driver. An uncle took me to visit Mom in jail when I was ten years old. She was doing forty-five days in the county jail for fighting. I don't remember how long it'd been since I'd seen her before that day. I never knew when I'd see my mother. I always wanted to see my mother, but to see her locked in a cage like a dangerous animal, hmm. That was a complicated internal debate, yet I took him up on the offer to go with. I remember the trepidation I felt on the drive to jail; I loved my mother, but this just wasn't right. Television moms wore heels and pearls; they never fought or went to jail. I'm thankful I wasn't allowed to go in; sitting in the car and imagining what it was like inside was hurtful enough.

The shame only increased with each of her incarcerations, including her last near year in jail for drunk driving, and the following fifteen months she was in a halfway house. I wouldn't visit Mom during that final lockup, but we did correspond by mail. It became more challenging when she got to the halfway house and truly worked the program. It was bittersweet to watch her awaken and begin to understand that her mama's house and environment were unhealthy for her.

She also asked for nearly more than I was willing to give; she asked me to bring my children to visit her on family day. I'd sworn to myself that I would never expose my children to the inmate environment. They'd already seen and heard too much within our family without adding that to their burdens. I wanted as much of a normal life for my children as possible. I'd never been to a halfway house; however, I worked for an attorney and dealt with many clients we sent to those programs. To me, the halfway houses were dirty and seedy, not anything I wanted my children to experience.

Ah, but Mom was making significant progress. It was important to her that I visit, Gran wouldn't and shouldn't go, and I desperately wanted a healed mother. I ping-ponged within myself and made the tough decision to put my mother's needs before my children's. (Don't judge me for that! You can't know what you would do unless you faced the same circumstances with the same history.)

I rationalized my children wouldn't be visiting their grandmother in jail; it was a house full of women, and other children would be present. I explained to my children that we extend our hand when people are down, we never kick them, and Grandma Lou needed us.

Seeing my mother being one of "those people" was hurtful. It was hard truth I already knew, but still, the moment wounded me deeply. That shame and embarrassment were rearing up again.

"Far from Folsom Prison, that's where I want to stay, then I'd let that lonesome whistle blow all my blues away."

But it never did. Remember that TV show *Cops*, with the "Bad boys, bad boys, whatcha gonna do when they come for you?" theme song? My husband was channel surfing and landed on that show shortly after it premiered. I heard the song from another room and walked in to see what it was. I felt sucker punched when I saw the introduction of the show.

Years before I married my second husband, two of Mom's siblings had a bitter dispute that destroyed the family. Dear reader, you have family. You know how that goes with people choosing sides. At that time, Gran sold her home and her business, leaving our family without a hub. There were no more family gatherings. She moved, I moved, and the outlaw moved. No more family gatherings, so we weren't exposed to whatever was going on in the lives of the outlaws. I hadn't told my husband much about my family because there was no need. I finally felt free of their baggage.

Unlike my former husband, my second husband wasn't a local. He wasn't aware of my people's infamy. Eventually, others told him tales of the family he'd married into, but he never experienced any of our gatherings or got to know our outlaws as humans, as beloved family members. He wasn't around them and had no idea of the lives we'd led. There are still many things he doesn't know (a lot my children don't know), but they'll learn some when they read this book and the next one. It's not like I intentionally kept things from him or them; I didn't want to pick at old scabs, and there was a lot I'd forgotten. I wanted my new, different life. Freedom from my people's story. (Irony strikes again. Now I'm telling the story I hid from for over half my life!)

Back to that TV show . . . I explained that I couldn't tolerate that show in my home because I'd lived that. I'd been one of those innocent little children in the background. The collateral damage children. The desire for voyeurism and judgment into the lives of human beings you don't know or understand just to make you feel better about your life is sad and hurtful.

When you judge those "bad boys," you're also judging every innocent person in that family who bears a weight not of their making or within their control. You don't know their story; you aren't going to learn their story, and my heart can't stand to have that in my home.

Sidebar: Who are any of us to judge another? People watch that type of show and condemn people. "If that was me, I'd blah, blah, blah," I call BS on that. We all have degrees of wonkiness; you have no clue how you'd manage in that situation when you aren't that person and don't have their life experiences that brought them to that moment. Imagine how hard that life is on those innocent little children in the background. Stop judging! (Off soapbox.)

Back to my blues, not long ago, I shared the story of the cousin prison pic and my prison blues with my older kids. (Due to the family collapse, my youngest wasn't around that side of my family very much; knows few of them or these stories.) Anyway, my older two independently told me about when Gran had taken them to visit a relative in prison. It was thirty years after the fact. I was incredulous and furious. I'm grateful Mom and Gran have passed; they wouldn't have appreciated what I had to say. At all.

My son said it wasn't so bad. Gran bought him an action figure on the way, so he thought it was pretty cool for a time. Then he said it worked as a great deterrent. Walking into the big meeting room with the inmates and families, the shouting because some are happy and some are angry, the armed guards and bars in the windows. It made him never want to be in such a place. Prison was a bit more normalized on TV by this time, and son saw that it wasn't the cool place it was portrayed to be. It was definitely not a place he ever wanted to be.

When I told him about sharing my experience in school and the teacher's horrified reaction, he said he wasn't dumb enough to tell. He then said he was actually told not to tell! Grrrrr. Innocence stolen.

You can't force inmates to learn, to grow spiritually, emotionally, or to change. But maybe we can give them some practical options to succeed. For the most part, they aren't provided with meaningful opportunities for growth and change. Whatever they've done to earn their sentence, when they've paid their debt (incarceration is to be payment to society for the crime), they should get a second chance at life. A REAL opportunity for a meaningful change. Humans are not disposable. Our society would be so much better if we allowed change, if we stopped pressing people down so we could rise above them.

Prison consists of race-based politics. No matter their age or crime, inmates are expected to join a gang of their ethnicity to survive, then do as they're told or become a shot caller themselves. They're repeatedly told they're worthless convicts by those in control and told they won't survive on the outside, that they'll be right back to the joint. On the inside, they learn how to be better criminals and learn more ways to avoid getting caught. Drugs, alcohol, and violence are rampant within.

Nonetheless, the incarcerated have hopes and dreams of what they'll do when they get on the outside. Every living creature wants to be free. In reality, where will they go when they're released? They'll have no job, no money, and are convicted felons. They're going to the only place they know. Home.

Home to people and places where they got in trouble in the first place. What kind of job will they get when they must admit they're a convicted felon on every job app? Who's going to hire them? You? Probably not. They've been labeled bad, worthless, and incorrigible. Most humans read the labels placed on others. It's so, so sad. The system is incredibly flawed.

According to the Bureau of Justice's statistics, "Spending per prisoner varies widely across states, from about $18,000 per prisoner in Mississippi to $135,978 per prisoner in Wyoming in 2020. States spent an average of $45,771 per prisoner for the year." The cost to house an inmate, one inmate, here in California was a whopping $106,131 in 2021-2022!

There are nearly TWO MILLION people incarcerated in the USA today! That figure includes military, tribunal, juvenile, county, state, and federal facilities. The recidivism rate (those who go back) is 64.7%, with 75% of them returning to lockup within the first sixteen months after release. The system isn't working people!

A for-profit business couldn't survive with a 65% continuous failure rate. Our country is spending around $60 BILLION (with a B) per YEAR, year after year after year, and failing every one of us. We're paying those bills and getting what in return? Failure. Abject failure. This absurd, wildly ridiculous waste of money is one thing; however, the waste and destruction of human lives is far worse. It's not just the inmates. Their families are also impacted. Society is impacted, you and I are impacted. NO human being is disposable! Not one.

Records show you fulfilled your obligation when you get a loan and pay it off. Other lenders don't hold it against you when you've paid your debt. When a person is convicted of a crime against "The People," the convicted one owes a debt to society, calculated by time served in confinement (sometimes there's a monetary debt as well). So, we deprive them of their liberty for the prescribed time, and even though their debt is paid, it continues to follow them throughout their life as though it's still owed. How is that right, fair, or reasonable? How does that serve society as a whole? Let me answer that. It doesn't.

Should we force those who don't have GEDs to earn one as part of their debt? Do we force further education, psychology, and job skills? I don't claim to have any answers. However, it's obvious what we're doing is failing. Do you have ideas on how to fix this mess? I'm interested.

All our lives would have been different and better if the outlaws in our family had real opportunities after they'd served their time. Thankfully, some former convicts have established prison programs to change lives and give felons the second chance opportunities they deserve.

My heart told me to stay far from Folsom Prison because that past was painful. After sharing the prison pic of cousin and I, we've both repeatedly told one another we weren't going back to prison. EVER!

Then I stumbled upon the *Roll Call with Chappy* podcast. Or truthfully, God directed me to Chappy, for my own healing. Host Peter Meyerhoff (Chappy) served twelve years in prison; his podcast is about overcoming addiction, prison, and succeeding in life. His guests are gritty and authentic; they share their stories and offer advice as to how others may overcome, from right where they are, including a prison cell. Thankfully, every inmate has a tablet, and *Roll Call with Chappy* is available to them. They just need to choose to listen, believe, and change for themselves.

Roll Call with Chappy's been pulling on my heartstrings and has stirred me to action. I attended a Women's Ministry Workshop hosted by Dr. Ann Hill in November of 2022; when I thanked her for her women's prison ministry outreach, she asked if I'd like to join the team.

I literally took two steps back and said, "Whoa, I don't know if I can do that. I have some history with family being in prison, and my mom being in jail. I'm going to have to think about that."

I went home thinking, "Nope, can't do it. Nope, not going to do it. Nope. Nope. Nope."

Then God whispered into my soul, "Do it."

I replied, "Are you talking to me? I can't do that. I'm too wounded. I'm not going back to prison."

I called my cousin, told her of the experience, and reaffirmed that I would not be going back to prison. She agreed she wasn't going back either.

Yeah, so then, God told me, two more times, to do it.

The greatest goal of my soul is to hear the Everlasting King of the Universe say, "Well done, my good and faithful servant." when my life has ended. Crikey. So, what could I do but face my wounds and join the Women of Love Ministries Outreach Team to love on the Chowchilla Women's Prison inmates?

Female inmates are harder on my soul than males, presumably because of Mom and her jail stints. I obeyed my God's instruction, thinking my service was for the inmates; turns out I'm the one being healed. When I see those women worshiping God, hands uplifted, tears streaming, hearts rejoicing, I am also moved to tears of gratitude. Their bodies are captive, but HE is setting their souls FREE!!

This past month (June 2023), I prayed for a message for them, then got slapped up beside the head with a message for me.

I said, "Whoa, Jesus. I asked for a message for them; this message is for me."

He responded with, "Child, you're no different than them. You're to teach what you most need to learn. You, too have man wounds, earthly father issues, adults who weren't trustworthy or reliable, so you learned to be self-reliant, wary of trusting, head strong, and unsubmissive. And girl, sometimes that gets in the way of you with me, and in their way with me. I want each and every one of you in heaven with me . . . so you share what I lay on your heart with your sisters, and then I want you all to do the work to come home to your true, perfect father who has loved you from before you were placed in your mother's womb. The father who knows every thought and every deed you would ever do, before you did them, and who has never loved you less for having done them."

Oof. God sent me to prison to heal me.

It's on my heart to do more than participate in a prison ministry in honor of my people. I must do something for the outlaws, and the innocents. As I'm developing the concept, I'm also looking for a place to implement it, perhaps a halfway house first. I look forward to collaborating with people like Peter Meyerhoff and some of his former inmate podcast guests who are also doing God's work with these wounded souls and families.

Anyone can change. Gran raised us up with, "As long as there's life in the body, there's hope for the soul." That's 100% truth!

GENEVA MARIE BRETT

CHAPTER 30
Spoons In the Drawer

I'm pretty sure it was a year or two before Gran passed, so I'm going to claim the main event I'll soon describe occurred in 1994. Two years before, I'd realized my grandmother would actually die, the grandmother who raised me, who wanted me when it seemed no one else did. The one person whose love I never doubted in all my life. I was her namesake and her "golden girl child." She was my rock.

I accepted that I couldn't change what would happen and that I would be left to deal with how I behaved during her last years and her passing. Rather than be sad and lost between the awareness and the event, I decided to get all of her I could while she was alive. I phoned her daily, visited her at least once a week, drove her to her doctor's appointments, took her to church, and slept in the hospital room with her when she needed a stay. It was a hundred-mile round trip from my home to hers.

The drive and inconvenience to my life (I had a job and a seven-year-old child at home) were minor. The bigger issue was her home environment, from which I'd distanced myself for some years. My recollection of her home (as far back as I can remember) was frequent chaos and confusion. Grandpa had alcohol issues, as did some other family members, and some others had drug issues.

Drug addictions created more chaos than the alcohol because dope is illegal and expensive. The drinkers were able to keep jobs, while the junkies spent a great deal of time hustling for cash, which affected their ability to work. Their hustle often included illegal activities, resulting in attorney fees, jail/prison time, chaos, and confusion. Much to our embarrassment, they all used our address when arrested. Gran often picked up the pieces, the attorney fees, and helped during incarcerations.

In addition to that, there were the occasional altercations among family members. If you didn't see it, you heard about it. She said, he said, and they tried to drag you to their side. Like I said, chaos and confusion, from which I distanced myself. I loved my people, we had great times, laughter, and love, but it just wasn't the environment I wanted.

Ah, but Gran would die, so I sucked it up, pushed the yucky old feelings away, and spent time with her in her home. I even helped her prepare taxes again, which I hadn't done for over a decade.

Now that you have the back story, I can get on with telling you about those spoons in the drawer.

I was visiting Gran one day, enjoying our conversation, when a couple family members unexpectedly walked in. These two had danced with heroin for decades, hustled for cash, and been charged and/or convicted of crimes ranging from burglary, pimping, assault, battery, pandering, armed robbery, extortion, being a drug addict, accessory to murder, murder, and had done tours of California's penal institutions; one was even on Death Row for a time. They were infamous in the county, and both had been on the top 10 hit list of the prison-based Nuestra Familia gang.

They were also family, and we all loved them. They would steal from you and fight you, but they would also literally give you the shirt off their back if you needed or wanted it. God help the fool who messed with anyone in the family because if either of them heard about it, the responsible party would be pleading for mercy. They had their own code of honor and sense of justice.

Anyway, at the time of this reminiscence, these two outlaws had been out of the joint for a few years, and both were allegedly clean (aka not using heroin). With all due respect, like with a dog who bit you once, you always wondered if they were a nip away or thinking about it. Having been around them for decades, most of us could tell when they were high. It was highly suspect when the two of them went for a ride together.

They'd come to Gran's on this day after going somewhere together, so my Spidey senses were tingling. My senses didn't let me down. They were both high. Not kite high, but butterfly high. I could tell by their voices that they were groovin'. Grandma didn't allow smoking in her house, so they stepped into the garage to smoke.

Within minutes, I opened the unlocked door and walked into the garage. To this day, I can't remember why. I might have been going to confront them about being high when they were supposed to be clean, particularly at Grandma's after her heart attack. Perhaps I don't remember because of the shock of seeing them fixing. One was tying off the other (wrapping a rubber band around his arm like the phlebotomist does before drawing blood). The fixee had the hypodermic needle in his opposite hand, waiting for the vein to rise.

"Whoa, Nev, don't tell her.", said the one tying off. "We're just having a little taste."

The other said, "Nev honey, don't upset the old girl. We haven't done this in a long time. We aren't bothering anybody. We're just having a little fun."

To say I was highly offended would be an enormous understatement. That they were using again, or still, was their own business, to disrespect our elderly matriarch in her home infuriated me! We all knew she'd had a heart attack. That's why we were all circling around her. I quickly stepped back into the kitchen and closed the door. That's when the internal debate began.

Gran had heart issues; I didn't want to upset her to cause another heart attack. I didn't want to break her heart with the disappointment of knowing they were using. If they were using, they couldn't be trusted. A taste of heroin often resulted in gorging themselves until the law intervened. How could I knowingly allow them to disrespect her? How could I respect myself if I didn't speak up? I accepted that I couldn't.

I told her the two of them were in the garage fixing.

She said, "Oh honey, you're mistaken. They're clean. They don't use drugs anymore. Neither one of them does. They told me."

I said, "Gran, I just saw them. I saw them with my own two eyes just a couple minutes ago."

"Sweetheart, I don't know what you think you saw, but I know they weren't using drugs."

I offered the truth once more, "Gran, I don't use glasses. I saw one tying off the other, and I saw the needle in the other's hand."

She walked out of the room, thereby ending the conversation.

Chaos perfectly describes my emotions. Confusion, anger, indignation, hurt, offendedness, disappointment, and shock are the major emotions I readily recall. At the time, I didn't understand how she could dismiss me, disregard me, and effectively choose them over me by not believing me. I'm not whining because she chose them over me; she chose a lie over the truth. I did not have a habit or reputation for lying then (nor do I now), but they did. She didn't go into the garage to confront them or ask them if what I said was true. She just walked into the living room, turned on the television, and sat down to watch it. I followed her and sat down in stunned silence for maybe five minutes before the torrent inside me required my exit. I told her I loved her and got up to leave.

"Why are you leaving, honey? Stay and visit."

I said I needed to go and would call the next day. My head was still spinning on the drive home.

I did phone her the next day but didn't bring up the junkies for discussion because it was pointless. She'd made her stand the day before. I didn't bring it up to the dopers, again pointless, and we got on as though it never happened. That wasn't unusual; that's how we'd always lived. "Keep moving, folks, nothing to see here."

After Gran passed two years later, I began to understand that, on some level, she realized her time was short. Those last few years, she was all about being right with Jesus, not making any waves or causing drama. Because of that attitude, she did, in fact, cause drama. It wasn't intentional . . . and it's another story for another chapter or book two. Maybe.

She crushed me when she didn't believe me about those two fixing in her garage. It baffled me that she was so naive as to believe them on their word when they'd lied so many, many times before. That she didn't believe my eyes or my word.

After she and Mom passed, I sold their house. While packing up the kitchen, I found where Gran had hidden most of her spoons in the back of a drawer. You see, heroin users cook/melt their drug in a spoon, which blackens and deforms the spoon. She said she believed they were clean (dope free) . . . yet she hid her spoons.

The spoons in the drawer were an "Aha!" moment for me. On some level, she probably did believe me when I told her they were shooting up in her garage. She just decided not to deal with it. That rolled around in my head and my spirit for some time, and as it did, I was thinking and feeling a bit judgy and critical of her. I always thought she'd been an enabler.

Then I had a look at the three fingers pointing back at me. There have been many times in my own life (maybe yours, too) in which I opted not to face the truth. Sometimes knowingly, sometimes unaware of what was going on under my surface.

Yep. I believe nearly all of us humans hide spoons in our drawers.

GENEVA MARIE BRETT

CHAPTER 31

#MeToo

Oh my, how powerful that hashtag consisting of six characters! Two tiny words plus one symbol equal six characters that tell the reader, "I was wounded." For most, add "shamefully wounded" because most of us carry the baggage of shame for what happened TO us. Six characters tell the reader, "I have deep dark secrets I'm now exposing to the light of day." Six characters that say, "I choose to be free of a burden someone placed upon me."

Six characters that cause an undiagnosed discomfort within the reader because one in three girls and one in six boys have been sexually used before they reach the age of eighteen. (Statistics widely vary.) Most never tell of their #MeToo incident(s), even to the one they trust most in the world, for their shame, their wound, is far too deep. Somehow, they blame themselves; they "woulda," "coulda," "shoulda." Or maybe they carry the wounds from the other side of the #MeToo; perhaps they were the one who directed the inappropriate behavior upon another.

I'm not going on the defense of the user here, but I am saying that the user may not have intended to inflict a wound. Perhaps the user was trying to fulfill whatever it was that drove them to do such a thing. Was it youthful curiosity and the belief that no harm would be done to the other? Was it a sexual urge and a seemingly compliant "partner"? Of course, there are the dark ones who have a "need" to hurt another. Not talking about those folks, because intentionally inflicting pain on another, especially a child (or elder), is something I will never understand and don't want to discuss within these pages.

Sidebar: I've deliberately chosen to use the term "sexually used" instead of "molested." Molested is a gentler term, a more whitewashed term. The word "molest" originally meant "to cause trouble or grief"; that's how the word is used in the old literature we still read today. It wasn't used to mean "sexually abuse or assault" until about 1950. Whereas "use" means "to take advantage of a person; to exploit." Exploit means "to use someone unfairly for your own advantage." I think you'll agree that in the #MeToo context, "used" is the more appropriate description. Stop and compare the terms for a moment. Which more succinctly illustrates the action? I hope the term "sexually used" catches on because it's a more accurate descriptor. It's ugly, and it's real. As is the sexual use of another, particularly of a child.

Of the nine times I was sexually used before I was eighteen, not one of those males had intent to hurt me. Nevertheless, I was wounded each time, and I carry the emotional, or better said, soulful scars of each incident. I hadn't planned on sharing this part of my story and hadn't remembered all those incidents until two days ago. I am skilled at burying and moving on! Interestingly enough, the second time around, I married an undertaker, a professional burier! HA!

As I typed those burying words, I flashed on a cartoon of a dog digging up the entire backyard, trying to find where it buried its treasured bone that it saved for later. Trauma isn't treasure but is often buried at the moment to later sort out. For most, later never comes because who wants to go through that again? Actually, it's not going through that "again," but work through it for the first time from a safe place and space. Nope. Nope. Nope, is what we say.

My statistics: I was sexually used by a male six times before I was ten. Three times by family, three times by "outsiders." I recollect four of those times relatively well; of the other two, one is vague, and the earliest is just a knowing without the details. At this writing, I've no need to dive deeper than what I have. I acknowledge and release the history here on these pages to help myself and you. You, precious unknown sister, or brother, with wounds as deep or deeper than my own. The Bible says, "Know the truth, and the truth shall set you free."

There were three other incidents when I was a teenager; two by family, the last one by an "outsider" when I was seventeen years old. I've freed all but one of those males who used me from condemnation. I do hold something against that last male, yet as I write this, I realize I must forgive him to free me. He was old enough to be my father, a trusted "family friend," whom I later learned had been accused of repeatedly sexually using his adolescent stepdaughter. He claimed her a liar, and me as well. She said. He said.

Sometimes the one who purports to have been used does lie. I get that. But when you tell your story, tell the truth, and you aren't heard or believed, it feels as though you're used again. According to research, those who tell and aren't believed are at greater risk than the general population for psychological, emotional, social, and physical problems often lasting into adulthood.

Your people, "authorities," are supposed to protect you. When you're used and speak out, they're supposed to have your back. When they don't, you're left feeling isolated, alone, distrustful, and self-reliant when you're unequipped to be self-reliant. It's a rough row to hoe friend. But life goes on, and so do we. Ready and able, or not. Life is forward.

If you're used and speak out, you can become "tainted" in the minds of others, especially if the user is family. Other family can't imagine or face the fact that the one who was accused was guilty, so they fearfully blame and exclude or exile the victim. The innocent child can experience the withdrawal of physical closeness with other family members because rather than face the uncomfortable truth of what occurred, they fear they, too, might be accused. Can you imagine how hurtful and confusing that is to a child who was used? The effects are long-lasting and far-reaching.

A child who is the victim of prolonged sexual use often develops low self-esteem, a feeling of worthlessness, and an abnormal or distorted view of sex. The child may become withdrawn and mistrustful of adults and can become suicidal.

I contemplated suicide at the age of eleven. I'm not saying it was due to the sexual use of my body by males. It was a whole lot of combined issues: my overall life. My best childhood years with #5 had crashed and burned. I felt unloved, unwanted, out of place, without hope, and so, so lost. I wanted free from my pain and anguish, and at the time, didn't think I'd be missed. I well remember riding my bike (a super cool yellow Sting-Ray) down our country road to its end at the busy US Highway 101.

I believed that if I closed my eyes and pedaled onto the highway,

I'd be struck by a car or truck and instantly be killed. It saddens me now to think of how sad, lost, and lonely I was and that no one knew. (Today, I know that many who die by suicide expertly charade, as did I. You can't blame yourself when someone ends their own life and has masterfully been hiding their pain, depression, and intention. If you've had suicidal thoughts or a loved one has died by suicide, please visit kevinhinesstory.com. He survived his mistake of intentionally jumping off the Golden Gate Bridge.) As for me, I didn't share my thoughts or feelings; that wasn't something we did. We each lived our parallel lives in my household. Oh, the secrets we each held!

I sat there on my bike for several minutes, watching traffic fly by and contemplating my future. Well, actually, I was contemplating my impending death and what I thought would be release. Poor, pitiful me. Five-plus decades later, I don't recall my exact thought process. However, I did change my mind about pedaling onto the highway. I have a hazy-on-the-edge-of-my-memory vision that I realized I might not die but instead be paralyzed like my cousin's dad, which would be even harder than dead. So, I pedaled home.

I was no less forlorn or no less lost. I hadn't embraced living; I'd just decided not to die that day.

There's no benefit in providing details about the sexual use of my body by older males. Some readers would be horrified, and others would say, "That's it? What are you whining about? I had it much worse!" None of my experiences were violent. There was one gentle slap to my face by an adult male relative when I was a teen that assured me I was to allow his "French" kiss. This was also from the one with whom I have no exact memory but the "knowing" of the inappropriateness of his touch upon me as a wee child.

Precious unknown sister, or brother, please know I feel for you and your wounds. You should not have known such a touch. That you did, whether you fought it or not, is not on you. Please be free of it, for that is all we can do. Nothing will change yesterday. All we can change is our perspective about yesterday. To remain in yesterday robs us of our joy, our life, our power, and our future.

I was once struggling, trying to come to grips with a devastatingly hurtful betrayal I'd just learned had happened a decade prior when a friend gave me some of the most sound and powerful advice I've ever heard.

"Nev, you've got one foot in yesterday, one foot in tomorrow, and you're pissing all over today."

Meouch. He was right. I didn't like what he said, but accepted it as truth. Don't victimize yourself by not letting go and moving on. Nothing will change what happened yesterday. Nothing. Period. Full Stop. Memorize that, beloved!! Nothing changes yesterday!!! Nothing. It will always be as it was. We must get beyond yesterday.

Statistically (again, statistics widely vary), over 90% of those who sexually use a child are family members. Eighty-five percent of the children never tell. Many of those who have sexually used children were sexually used themselves.

The link between being used as a child and becoming a user isn't clear. Fear is a liar, so you can't trust that the sex offenders telling their childhood stories don't embellish or create a history to gain sympathy, rationalize or minimize their actions, or even secure a more favorable sentence.

It's impossible to look at another human being and know their story. If you know me, had you ever thought I'd been sexually used nine times before I was an adult? Of course not. I can't see your story either, but I'd love to hear it. Each human has their own unique story.

Sexual use of a child crosses ALL, and I do mean every single socio-economic boundary. Being sexually used as a minor can, and does, cause a host of issues throughout life. Each of us deals with them differently. Most of us bury them, and we 100% do have unacknowledged, undiagnosed, post-traumatic stress for the rest of our days. We don't understand the origin or realize it's post-traumatic stress. But let me tell you something folks, we can sense a "creep" or someone with "bad intentions" from quite a distance. We may not be able to put it into words, even within our own minds, but our body knows that ugly energy, and we move away from that soul.

I know this is hard and ugly to read, but I'm all about being real and healing, so I'm going to share a few facts about some common consequences of being sexually used as a child:
Traumatic memory loss
Mental health problems
Physical health problems
Substance abuse problems

Distrust of family/authority
3 to 5-fold risk of delinquency
Inability of adult sexual intimacy
Twice as likely to run away from home
Delinquency and crime are more prevalent
More likely to be arrested than non-used peers
Poor school performance and dropping out of school
Obesity and eating disorders are more common in women
Over 75% of teen prostitutes have been sexually used as children
45% of pregnant teens report a history of being sexually used as a child
Behavioral problems, including physical aggression, non-compliance, and opposition
Sexually used young males are five times more likely to cause teen pregnancy, three times more likely to have multiple sexual partners, and two times more likely to have unprotected sex

Some of those who've serially sexually used children said they looked for passive, quiet, troubled, lonely children from single-parent or broken homes. In other words, they sought children looking to be loved, children longing for the comfort of a loving touch. They often seek out children who are particularly trusting. The predators prey on children seeking love and acceptance, the most vulnerable ones:-(

I'm a kind and gentle soul, accepting of others, always trying to understand where people come from, and leaving the judging to the Almighty God. HOWEVER, it sickens me that pedophiles now demand to be referred to as "minor attracted people." They want this because of the stigma attached to the term pedophile. Um, hello. THEY KNOWLINGLY HURT CHILDREN!! They cause lifelong harm to an innocent soul, which can damage a child's future generations, AND they demand this "woke" world side with them and their feelings regardless of their bad and abhorrent behavior.

It infuriates me that some of society, including "well-educated," support this so as not to hurt the feelings of the pedophile. IT IS OUR RESPONSIBILITY TO PROTECT THE CHILDREN!!!!! Some of those "educated" folks also say it isn't immoral to be attracted to children. Wrong, wrong, and triple wrong! Sexual use of a child wounds a child. Period. Full stop.

Some people recently voted to support a publicly acknowledged pedophile to represent them as an elected official. That individual has an acknowledged desire to break the law and hurt innocent little children; such a person is NOT trustworthy! How can anyone other than another pedophile overlook the intent of a pedophile? A child cannot give consent to sex! Under no circumstances is it healthy for a child to experience any form of sex with anyone!

I'm not going to throw my own cuss words into this writing, but making statements to the effect of, and the belief, that pedophilia doesn't harm a child is worse than a dog returning to its vomit! I hurt for the hurting.

Now, I don't know what happened to the pedophile to cause them to become a pedophile. An individual is not born a pedophile; he or she was somehow wounded, which resulted in their abhorrent behavior, as in unnatural, against the laws of nature and God. I'm sorry and saddened for the wounded pedophile; however, it is reprehensible for anyone to place hurt adult feelings (caused by their own bad behavior) over the future of an innocent child.

Sexually using a child is wrong. Period. Sexualizing children is wrong. Period.

Out of the 329,500,000 people in the USA, it's estimated that 92,260,000 (a little shy of 1/3) of us were sexually used when we were children. Woof. Not quite a third of our people live day to day with devastating childhood wounds most NEVER mention. It's no wonder we don't monitor our elected officials better than we do; we're just trying to survive!

Let me toss a little more fuel on the fire of our woundedness. The statistics for the sexual use of a child and domestic violence are very close; not saying one has anything to do one the other. Just saying we're a much more wounded nation than we let on.

One in four women and one in seven men have experienced SEVERE domestic violence by an intimate partner. (You've read of such violence in my family.) Domestic violence, like the sexual use of a child, has no socio-economic boundaries. Please realize those domestic violence stats don't consider the children who witness said violence. Adding the children who witnessed the violence would easily quadruple the statistics!

So, roughly a third of us Americans suffer post-traumatic stress from being sexually used as a child, and another third from witnessing violence in our homes. Yeowza! That's a whole lot of wounded people! I don't know if I'm entitled to win a prize for being in both groups, but I'm definitely in both groups. Actually, I did win a prize. I overcame. You can too.

I don't consider myself a "survivor" because to survive means to continue to exist despite danger or hardship. I chose to do more than exist despite the very hard challenges in my life. I chose to overcome. I chose to believe that where I came from, what I witnessed, and what happened to me did not define me or what I could accomplish in my life. I chose not to be bitter, not to hate, not to quit, not to be mean, and not to blame the world for my circumstances.

Oh, friend, I'm far from perfect, and I've had my struggles. Shoot, I struggle today. My life's not perfect. Like the Israelites, I wandered around in the desert for decades, trying to find my way. I did a little dance with alcohol and some light drugs, but then I was a child of the '60s. A little later, I did live in the danger zone for a spell until I recognized what such a life would cost me. The bottom line, my bottom line, was that I couldn't stay there. I knew I was meant for more. I knew I couldn't be like that which harmed me.

Like Dory in *Finding Nemo*, I've just kept swimming, not always knowing where I was going or how I would get there. I just knew I had to keep on keeping on. I have and will to the end of my days.

Dearheart, the most important person to tell what happened to you . . . is YOU! Face it, in mini bites if need be. That's the only way to get through it and release it. Write it out and burn it if that's what you need to do. So long as it's buried within, you're still being used!

People can minimize what happened, "it was only touching" . . . If you've been touched inappropriately, you know it was more than "just a touch." Someone stole your innocence, and you never get that back. Ever. Children feel energy, and you felt that older person's energy wasn't right or "normal."

Perhaps you couldn't name what was wrong, but you felt it. It's the same if you weren't touched but instead made to look at anything sexual, including an older person's body parts. Your innocence was taken; you felt tainted. You might not have said anything because it felt wrong. You didn't want to get in trouble, get another in trouble, or cause a grown-up in your life to hurt that person. You might have thought you were protecting someone you loved. If you haven't before, make today the day you begin to protect yourself. Make today the day you begin to heal your wounded self, beloved sister, and brother.

Do not blame yourself. Do not. Do. Not. Blame. Yourself. Your trust was shattered, and your world was confused. You need to trust again. Start by facing your wound. Then, love yourself no matter what happened to you. You'll learn to trust that you'll take care of yourself. Someone needs to love you most, friend. YOU must be that person! If it's happening today, tell someone. A trusted adult.

I can't promise you it will change anything. I can't promise you will be believed or that they'll do anything about it. I don't know if it hurts worse to tell and have no one believe or protect you or to remain silent. Three times, I told. I was believed once and told to be a lady and never discuss it again. I am a lady. Moreover, I am an overcomer! And I'm discussing it!

I've just realized there's another group of my sisters and brothers who need healing. If you've touched someone inappropriately in your youth or perhaps coerced someone to be intimate with you, you, too, need to heal. Many teens and adolescents have had another say to them, "If you really loved me, you'd . . ." Yeah, if you said that, you coerced someone.

If you had youthful sexual curiosity and touched someone younger, thinking it wouldn't hurt them, you were wrong. It did hurt them, and it hurt you too. You knew it was wrong, and it's sat there in your soul and theirs. Pressing it down and denying it doesn't serve or heal YOU. It prevents you from complete intimacy with another because you don't want that hidden corner found. Be completely honest with yourself. You don't have to hate yourself. Jesus loves imperfect and flawed you. He'll forgive you if you ask. You do need to admit the truth to yourself. Say it out loud to yourself, write it out, and burn it. Beloved, get it out of you so you can heal.

Your healing will be more complete if you apologize to the other person. You could say, "I've recently realized I hurt you. I didn't mean to hurt you. I'm sorry."

The thought of admitting such behavior today can be truly terrifying. "If I admit what I did, my life will be ruined. I'll be sued, hated, feared, canceled, etc." Any of those are possible consequences in today's world. But you need to heal, and so does that other person. If you can't face the person for one reason or another (perhaps they've died, or you lost contact long ago), at least write out your apology and burn it. Sister, brother, you, too, need to heal. You need to forgive yourself; God will forgive. I promise.

I don't recommend you ask the one you used for forgiveness. Accept it if it's offered, but don't ask for it. You've wounded someone, and now you want more from them. I learned this about two years ago. I'd misjudged a family member and accused (thereby insulting) her of something. When I realized my error, I immediately apologized but chose not to ask more of her. Asking for forgiveness is about you, not the other way around. (Unless you're talking to God.)

Before publishing, I read this chapter to an 80-ish friend. He responded that he could relate; then told, for the first time ever, about inappropriate touching in his life some seven and a half decades ago! My friend was touched for maybe a minute, over his clothing, but it was enough to rob him, to make him feel dirty. It spoiled an otherwise wonderful adventure for him and caused him to relive that moment every time he saw the type of vehicle they'd been in. It's bothered him and wounded him for nearly 75 years. He told! And now he's free of it!

Pre-publishing, I read this to a female friend who shared an experience she'd never told anyone. Then she told me about the old single man who sat on his porch in their neighborhood and invited kids to sit on his lap and eat the candy he gifted. When the child was into the sweet treat's deliciousness, he'd touch them inappropriately. One day, a child told a mother about the deviant behavior. That neighborhood of women didn't wait for their men to come home. Together, they went at him with broomsticks, pots, pans, pipes, whatever was handy, and they chased him out of their neighborhood. Bravo mothers! Bravo! Well done!

My friend's story caused me to remember there was a ninth male to use me, which made my before ten stats grow to six times. Old man, family friend, with candy and a similar modus operandi.

It's much more common than you'd thought. It's much more devastating than you can imagine.

Let me repeat ~ If you've had suicidal thoughts or a loved one has died by suicide, please visit kevinhinesstory.com. He survived jumping off the Golden Gate Bridge. As soon as he let go of the railing, he knew he'd made a horrific mistake.

Kevin is a wonderful storyteller who has looked great adversity and abject despair in the eyes. He's faced the deepest of regrets and found love and acceptance. He will help you. All you have to do is reach out. He's been there, and he truly cares. So does Jesus!

GENEVA MARIE BRETT

CHAPTER 32

The Broken Letter

After high school, my father's father went to business school. He developed a record-keeping mindset and beautiful, flowery penmanship. Upon graduation from business school, Grandpa accepted a job with Prudential, where he worked for forty-five years before retiring.

After Grandpa passed and the time came to sell the family home, his youngest daughter assumed the responsibility of doing so. If you've never faced that daunting and emotional task, I'll take a moment to explain. It's hard. It hurts. You must touch everything in the house. You must carefully review every single item and every saved paper/document to decide its destiny. You feel like an intruder violating the privacy of another. Yet you must.

Grandpa was a record keeper; he had decades of bank statements, expense records for his home, expense records for his rental, his sister-in-law's home, my father's letters to him during his military service, and all the correspondence between him and my mom's family regarding me.

My grandfather made copies of every letter he and my grandmother wrote to my mother's family and me. Dad's parents hadn't met my mother before Dad's death; they didn't meet her until my first wedding. Grandpa said he made and kept those copies because he didn't know my family and didn't know if they would share his outreach to me, with me. He wanted to make sure he had proof that he had tried to have a connection with his oldest child's only child in case I ever questioned him as to why he wasn't involved in my life. I appreciated that he kept copies of the back-and-forth correspondence.

I'm eternally grateful my auntie reviewed each of those saved documents and sent them to me. She gifted me glimpses of my father as a man and a son by doing so. The communication between my mother's and father's families gave me an understanding of how deeply I was loved and how far out of their comfort zones my grandmother, aunt, and mother ventured for me. Given their discomfort with letter writing and then writing to people they didn't know, for ME saturates my soul with love, somewhat akin to the Christ's love for me. It was utterly selfless.

They never expressed their deep abiding love for me in person, or on the pages they wrote, yet the pages they wrote expressed more love for me than their words to me ever did.

Again, I digress. Nah. You needed the back story or side story, whichever it is.

Except for one letter, that last letter, each of my father's letters to his father lay flat, stapled to the envelope in which it was mailed. That was how Grandpa kept his records. Grandpa didn't keep copies of his replies to Dad's letters as he did of those with my family. I get that. He had something to prove to me.

The last letter between my father and his father might not have been their last communication. However, it's the last written communication I have between them.

Dad's earlier letters are typical of those of a soldier to his family. "Hi, I'm at 'x' location. My daily duties are 'y. I'm striving for 'z,' how are things at home?"

But that last letter, it's a hard one. Dad was emotionally wounded, and he vented. Dad's mother had died about five years earlier; a year later, his father remarried. A year after his second marriage, Dad's father had a new child, followed by another child a year later. Dad liked his stepmother well enough. He even served as the best man at their wedding. He loved his baby sister and brother.

What wounded Dad and prompted his letter was receiving a Christmas card signed, "Annette & Joe." Dad didn't know what a Banty rooster was; however, he was Banty rooster mad and deeply hurt. I could almost see the smoke rising off the pages as he fumed to his father, "That's how it is then, you're 'Joe' to me?"

Oh, I get it. I understand his woundedness, although I doubt his father did. My father was far away from home, going through a divorce he didn't ask for; his beloved mother was five years in the ground. His dad's remarried with two new kids, one of them a son, and now his dad is no longer Dad, but "Joe." I call that life lasagna: one little thing layered on another. If you leave it long enough, it starts to ferment.

So, my dad wrote a letter to his dad, mentioning the, "Now you're Joe to me," and haranguing his father with his shortcomings. My father was twenty-six years old, a man who should be recognized for who he is, what he's accomplished, and who he can become. He stopped short of saying, "I'm done with you!" but there were plenty of other wounds my father inflicted upon his father. So many of us have done such a thing! I certainly did so to my mother.

That letter wasn't laid flat and stapled to the envelope as were the others. That last letter was returned to live in its envelope . . . and it was pulled out, opened, read, refolded, and placed back in the envelope for over three decades after my father's death, until his father's death. Its pages are cracked and worn, at risk of imminent decomposition. The letter is broken, as I'm sure was a father's heart every time he reread it, which he must have done for over thirty-three years before his passing. I won't share Dad's words, but I have shared an image of the broken letter at the end of the book.

Oh, beloved sister or brother, be careful what you say and how you say it, even in your most wounded state! We never know the last moment between two humans. We never know when the words we speak or hear will be the last ones said before a life ends. Each of us gets wounded, and then angry within our relationships. Oftentimes, the deeper the wound, the more intense the anger. When our most vulnerable self is hurt, many choose to hurt another in return. It's said that hurt people hurt people. That was certainly the case between my father and his own father. Had they more time, I trust they'd have moved on. Since Grandpa didn't keep copies of his letters to Dad, I can only wonder what he said in response.

In all probability, the card my father received was signed amidst a slew of other Christmas cards, and it was sent innocently. My grandfather typically signed and addressed all cards, as his handwriting was beautiful and was always complimented. It was a source of great pride for him. Perhaps he was dallying in December of 1953, so his bride took charge of sending the cards to ensure their timely arrival. My dad's father and stepmother didn't mean to hurt or insult him, but that's how he interpreted the card. How very sad for his father.

Since I've figuratively splayed my ribs and offered my heart for inspection, I'll go ahead and confess that I wrote a much worse letter to my mother than what my dad wrote to his father. I didn't know of his broken letter at the time, which might or might not have made a difference in what I said to Mom.

I was in my early 30s and had asked her what it was about me that she couldn't love because she'd kept my brothers and not me. (You already read that.) Although in the moment, I appreciated that she owned up and told the truth about being selfish, and it was her, not me . . .

I later got mad over her truth. Not Banty rooster mad but brooding mad. I hadn't planned my first child, yet I couldn't bear a moment's thought of not raising her, so the more I thought about Mom's selfishness, the more hurt and angrier I became.

Mmm, mmm, mmm, I stewed in my woundedness for a bit and then sifted away the pity and replaced it with anger, which I wrapped around myself like a burrito. Steeped in those emotions, I decided to tell my mother exactly what a failure of a mother, a daughter, and a human she was. Oh, I'm not proud of that, at all. Nevertheless, we can't change yesterday.

I filled page after page of her transgressions as I saw them. When I got out all my hurt and anger, I addressed the envelope to her . . . using all the men's surnames she'd used up to that point, which was indeed thirteen. And then I mailed it to her. Today's gentler, more considerate, understanding, and forgiving me feels shame for having wounded her by thrusting my pain upon her.

Mom responded by saying she owned her past, some of what I said was true, that I also wasn't perfect, I'd made some big mistakes, and she hoped my daughter never did the same to me. She said she was going to save the letter for my daughter (who adored her).

I'm very grateful we were able to get past the hurt I laid upon her. And by the way, I didn't find that letter when I went through her belongings after she died.

Lead your life with your soul, my friend. Be kind and considerate, for your own soul's sake. The Bible says to be slow to anger and quick to forgive. That's most excellent advice.

Do forgive others for simply being the imperfect humans that they are; we are. We quickly point our finger at others and their erroneous ways, condemning them for falling short of some mark we set for them. Please look your own self in the eyes in the mirror, and be honest with your own shortcomings, then remember every other human is also a flawed human, same as you.

Beloved, please look at my father's broken letter to his father at the end of the book. Do you want that to be between you and someone you love? If you're holding out from someone today, trust that if they go before you and there are wounds between you, YOU'LL be hurting for the rest of your days. If you're raising children, you're modeling unforgiveness, which will hurt their lives, relationships, and future generations. What you're planting and growing in your children by modeling such behavior will bring you seemingly intolerable pain if they choose not to forgive you or one of their siblings for something. Children learn much more from what they see and overhear than what they're taught.

So, your feelings were hurt, and you've talked so much trash about that person to others that you can't back down from what you said for fear of what others might think of you. Frankly, your "pride" is meaningless.

Stop whining. Stop acting immaturely. Grow up! Forgiving another for their shortcomings is really freeing you from the burden of hate. When you harbor a grudge, it's your soul that carries the burden. Holding a grudge is like drinking battery acid and waiting expectantly for the other person to die. I plead with you to be free of YOUR pain. I pray for YOUR freedom and healing.

How can you leave this life and leave someone with a burden between you? YOU are not perfect. You've hurt others yourself, accidentally and purposefully. Love you, be free! In your time of judgment, God will judge how YOU behaved when another said or did whatever it was that grieved you so much. He will say, "This is about you, how YOU lived, not them. I'm not your earthly parent; blame shifting doesn't cut it with me. You, and you alone, own your behavior."

Remember, if you don't forgive . . . come Judgement Day, what you gonna say? More importantly, what's The Most High God, THE JUDGE, going to say? You don't get to have two sets of rules, one for you and one for others.

CHAPTER 33

Liar, Liar, Pants on Fire

Two months ago, I read *The Entrepreneur Evangelist* by Bryan Dulaney. About a third of the way in, I again felt like I was a fly sucked out the window at 89mph. To make it clear, I am not fond of that ride.

This time, the shock and spinning felt like it resulted in a Sunday punch to my gut, and then a heart stab. I *felt* the words, "Liar, liar, pants on fire" in my gut, my heart, my head, and my lungs. Ooof.

What caused my reaction was Bryan's sharing his experience when God told him he had to forgive his father completely, receive his forgiveness, and then go out in the world and freely share his story with others. Bryan's instant reaction was pride, followed by defensiveness, and then anger. That same anger he had yet to release.

The anger stemmed from Bryan's youth, when his dad had been a drug addict, repeatedly choosing drugs over his family, endangering his life by taking drugs and all the mess that goes along with addiction. Although his dad had been clean for years, had given his life to Christ, and really turned his life around, those childhood wounds of Bryan's festered beneath the surface. He did what many of us do; he built walls to protect his most vulnerable self. We build walls to avoid feeling the pain; however, those walls also keep us from truly feeling all the good stuff.

Bryan locked himself inside the walls, which prevented him from fully forming healthy attachments with others. Kind of like not allowing oneself to get too close to a flame once you've been burned by fire.

Now, God's telling Bryan he must apologize to his father to move forward! Wait a minute! It should be the other way around, thought Bryan, and almost every one of us. Bryan's the one who was wounded by his father's actions, and his father's bad deeds. Bryan's dad should be the one to apologize first and foremost! But being the loving father he is, God showed Bryan that he was a partner in the festered wound. Whenever we point our finger at another, we must remember there are three pointing right back at us.

As Bryan spewed out the wrongs committed against him, God gently reminded Bryan that it didn't matter what his father had done. What mattered was what God had done for Bryan. The repeated forgiveness and unconditional love.

Upon examination and reflection, Bryan recognized he'd been short with his dad, quick-tempered, not as patient as he should be, and truthfully: bitter and angry. Bryan acknowledged all those unconscious and unrecognized feelings had affected his relationship with his father. He was keeping his father at a distance, which prevented him from getting the closeness to his earthly father and to his heavenly father that he hungered for.

Although he knew he had to apologize to his dad, it took him a little time to work his way through his thoughts and feelings to be authentic with his father. He had no idea how his father would respond, which didn't make a difference. He was to apologize and free himself every bit as much as his father. So, Bryan called his dad, said he needed to tell him something . . . you know his pops was feeling dread in that moment.

A wound like Bryan's that's never been cleaned out is very sensitive for all, like a deep bruise or a sore toe. Bryan shocked his dad with his tearful, heartfelt apology, which opened his dad to apologize, and then the floodgates of years of unspoken feelings and words opened up between them. Peace and freedom washed over both of them.

My reaction to that, the sucked-out-the-window gut punch, was the realization that I felt God was telling me I needed to do the same thing! No, not apologize to Bryan's dad, but to my husband. In thirty-five years of marriage and thirty-eight years of togetherness, I realized that although I'd told my husband *and myself* that I'd forgiven him for some ancient and not-so-ancient wounds, deep down, it wasn't the truth. I was a liar, liar, pants on fire, and I did not like that one bit. I didn't like the truth of it. I didn't like the implications of it because I knew what I would have to do. I would have to do what Bryan did. I did not want to do what Bryan did. I did NOT want to apologize when I was the wronged one. But . . .

You see, I fully acknowledge and accept that I'm in the fourth quarter of my life. More of my life is behind me than in front of me. There's no escaping that I will die and face judgment from Almighty God, the Everlasting King of the Universe, for what I have and have not done. There isn't a single thing I can do to change my yesterdays, but I'm doing what I can to use the talents gifted me, live the purpose intended for my life, and do what Jesus would do. Jesus, Yeshua, was perfect. I'm not trying to be perfect; that's impossible while I'm living, but I can do my best to be my best.

Liar, liar, pants on fire. That's me. Geneva Marie. Preaching to you, to family, to friends, to inmates, about forgiveness when, at my deepest self, I hadn't truly done so. Hadn't truly let go. Doing the internal work to be free of it was one thing, but facing my husband, admitting I'd unconsciously been holding on to some ugly was a horse of a different color, and not one I found attractive. Apologizing when I was the wounded one, ptoey!

Aah, but the truth will set you free. So, while my doggo and I walked, I talked to God and searched my soul. I tried to justify why my husband did what he did; well, not exactly justify his actions. I think understanding is the better word; I was telling myself, perhaps this or that caused blah, blah, blah. But that wasn't getting me any closer to the freedom I needed and then the apology I needed to make.

Finally. I figured it out. I asked Jesus to help me because it was obvious; I had not, could not, do it alone. I asked him to hold my hand (which I felt) and walk along the beach with me. The beach has always been a healing place for me.

So, I visualized Yeshua and me holding hands on a warm and windless day at the beach in Marina, near Fort Ord, where I was born. The weather was perfect, and the water was warm . . . which is proof this was a visualization – that ocean water is never warm!

Our backs were to the ocean, and I could hear and feel the warm water gently lapping at our bare feet as we faced the shore and looked at the sandcastle of my husband's wrongdoings that appeared out of nowhere. Wrongdoings isn't the right word; it was a sandcastle of my wounds from the decades of my relationship with my husband. The wounds imprinted on my soul like old childhood memories, like little scars you see on yourself and remember exactly how you got them if you stay focused on them long enough. Yeah, I needed free. I wanted free. For me, he, us, God.

As Yeshua, Jesus, and I stood there holding hands, a little wave rose up behind us and washed over the sandcastle, flattening the outside walls a little bit, and then gently returning to the sea. As it washed over the sandcastle, I internally felt it wash over me, some of those scars washed out to sea with the water, and I felt a little lighter. I felt a clutch in my chest, so I held his hand a little tighter as I sensed the next wave, a bigger, stronger wave, rising up behind us.

Quickly, I cried out, "Jesus, hold me tightly!"

I wasn't fearful of the wave dragging us out into the ocean; I was with Jesus, after all. Instead, internally, I'd just felt the sensation of those deeply buried feelings leaving my body like a hoodie string being pulled out of its garment. They weren't wonderful old memories, but they were a part of me, and they'd just been pulled out and washed away.

I knew the incoming wave wasn't powerful enough to move us from where we stood, but it was tall enough to reach the middle of our calves. It rushed past us as it proceeded on its mission to dissolve more of the sandcastle of wounds and bitterness of disappointment. That wave splashed up almost a foot in the air; it reduced the castle to half its height, then slunk back to sea. More of my scars flowed with it.

I can still hear the wave swooshing up behind us and see the sun sparkling on the water as it splashed high above the sandcastle; I can taste its salt on my tongue, feel it on my skin, and then I hear the gentle thump as it falls and flattens the sandcastle. As the water gently ebbs back to its own realm, I hear it, can practically feel it, grating along the sand, almost like the muffled popping of packing bubbles. More of me is freed. I feel tears of release welling up behind my eyelids. I feel lighter, my chest opens, and I'm filled with oxygen, which I feel coursing through my veins, delivering life and freedom from a prison of my own making.

Two more waves and all evidence the sandcastle ever existed was gone. The sand was flat and smooth. Perfect. I had truly forgiven it all, at my core. As I looked at the pure and perfect shore where decades of wounds and scars had just existed in multiple towers, I acknowledged that's how God, how Jesus, forgives sin. Not how I'd lived it.

I'd forgiven but hadn't forgotten, which meant I hadn't forgiven. Looking at the sand, it was as though the wrongdoing, the wounds, had never been there. Completely erased. Winning the lottery couldn't provide such bliss (although I'd like to compare).

Newly freed me was elated and joyful . . . for about a minute. Then I realized I needed to make another sandcastle to free the wounds from my dead people, to forgive them all the way to my core. So many people . . . tender me had felt so many, many wounds that arose every now and again, especially while writing this book. So, my people got their own sandcastle and village, complete with a moat! There was a lot that needed releasing!

Jesus never let go of my hand as I went through the same process of the waves washing away the wound, of forgiveness making perfect, unflawed sand. Hallelujah! I was done! Free and forgiving.

But wait. Just when you think it's safe to go back in the water. There's more! I recognized I needed to forgive me, Geneva Marie Brett, for not forgiving, for falling short, for hurting others, for not living up to my potential, my purpose. And so, I did.

Friend, I was walking on sunshine and be-bopping for the remainder of my walk. My doggo gave me a side eye, then the sidestep, wondering what had come over me.

I did apologize to my dead people, who thankfully didn't respond, and to my husband for my unknown harboring. Since then, when a scar is touched, a wonderful memory evoked . . . I see that pure and perfect sand; I feel myself there with Jesus and I let it goooooooooo!

Preaching to incarcerated women, some of whom may never obtain physical freedom, I'm very aware that freedom is a glorious thing. I encourage you to do some searching within, hopefully finding you are truly free of those ancient wounds and the one(s) who caused them.

If you aren't, you're welcome to find your soul's freedom at my beach. Jesus will be there with you. Just ask and allow yourself to be set free. It is glorious!

GENEVA MARIE BRETT

CHAPTER 34

From There to Eternity

As I write this chapter, my two-year-old grandson is in the hospital. I'm at his home, watching his older brother while their parents stay with him in the hospital all day. About 9:30 each evening, my eight-month-pregnant daughter comes home to rest as best she can while her husband stays the night with their son. Son-in-law comes home to shower and nap daily. I overheard him update their five-year-old on his brother's condition, then ask if he had any questions. It moved me to tears with love and appreciation that my youthful hardships have not been, and will not be, perpetuated upon mine and theirs. No one even told my brother and me that our little brother was injured or that he'd died; we overheard adults talking. My people didn't mean to disrespect us. That's just how it was, how they knew to be.

I leveled up with my children, and they're exceeding my efforts, which is how it's supposed to be, and was my great desire. Functional families at last! I don't live within those families; however, they are my offspring, so I rejoice in their loving and nurturing environments. I believe I have won, as I didn't continue along like my elders.

I can't imagine how different all our lives would have been if either of my grandparents had said, "About me shooting at my spouse, I want you to understand that's not how people typically behave. How did that make you feel? Were you scared? I apologize for scaring you. I shouldn't have done that."

If I'd had suggested my Gran talk to me like that, she'd probably have said, "You talk like someone who fell out of a well!" I think that means, "Are you crazy?" but to this day, I don't totally get that reference. My people didn't talk to us that way because they didn't have the skills. I wonder how many of that era did speak to their children about feelings and family goings on. We just lived through whatever. You don't know what you don't know.

Sadly, millions and millions of girls and boys are growing up in such environments to this very day. It's not their fault; I don't even know if I'd say it's their parents' fault. Just how far back does it go? Wherever it starts isn't as important as when and where it ends. Beloved, if you're living such a life, know, believe, and TRUST that you can overcome and change your future family generations.

YOU can be the one to do so. It doesn't take a high school or college degree. It takes making the decision to change and being in the moment, being mindful, continuously checking and questioning yourself until you've left the old ways in your yesterdays.

Watching my five-year-old grandson today, I thought about how different our life experiences have been. I acknowledged how grateful I am that he nor any of my children or grands had life experiences like mine by that age. I'll repeat that I accept that what I experienced brought me to who I am today, and I love the imperfect me that I am. Lemme tell you, though, I'm no pansy. I've got the grit, friend. However, truth be told, some of my cousins have twice the grit as me. I had a tough time, yet some of my cousins had an even harder life than me.

There've been times I thought my children were a little on the soft side, especially as parents. Yet I'm grateful not one of mine or theirs can imagine my life. Even with this writing, there's much left unsaid. With all the pressure and irritations my people and I endured, we should be diamonds and pearls by now!

By my grandson's age, I'd had a couple of hospital stints and was left alone in that foreign, scary place. They humiliated me by placing me in a crib, a baby cage, and I was far from being a baby. Gran and an uncle visited for a few minutes every other day or so; they'd promise to come back later or the next day and not do so. I'd already been sexually used twice. I saw my grandfather grab a rifle to shoot my grandmother. Our family home burned. I didn't live that wild life with my mother; however, my home life wasn't stable, safe, or secure.

When I was five, my seven-year-old brother and I stayed with Mom for a minute or two during her marriage to #4 (little brother's father). One evening #4 was watching us while Mom was working. When my older brother made the mistake of reaching across the dinner table for something, #4 stabbed him in the hand with a fork.

Not long after dinner, #4's child used the toilet and forgot to flush. Number four pulled the feces out of the toilet and forced his child to eat it.

That's when my big brother grabbed my hand and snuck the two of us out of the house, leaving our 2-year-old brother with his father and half-brother. We ran to a nearby market, where brother called Gran, who'd made him memorize her phone number. Gran was no fan of #4. She didn't trust him and had told brother if anything ever happened, he was to call her, and she'd be there pronto.

Brother called and told her what had happened; she instructed him to hide us behind the dumpster until she could get to us. Thankfully Gran was only twenty-five miles away. Brother held me tightly to his chest and told me I was safe with him. He promised he'd always protect me and would always be there for me.

We never stayed with Mom and #4 again. Surprisingly, the events of the evening didn't cause Mom to leave #4. I don't recall what his version of that evening was. I do remember that my brother's hand carried the scar from the fork stabbing for quite a long while.

After Mom's unsuccessful attempt to de-penis #4 by gunshot, #4 decided his bride might not ever forgive or forget his cheating ways. He knew he'd cheat again; maybe the next time she caught him, her aim would improve, so he was the one who said adios. He didn't press charges; however, the attempted de-penis story continues to be told by several family members over six decades later. It wasn't a story Mom readily told, more of a story told on her, accompanied by laughter that she was such a lousy shot. Mom would always say that she really loved #4; she just couldn't tolerate a chippy chaser.

Again, my gratitude that my people's times were pre social media. Mom would have been infamous in more than just one county, probably the country! Undoubtedly, she'd have her own memes.

My brother has three siblings on his dad's side whom he loves deeply and who he lived with off and on during his growing years. However, he and I have a different kind of closeness for what we lived through. So much unspoken history that words couldn't describe then, or even now, that it causes me to shake my head at the bizarreness of it all. And no matter what, I know I can call upon my brother, who would move heaven and earth to do whatever I needed.

I was having a rough time with something a few years ago; my brother pulled me close to his chest, held me tightly, and said, "I got you, little sister. Do you remember the night we ran from #4? While we were waiting on Grandma to come and get us, I held you close and told you I'd protect you, I'd always be here for you, and that I love you. I'm still here. I got you, sis."

Truthfully, I'd forgotten the moment, but as he spoke of it and held me to his chest, I felt it wash over me again. I remembered the feeling of comfort, being loved, and trusting I was safe with him. It was a moment of security I desperately needed. A moment I will cherish forever.

By the time I was my seven-year-old granddaughter's age, I'd witnessed my grandfather throw a hatchet at my nine-year-old cousin. Grandpa missed; the hatchet stuck in the door. Grandpa did that because my nine-year-old cousin, eight-year-old brother, and eight-year-old cousin had found Grandpa's hidden wine and got drunk. Grandpa wasn't mad they were drunk; he was mad they found his stash and drank it. Grandpa had shot at Grandma's date, and I'd chalked up another #MeToo. I'd visited family at the Preston School of Industry (a reform school) and the California Youth Authority, a penal institution for youthful offenders.

I remember watching Gran chase and beat my brother and boy cousins with what she called an ironing cord, but was actually a coffee pot cord. I'm sure I saw her do the same to my aunt and uncles when I was a wee one.

An uncle, aunt, and Mom told me she'd beat them until their legs were raw. Uncle said his jeans stuck to that bloody raw skin. They all told me that today she'd be in jail for how she beat them. Remember, though, those were very different times, so don't be judging her by today's standards. She never hit me with the coffee pot cord; the worst she ever did to me was slap my face once when I smart-mouthed her as a teen. I deserved it.

A memory just flashed through . . . I remember Gran chastising one of her daughters because she whipped her children too hard with a belt. There's a little dish of irony.

Not surprisingly, I didn't feel safe or secure at home, well, anywhere, for that matter. I remember being in kindergarten and told to lay on my rug and take a nap.

That was falling out of a well talk! Lay down, sleep, be vulnerable, susceptible to physical or emotional attack or harm from these strangers? Grandma always said to be careful of outsiders. No way was that going to happen. It was dangerous enough with family! Those other kids were fools or chumps! I never napped in kindergarten. I was always alert.

There was no one in my life whom I completely trusted. I'd learned hypervigilance to survive and minimize whatever tornado might swirl about me and suck me into its vortex. You always had to be ready for the unexpected. My people walked out into the world like it was all okay when our home life was off the charts. But that was all the life they knew. We all had grit.

A few great lines in a recent episode of *Yellowstone* sum it up succinctly. "Fighting is all my people knew; it's how they kept what was theirs and their dignity. Today that's a liability. Cowards rule the world these days. Coward rules and coward customs. To succeed, all you need to know is how to blame and complain."

My people just did it long before Nike and its slogan were created. Home was freaking chaotic, to say the least. I think us cousins "white knuckled" a great deal of life. That's not to say we didn't laugh or have fun; of course, we did. We truly loved one another and had great times. There was just a mountain of bigger stuff to ignore. I am genuinely grateful to have grown up with my people, to have learned grit, kindness, never quit, don't kick someone who's down, you'll never learn any younger, and there's nothing I can't learn. I know that no matter what comes my way, I will manage and that I will be a rock for myself and my people. That my word will be my word.

My husband hadn't spent enough time around my family to really know them as we know our people when one of my cousins visited.

My man later said, "Wow, that cousin of yours wants everything you have, she kept saying she loved this or that, wanted this or that. It made me uncomfortable."

I explained we've always been that way with one another. My people are loving and generous. We compliment what another has; if we love it, we say we'd love to have it. If the owner is tired of it or thinks the other loves it more than they do, they give it to them. Literally, the shirt off your back or the shoes off your feet. It's a natural act for us. That goes for expensive clothes, accessories, furnishings, horses, tack, and maybe even a vehicle. No one ever gifted another a spouse or child though, there must be some lines . . .

It was easy for me to see and accept others, outsiders, as the flawed humans they were. Jesus was the only perfect human. As I explained to my children many times, "parent" is a job title, like bus driver or teacher. We're all humans with histories before we attach those titles to ourselves.

Eventually, I grew to see Mom for who she was as a human being, regardless of her past and my childhood wounds. I accepted that like every other human, she was a product of her raising and life experiences. Who was I to judge her, the human, for how she managed her life experiences? I've made a myriad of mistakes myself and wounded others in the process, mostly unintentionally, on very rare occasion, intentionally. It was good for me to free my mother from condemnation for her imperfection. She was the best parent she could be, and hard as it was, my best and safest place was indeed with her mother.

From the time she was a wee child, Gran carried a feeling of being unwanted and unwelcome. She was like a mother hen, wanting her flock gathered around her, maybe not so much to protect them, but to keep their love close. I don't think she ever got enough love to fill her need; some folks are just like that.

I always loved my mother and wanted to be with her, yet I felt guilty about hurting Gran with that love, although I did so the two times I left her to live with Mom. Gran had indeed sacrificed a great deal for me, my brother, and the cousins she raised. I felt like she expected the most from me; I was her namesake, after all. In reality, we were never told of any expectations upon us. I probably placed her expectations upon myself.

I just flashed back on the memory of driving Gran to Reno so she could enjoy a weekend of gambling with an out-of-state daughter-in-law. This was while we were circling the wagons. I don't enjoy gambling, but I was doing all I could to please Gran before she exited this world.

Gran played progressive slots almost exclusively and would play two at a time, refusing to walk away to relieve herself because the one-armed bandit surely had to be about to pay off. I mostly stayed in our room and read, checking on Gran periodically. Late at night, I offered to watch her machines while she went to the toilet. She was very possessive of her machines but trusted me enough to let me play in her absence, so some other soon-to-be winner didn't win on her past play. She was shocked I didn't enjoy gambling, saying, "And I thought you were just like me."

Woof. That caused turmoil within. Hmm, I peeked in that window but never opened the door of discovery. I will be examining myself to see how much truth there is in her words. I'll let you know how that turns out in the next book, maybe. I didn't want to be like any of my people. I wanted to become the best of each of them and leave their worst in yesterday.

After Gran died, I no longer had to worry about hurting her feelings because I loved my mother. It had felt like Gran was between Mom and me, so we always treaded lightly so as not to hurt her tender feelings. Mom and I got to know one another as women and became very close for the four years between Gran's and Mom's passing. Before Mom died, I knew I was her favorite and most trusted person on the planet, which was healing for us both. (Sorry, not sorry, to usurp your seniority, brother.)

Gran passed in 1996, and two years later, #10 died from cancer. I'd been running hard for several years at this point, first transporting Gran to doctors and hospital stays. I'd drive from my home in Los Banos to San Jose to pick up her sister, drive my great aunt to Salinas so we could all go to church and lunch together, then take Aunt Rita back to San Jose before heading home. (A two hundred thirty-mile round trip.) After Gran passed, I'd meet Mom in Gilroy to pick up #10, drive him to the VA Clinic in Palo Alto for his chemotherapy, and take him back to their home in Salinas before heading home to Los Banos. Each of his treatments took 4 hours, plus 5 hours of driving (about two hundred fifty miles per trip) for me. Being so busy with that, my real estate career, and an eleven-year-old child, I hadn't paid attention to Mom's weight loss and weakness.

Mom tipped over in September 1999 and succumbed to COPD in January 2000. She didn't want to die in the hospital, so I took her to her home and went through the end of her life with her.

Forty-five years before, my mother had accompanied me, a fetus, to the very edge of the unknown world I was about to enter . . . then it was time for me to go it alone. I left Mom. I shared Mom's journey as far as I could, then it was time for her to go it alone. Mom left me that final time on January 4, 2000.

Unlike Forrest Gump, that's not all I have to say about that. As you've noticed, I'm a talker. There is more to be told and more seeking release; however, I'm going to wrap this up fairly soon. When I picked up this promise in May 2022, I committed to completion by year's end, for me. Now I need to find all my cousins, or the offspring of those who've passed, to inform them I'm sharing our people's story. I don't want to give my people that same "fly sucked out the window at 89 mph" experience I had. It wasn't fun, so I can't thrust it on another.

Although my intent hasn't been to rip your nerves to rags, I'm confident you've been feeling me and experienced a few ragged moments with me. My son isn't looking forward to reading this; he said he expects it'll hurt him to learn details about how much someone he loves suffered. Yet he will because he wants to know me, to see me. He expects it will answer questions about why I'm me. Hey, sounds like that should be part of the title! The why I'm me:-) Dang, I crack me up! I hope you've had some laughs along with my people and me.

Beloved, it isn't about the suffering. I don't want you to suffer. I've written from my favorite storylines, those of redemption and overcoming. The only thing over which you have control in life is your attitude. Life happens. YOU alone choose to be bitter, or better. Yes, some of my people were badass outlaws who committed some felonious crimes. However, they weren't 100% bad. No human is. One of them reached into a burning car and saved a stranger's life when he was a teen. Another saved a life when he was doing time in San Quentin, which resulted in him being on Death Row for a spell.

They stood in the gap for us. People didn't mess with us, or if they were foolish enough to do so, they paid a price. A man tried to rape a teenage family member, and that young man had a reputation for doing so to other young women. When one of our outlaws learned of it, he went directly to the guy. He told him the only reason he didn't kill him was that our families went back too far.

However, from that day forward, if the guy saw the family member he'd tried to rape, the guy was to cross the street and avoid eye contact. If he didn't, he would pay with his life. The man took him at his word and behaved as instructed.

As bizarre as it might sound, that was a source of pride within our family. They had your back, no questions asked. Their bite was far worse than their bark. When it got down to the nitty gritty, they were there for our people, wrong or right, believing blood was all that mattered.

Years later, when I learned a young family member had been beaten by her man, my first thought was to inform one of the outlaws. I wanted the cowardly man to know what it felt like to be beaten by someone much bigger and tougher. I can't tolerate a bully. I wanted him to feel helpless and frightened.

I wouldn't ask our outlaw for justice. I wouldn't have to. Well, I didn't call, I couldn't call, but it came to mind. In times of stress, we revert to habit. Realistically, being beat man to man wouldn't be like getting beat by someone you loved and trusted. Those fists he threw at her resulted in temporary nerve damage, but that was nothing compared to the damage to her heart, her trust, and her soul.

Remember I told you there'd been a bitter dispute between two of Mom's siblings that lasted for decades? One of the most glorious days of my life was when one sibling was on her deathbed, and the other visited.

When he walked in the door, she said, "Oh brother, it's so good to see you."

Not one of us present had a dry eye. They spoke not a word of yesterday, and we all healed. That's the good stuff right there and where I'm trying to take you. Healing and redemption.

Auntie suffered a widow maker heart attack and hung on for a month. I believe God gifted her the opportunity to say goodbye to her children and her brother. When the doc explained there wasn't anything else they could do, I faced the fact that this beloved woman would die soon. A tear leaked out of my eye and rolled down my cheek.

She turned her head to look me in the eye and said, "Stop that. Don't cry. There's no need to cry, honey. What are you, some kind of pansy?" That admonition dried up my tears just as it had in my youth.

I've just now realized Auntie knew there was no need to cry. She'd been with her oldest sister as she passed. She witnessed the peace, calm, and joy her sister experienced as she left this world for her heavenly home with the Lord. Both Aunties knew where they were going.

About a year after her passing, one of Auntie's daughters called me and said, "Nev, I think you should get a tattoo."

I told her I was born with all the tattoos I ever wanted.

"Oh, but this is a good one. You should get a classy little tattoo on your wrist that says, 'I'm no pansy,' and you'll think of Mom every time you see it."

Surprisingly, I seriously considered it. Actually, I considered one for each wrist, with the other saying, "Or am I?" because I do cry now, well, a little bit anyway. Do you remember when I mentioned the tattoo much earlier? I told you it was a quiz!

Grandma's unspoken message was if you rise too far above your raising, you'll be ostracized. Me, the stray, had one foot out the door and the other on a banana peel. I couldn't allow myself to be like my mother, the outlaws, or those caught in the cycle of dependency for love and/or money. I didn't maintain generational relationships with like families from Oklahoma. I wanted more. I wanted better.

I was criticized as "Miss Goody Two Shoes" for my outreach and desire for betterment. I was accused of thinking I was better than the others. Decades later, I was told at least one family member had plotted to take me down from my "pillar of goodness."

I stopped asking, "Why me?" a very long time ago, instead asking, "Why not me?"

To whom much is given, much is required. I have risen above my raising, but only so far. First female to not marry before the age of eighteen. (I was still too young when I married at nineteen.) First female to graduate high school and go to college. I recently registered for college to complete my degree and joined a women's prison ministry team.

If you're reading this, I'm also a published author. (With your help, a *New York Times* bestselling author:-) Although twice married, this second time it's been 35 years. My second husband and I haven't divorced one another, but we have married one another three times. My children are awesome people and solid parents. They have risen above their raising, which pleases me immeasurably.

Imma tell you, though ~ the writing of this book hasn't been easy. The plan was to tell my people's story. Instead of simply telling their story, I ended up plunging into the depths of my soul. Meouch! I didn't realize how much I needed it and how much some of you need it. As different as they are, our stories connect us. They evidence our sameness under it all. And that's what we should look for in one another, sameness. Our stories can help us do that.

In the early '90s, my husband and I owned a flooring store in Hollister. We were doing well until the recession hit, then things got grim. Our landlord was going to double our shop rent while we were barely eking out a living. We thought we had no alternative but to close the store, but then wondered how we'd survive; it was the only source of both of our incomes. We feared losing the home we built after our old house had burned. It was quite depressing and scary. I think three of our five kids lived with us then.

Not knowing what else to do, I decided to throw myself a party. A pity party. Imma tell you, each day, I got a little more into the party, feeling helpless and hopeless. I wanted to quit. Quit what, I don't know. I just wanted to quit. And that's when Francisco walked by on his way to the corner market three doors down from us to buy himself a bottle of booze.

Francisco lived at "The Church in the Alley" behind our shop. (A local minister had converted a detached garage to a men's homeless shelter, which folks called The Church in the Alley.) Francisco had been a successful man in a managerial position at the cannery, had earned some success as a boxer, was married with children, owned his own home and rentals . . . until the drink got the better of him

He lost it all and ended up living at The Church in the Alley. He'd often stop by our store on the way back from the Brother's Market and ask if he could give my youngest a package of Chicle gum he'd purchased for her. He was a polite and honorable man with me, never asking for anything. He was a lovely human being, and I considered him a friend.

One particular day, I was deep in my pity party, staring out the window, watching traffic go by on San Benito Street while contemplating my ever-increasing desire to quit. That's when I saw Francisco come around the corner of the alley and wobble to the tree in front of our store. His legs were rubbery; he had to rest mid-way between his place and the market, so I knew he'd been at the bottle and not eating for several days.

Watching him, surely sent by God, I got the message loud and clear. Of course, you can quit life any time you choose. But life doesn't quit you. Life continues on, and you're still in it. Francisco had quit, yet there he was. I realized that if you don't die, in all probability, one day, you'll decide to get back in the game again. I acknowledged it was far too big a step back to the sidewalk from "the gutter" where Francisco was. I never wanted to take such a huge hard step as he'd have to make to get back into the game of life as he once lived. When you fall, when you fail, get up and give it one more try, even if you must crawl to do so.

I immediately stopped feeling sorry for myself and recognized we had to minimize our losses, close the store and trust in the unknown future. We closed the store shortly after that, and within months we found a fish farm in Los Banos that we leased to operate a private water ski pond. It was something my husband had dreamt of doing for over two decades.

Dearheart, where we come from does not define who we are. Our life experiences do not dictate that we must remain where we were. We choose, every single day, who we are and where we're going in life. When we choose not to act, not to grow, not to reach, not to strive to be our best selves, we go around in circles instead of forward. Been there, done that, for far too long. From this moment to the next, we are always free to change. As Gran said, "Nothing beats a trial but a failure . . . and you'll never learn any younger!"

We all watch the Olympic athletes, their drive, struggles, and determination toward the goal, and we respect their path to greatness. How dare we disrespect our own paths! Those Olympians fall, they fail, they get injured . . . they just don't quit. They, too, have family issues, financial issues, and employment issues. Come on now! Let's do this thing called life!

I've never met a person who doesn't have some family issues or "wild ones" in their lineage, regardless of their socioeconomic status. Don't make family or environment your excuse; they are them. You are you. You alone are responsible for your choices, decisions, and actions. You get to decide what you want from life and then act on that decision. As the title of ET's (Eric Thomas, the Hip Hop Preacher) latest book says, *You Owe You* (Read that book; it's powerful!)

It's through those hard things we've lived through, those things that are so huge we can't talk about them, that we often find ourselves. The things that are so big and obvious they allow us, or force us, to talk about our yesterdays, even if we just talk to ourselves by writing them out. Those tiny yet huge memories resurface and are brought into the light of day so we can see we're safe after all. It's daylight, the nightmare is over, and the monster(s) have fled in the light of day. We've survived 100% of our yesterdays.

For far too long, I felt shamefully hidden behind my family. The truth is I loved them; I love them. My people did their best with what they had to work with. Their work, efforts, imperfections, and shortcomings lifted me. I stood on their shoulders to see beyond the horizon. I was inspired by the newspaper articles about their athletic prowess. I determined I, too, would have positive news articles written about me. (There've been many.)

Our life was hard, yet we all felt the love of family. Today, I am proud of my people, and I know my people would be proud of me. I am grateful for my people's story, and it's most likely why I'm me.

We all have bad memories; we can't do anything about the moments that made those memories; however, we do have a say about future memories. Hopefully, *My People's Story* has stirred up some of your emotions and memories, and you resolve to work through them. Get professional help if need be; this is important work for you! You are worthy and deserve freedom from your wounds.

Until we meet again on new pages, remember that you are a phenomenal winner. The fact that you exist is nothing short of a miracle. The odds are greater for you to win the lottery than to be born. From where you are, perhaps serving a life sentence in a prison cell, you can still be the 1% that succeeds. You've beaten the odds by surviving to today, no matter the odds against you.

If you're incarcerated, listen to the *Roll Call with Chappy* podcast that's on your tablet; you'll hear from others who were where you are, others who found a way to truly live and thrive regardless of their environment. People who've walked in your shoes want to help you live your best life. They want nothing from you except your personal success, which will affect the lives around you.

Your life change will positively affect your mama, your daddy, your children, and your siblings. Being a felon doesn't have to be the end of your story or a continuing saga. YOU get to choose! I wish our outlaws, my beloved people, would have had the resources offered to you.

Whether or not you're incarcerated, listen to *The Ed Mylett Show* and dare to grow into your best self. You are worthy and deserving sisters and brothers, yes, Y-O-U!

You, beloved reader, will find peace and the opportunity for life everlasting with Jesus Christ. You will find the love you longed for as a child, security, and your purpose. Jesus came to earth for us sinners, not the saints. Oh, to be held in such arms of forgiveness and love! He believed you, YOU, were worthy of his enduring humiliation, torture, and excruciating death. Imperfect you. Imperfect me.

Might you be one of those who knew God, and something happened in your life that caused you to turn away from him? Perhaps you're hating on him for some hurt or injustice. A grudge is a grudge, friend; you're hurting and denying yourself freedom and love when you harbor a grudge. Hugging that grudge is like drinking battery acid and waiting expectantly for the person you're hating on to die. It won't happen; shoot, they might not even know how you feel. Say what you have to say, forgive them for being human (as are you), and LIVE freely! Accept that life isn't fair.

We can't understand The Master's Plan any more than a two-year-old child understands how an internal combustion engine works. Choose to be free of hatred and grudges. Look around you; there is no way all you see was an accident. A brilliant creator created it all, the universe and all it contains, to share with us.

Watch *The Chosen* to see the Apostles as the imperfect humans they were, to see Jesus as a human, and to feel the Words in Red come to life. It's the first crowd-funded, multi-season series about the life and ministry of Jesus, and it is magnificent! Get to know the man behind the story. Jesus wants a one-on-one relationship with YOU; you don't need a middle person to interpret.

God doesn't call the qualified. He qualifies the called. He's calling you as he's called me. Allow yourself to feel that hunger within, that longing for connection and greatness that was instilled within you before your birth. Embrace your greatness and step into your best self. You won't be sorry. There is something that YOU can do to change the world. YOU have unique gifts and talents. Changing the world starts by changing yourself. When I say change the world, I'm not talking about making grand discoveries, creations, or millions.

Love God. Love people. Smile and be kind to strangers. Don't be judging people to make yourself feel better. That will change the world. If you're not with God today, work on simply loving people, for who they are, and where they are, as a start. You too are flawed.

I don't know where this new path will take me, which is fine because I do love adventure. I trust in God's plan and purpose for my life.

For a time, I was beating myself up for taking so many years to share *My People's Story*. Then I accepted that I'm doing so now because THIS is the time. I'm ready to be the best version of myself to serve humanity and honor our Creator.

I hope you've enjoyed my people's story. I think we all agree it's why I'm me.

Blessings upon you, dear sisters and brothers. May you search and find your own best self. Jesus loves you, and so do I.

Holla back at your girl, I want to know YOUR story! Wait. Don't "holler" at me, I do not like to be yelled at. I was trying to sound hip. Let's get real and heal. GMB@GenevaBrett.com

Acknowledgments

To **Abba (YHWH), the Creator of All**, with love and appreciation for the breath of life, your mercy, your grace, your unconditional love, and the promise of life everlasting. Thank you for giving your son's life for mine. And **Jesus**, sweet Jesus, thank you for taking my place, for dying for flawed me. Thank you for never giving up on me, even when I did or didn't see or acknowledge you. You were always with me, and I will always be with you. Thank you for the guidance in writing this book. May it heal wounds, touch hearts and souls, and inspire my earthly sisters and brothers to become their best selves, to find and follow you. Thank you for taking my father before my birth so I could have all these experiences. The experiences equipped me with what I needed to do your work as you had planned before I was knitted in my mother's womb. Excellent job on the knitting, by the way. It foiled her attempts to off me before my first breath. I appreciate that!

To my people who have passed. What a ride! From today I thank you for all the yesterdays, even the hard ones. I've learned to look past actions and try to understand what wounded your souls. I love each and every one of you. I admire and appreciate you for who you were. You were awesome! I thank you for being you and loving me. Under it all, each of you had beautiful hearts; I trust you are united in God's presence. That's so cool!

To my people who are living. Whew! Even with this telling of our story, no one else can understand what we went through together. They won't believe it. Cousins, I'm grateful to have gone through it with you. We're no pansies! We've had so many grand adventures! I love, want, and need you in my life. All of you. Let's do another reunion and maybe gather more stories for a sequel.

Beloved brother of mine, thanks for sharing so much of this with me. Thanks for your promise to my little girl self to always be my protector. I'm so proud of you for keeping your promise to your nine-year-old self. Thank you for believing in me and for encouraging me in this endeavor. I love you unconditionally and beyond measure. "Hold his head up! He smells alfalfa!"

To my five children, bio, and bonus. This isn't exactly a book of useless facts, you precious twits of mine:-) All that diverse info I provided over the years makes great conversation fillers! Oh, how I wish my mom would have gifted her story to me to help me understand her, her life, and myself. Now you see me and so many whys. We're all wounded, imperfect people. I pray you, too, find some healing of your own wounds. You've all done well with your lives, and I'm very proud of your successes. I'll love you forever; as long as I'm living, my babies you'll be. Thanks for the input and the encouragement.

To my man. We knew it from that first business lunch. Looking back, it's been like that virtual reality ride at The Ark Encounter. Despite our racing hearts and sweaty palms through the scary parts, holding hands made it so much easier. Here's to more grand adventures, my love. Buckle up!

To my precious Uncle, thanks for being an older brother, mentor, and friend. You are the best of the clan; always my favorite! I love you tremendously! All us cousins do! "Pump the brakes! Pump the brakes!"

To my beloved dad of heart, Lee Romines (#1). Thanks for being a man of honor. For your promise to my father, love of my mother, and acceptance of me as family. The joy on your face and love in your eyes every time we greet brings my father alive for a moment, for both of us. I appreciate the glimpses of my parents through your eyes and memories. Thank you for your encouragement every step of this journey! I love and treasure you!

Thanks, and love to my Aunt Maryann for saving all my father's communications, his belongings left at home, and his casket flag and for sending them to me. I'm forever grateful to you for gifting me a few more pieces of my daddy. You've been a wonderful Auntie my entire life!

Aunt Dot, I treasure your love for your big brother, my father, for all your days!

Cousin Carol, thanks for keeping our connection. I appreciate you saving all those treasures your mommy kept of her big brother and knowing that someday they will come to me, and I'll have a few more pieces of my father. I love you tremendously, and I am incredibly proud of you!

Much love to **my sisters-in-law** for all the late nights, listening, wine, advice-giving, fun, and love.

JP, thanks for your powerful advice when my soul was devastated, and I needed a true friend who would tell me the truth, whether or not I liked it. I desperately needed your friendship and those words, "Nev, you've got one foot in yesterday, one foot in tomorrow, and you're pissing all over today." It was lifesaving, brother!

Thanks to my beloved **Pastor Bruce Rivers** for being a great man of God, an outstanding mentor, and a beloved friend. PB, I wasn't ready for you to go. Still, I'll forever appreciate your parting gift of a beautiful friendship with your bride and my treasured sister, **Emily**.

Thank you to my Wellness Coach**, Lisa Roper**, Myofascial Release Therapist, **Christon Eslinger**, and everyone at Complete Body Wellness for kick-starting my internal and external wellness journey.

To my favorite **Marg Benton**. Girlfriend, I'm so saddened you can't see this. I cherish us, your motivation, acceptance, and our sameness. You'll be with me until my end of days.

To my precious friend, **Victoria Faktorovich**; I admired you before I met you due to Arkady's adoration of you. **Arkady**, I appreciate how our friendship has grown to that of a brother and sister.

To my beloved bestie **Sandie Helmrick**, thanks for everything, sister. You taught me much with your own book!

Thank you, **Linda Higby**, for your service to America, friendship, and service to me by reading my manuscript and giving me precious feedback!

To my **Cher Parker Grogan** ~ my, oh my. From our first meeting of disliking one another to decades of love and friendship. You're amazing. Thanks for the love, the support, for always believing in me so much more than I did, for everything. I love you tremendously!

And my best gunfighting gal pal, **Arlene "Cardoza Kid,"** I love our decades of friendship, Ming's Chinese Chicken Salads, and hot dog lunches!

Barbara Douglass-Scherer, thanks for being the best travel companion EVER! I cherish you and **Honey**. I'm very proud of your well-deserved and well-earned success, my friend.

Sue and Will York, I love you and our delightful road trips; we are family. **Will**, thanks for doing God's work and spreading his word. He has something great planned for you, brother!

Former husband ~ thanks for the children! I will always love you friend. Always. Even if we ever have another round of not liking one another.

Papa G (**Greg Custodio**), Tawodi (**Will York**), Sundowner (**George Narasaki**) thank you for the introduction to Cowboy Fast Draw! Together we played 1800's dress up, used pretend names (aliases), shot wax bullets at round circles, talked a whole lot of trash, created a phenomenal California State Championship, introduced many to our sport, nurtured some world champions and changed lives! I'm so grateful! And Papa G, you know it was true from the moment I said it; we were lifelong friends just waiting to meet. Love you forever little brother!

Thanks to my worldwide adaptive water ski family for your love and acceptance of me, as I am, from day one. Ya'll rocked my world, challenged me, and allowed me to serve and represent you. **Matty O**, you da man, and I love you immeasurably! And **Doc** ~ thanks for your words of wisdom and for caring for adaptive water ski athletes worldwide. No more shame because I was a victim. No more victim here!

Thanks to **Portagee 1** from Portagee 2 (aka Irish 1) for hauling my hog car, being a dear friend, and encouraging my writing by publishing my works in your newspaper. Heartfelt thanks to you and **Barbara** for all you've gifted to my beloved Los Banos over the decades.

Thanks to my dear friend, the remarkable **Margaret Sliger** for the encouragement, I wish it would have been published before you left. We'd have shared many more laughs, and maybe a tear or two.

North Salinas High School Class of 1972, I cherish you one and all! Thanks for the love, the acceptance, the memories, and the reunions. You lift me up!

Maxwell Leadership, thanks for the training to take me to the next level as a speaker, coach, and trainer.

Huge thanks and love to Linda Potgieter and her Power of Personal Style program for helping me up my style game and my life. To my global sisters in the Dress to Connect group, thanks for loving, accepting, and encouraging every other woman and me. You rock!

Props and thanks to Peter Meyerhoff for doing God's work to help those incarcerated have hope today and have opportunities upon their release. *Roll Call with Chappy* helped my Folsom Prison Blues wounded heart, and stirred my soul, so I must go back to prison to help others.

Precious Dr. Ann Hill, Woman of God, thank you for founding Women of Love Ministries and accepting me into your women's prison ministry. I am healed of ancient wounds and love the opportunity to share God's love and grace to the female inmates. Chaplin M. Gwasira, you are a precious gift of God!

Thanks to Ed Mylett for also doing God's work; I'm grateful I found your *Ed Mylett Show* (podcast) which drives me to give everything *One More Try*.

Kevin Hines, thanks for being a fabulous storyteller and saving countless lives by sharing your story of the mistake you made when you jumped off the Golden Gate Bridge. God definitely saved you to save others and heal hearts! Kevinhinesstory.com

Huge thanks to Andy Frisella and his 75HARD challenge. Thanks for reminding me and challenging me to find the grit and drive that's always been beneath my surface! I appreciate those letters of congratulations and encouragement included with the 75HARD merch my kids bought me upon completing the challenge. It just might become an annual challenge for me.

John O'Leary, God saved your life so that you can minister to others, saving souls, guiding people to our Lord, and providing perspective. JohnOLearyInspires.com. I, too, hope to die with ugly feet in service to Our Father.

Mr. Jim Kwik, thanks for writing *Limitless* for us, especially me! Learning how to learn is life-changing! I'm on my way to a limitless life!

Creators of *The Chosen*, thank you immeasurably for your gifted work. It is desperately needed because The People Must Know! new.thechosen.tv (There's also a Chosen app.)

Every human I've ever encountered has impacted me in some way or another. Thanks to each of you.

And last . . . thanks to my publisher. As I began writing, I said God would direct me to THE publisher or send THE publisher to me. I thank God for you! Which it turns out, is me:-)

Images

Stringtown, Oklahoma, Circa 1940
Gran, presumably pregnant with their youngest
daughter, with one of Grandpa Kennedy's sisters.
Not sure who the child is.

Salinas, California lettuce shed. Nor sure of the year, probably 1942 - 1946. Gran's the shortest one; she worked as a lettuce trimmer. Gran's youngest daughter would throw a fit when Gran left for work and would remain inconsolable all day long. They believed the best solution was for Gran to take her to work with her. She'd leave her two year old daughter in the car, alone, all day, except during her breaks and lunch time. It worked for them. Today, the law would be called, Gran, maybe Gramps too, would face criminal charges and their child would be taken away from them.

Grandma and Grandpa Kennedy - Easter Sunday 1946 at the Pinecate Rocks, North Hwy 101 between Prunedale and the San Juan Bautista exit.

It was the site of numerous bandit hold ups in the wild west days. After becoming US Route 101 in 1932, it became a free picnic area with firepits, horseshoe pits, BBQ, and playground equipment.

It became a four lane in 1959, isolating the spot between north and south bound lanes at the eucalyptus grove. Years later the big rock became a place to tag and taunt, often between rivaling high schools.

This area has since been blocked off by cement barriers and made inaccessible, due to the danger of vehicles merging back into traffic.

"The Rocks" New highway near Salinas, Calif.

Thursday, July 18, 1951　　SALINAS CALIFORNIAN—5

Truman Ready to Demand Law to Punish Persons Hiding or Hiring 'Wetbacks'

WASHINGTON (AP) — Rep. Emanuel Celler, (D., N. Y.), said yesterday after a White House visit, that President Truman is ready to demand legislation to punish persons who conceal or hire "wetbacks" who slip across the Mexican border into this country.

"Wetbacks" are Mexican laborers, so-called because they wade or swim across the Rio Grande and enter this country illegally.

Celler, chairman of the house judiciary committee, said he discussed with Mr. Truman a bill which would make it a misdemeanor for anyone to harbor, conceal, or employ aliens who are in this country illegally. The bill is aimed at barring the "wetbacks."

Mr. Truman last week signed a bill under which his government will negotiate with Mexico a six-month agreement for hiring Mexican farm labor brought into this country lawfully.

At the time, Mr. Truman said other legislation was needed urgently to stop the flow of unlawful labor into this country.

Celler said Mr. Truman told him that if opposition by congressmen from states which employ "wetbacks" kills the Celler bill, he will not try to negotiate another agreement after the projected six-month pact expires.

* * *

MEXICO CITY (AP) — The foreign ministry said yesterday Mexican-American negotiations on a new migrant labor treaty are being carried out with "the fullest spirit of understanding and good will."

At the same time it said the agenda includes salaries, guarantees, transportation, means of contracting, investigation of complaints and places not eligible for export or Mexican "braceros."

Employment of "wetbacks" or illegal workers and punishment of employers hiring these workers also was discussed by the five committees of the international conference.

Sen. Allen J. Ellender, (D., La.), and David Stowe, President Truman's special assistant, arrived by air from Washington and immediately joined the U. S. delegation as advisers.

A Mexican spokesman said participation of Ellender in the problem of contracting of Mexican farm hands is of the "highest importance," since "he has favored Mexico's points of view in the United States congress."

U. S. representatives visited Acting Foreign Minister Manuel Tello, who reiterated this country's position on the "braceros" question and expressed "full confidence" that Mexico's viewpoints will be incorporated into the act.

Youths Involved In Big Barn Fight Ask Jury Trial

Jury trial has been set for August 28 for 14 persons accused of battery and disturbing the peace in a brawl at the Big Barn Thursday night.

Louise Kennedy Simmons, 18, and another 17-year-old Salinan girl charged 11 youths with knocking them down and beating them during the fight.

The suspects are [...]

[...] 21, of [...] and four minor girls. Later the [...]

two complainants also were charged with battery and disturbing the peace. Mrs. Geneva Kennedy, 18, of 1061 Garner avenue, is accused of peace disturbance.

All 14 of the accused have pleaded not guilty. The trial was set yesterday by Justice of the Peace J. A. Jeffery.

Australia Cables Sympathy to U.S.

CANBERRA, Australia (AP) — Australia has sent a message to Washington expressing this country's "profound distress" over the loss of life and damage caused by the Kansas floods. External Affairs Minister Richard Casey announced yesterday.

The note expressed sincere wishes for early recovery of the devastated area.

7 Youths Plead Not Guilty to Battery Charges

Trial of seven youths arrested by sheriff's deputies who broke up a gang fight at the Big Barn Thursday night will be set on the calendar by Justice of the Peace J. A. Jeffery Wednesday.

The seven battery suspects appeared in court this morning and pleaded not guilty. Four minor girls, arrested with them, will be held by juvenile authorities pending the outcome of the trial.

Complainants are Sue Kennedy, 17, and Louise Kennedy, 18.

The suspects are

Five males:
Two aged 19
Two aged 20
One aged 21
One female, aged 22

They are all free on bail pending the trial setting.

Mom was married, and two month's pregnant with my brother at this time; don't know if she knew about brother. Number one doesn't remember the event, but he remembers how quick Mom was to fight..

Mom and #1 met at a dance at the Big Barn.

8 Sentenced By Jeffery in Battery Case

Gang fight at the Big Barn in the Alisal district July 12 resulted in eight young persons being found guilty on battery and disturbing the peace charges in Justice of the Peace J. A. Jeffery's court this morning.

All eight were sentenced following the court's verdict. Charges against a female 22, of Hebbron avenue, and two juvenile girls were dismissed by the court. Two other juvenile girls involved were certified to the juvenile department of the superior court.

Three males; 19, 20 and 21 years of age were found guilty of battery.

guilty of battery. and received 30-day jail sentences, with one day of each sentence suspended. was sentenced to 30 days in jail, suspended for two years on condition he pay a $20 fine. He was remanded to jail when he failed to pay. .

Louise Kennedy Romines, 18, of 1041 Garner avenue, Mrs. Sue

Mrs. Sue Kennedy was Mom's older sister. Three males: one 19, and two 20 years of age were found guilty of disturbing the peace.

found guilty of disturbing the peace.

, and the two girls received 30-day jail sentences suspended for two years in each case. The girls each paid a $20 fine as a condition of probation. was sentenced 30 days in the county jail, one day suspended.

Judge Jeffery warned all the defendants following the sentencings that future gang fight convictions would result in straight jail sentences on conviction. Attys. Michael Panelli and John Muller represented the defendants. Deputy Dist. Atty. Joseph A. Stave prosecuted for the state.

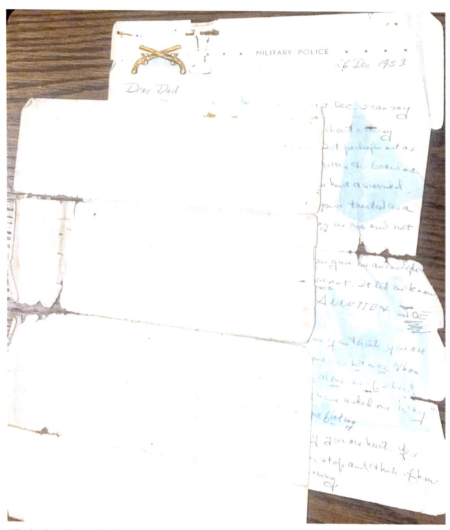

The broken letter ~ Dad was hurt and angry with his father, so he wrote him a scathing letter. Written the day after Christmas, and nine months before Dad's death. It's the last letter I have from Dad to his dad. His father opened and closed this letter for over thirty years before his death. All Dad's other letters lay flat, stapled to the envelope. This broken letter is symbolic of a father's broken heart over harsh words they didn't have time to heal.

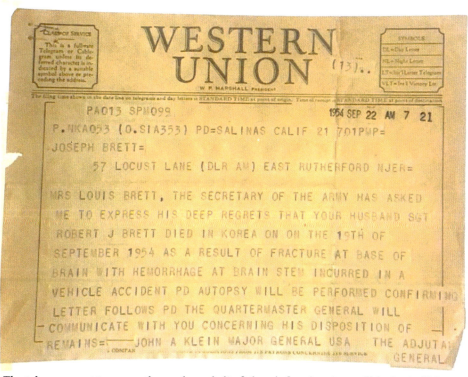

The telegram sent to my mother and my dad's father, informing them of his death. This is Grandpa Brett's copy; Mom's burned in a house fire along with all of Dad's personal effects sent home after his death. Looking closely, you can see the telegram consists of individual rows of typing, pasted onto a sheet of paper.

Salinas Woman's Husband Passes Away in Korea

Funeral services for Sgt. Robert J. Brett, 26, who passed away Sunday in Korea, are pending in East Rutherford, N. J., until the arrival of his body at Oakland on Oct. 14.

Mr. Brett's wife, Louise, who lives at 1041 Garner street, was notified of his death last Tuesday. On Thursday, Mrs. Brett gave birth to their first child, a daughter, which was named Geneva Marie. Mrs. Brett now staying with her parents in Salinas, Mr. and Mrs. John Kennedy.

Although details of his death are not known, the U. S. army informed Mrs. Brett that her husband was injured in a vehicle accident. She believes he was injured sometime after Sept. as that was the date of his last letter.

Mr. Brett was a veteran of both World War II and the Korean conflict. He enlisted in U. S. marine corps when 17 years of age, served overseas and was honorably discharged.

He entered the army in and served in Korea. He was discharged last January and re-enlisted, going overseas for the third time in July. He was a criminal investigator at the time of his death.

In addition to his wife and daughter, he is also survived by a step-son, Ronnie; his father, Joseph Brett, mayor of East Rutherford, and a sister, Miss Dorothy Brett of New Jersey.

Both the news clipping and the sock Dad bought for me when he learned Mom was pregnant were kept in Granny K's Family Photo album.

Dad's casket at his service in New Jersey. I received the folded flag after Grandpa Brett's passing.

What I have of my father are a few photos, the flag that draped his casket, and a few stories told by Mom's family and Dad's family. There are tens of thousands of Gold Star Children like myself, whose mother or father died or was killed while serving in the United States military

Mom ~ Easter Sunday Picnic, 1946, at the Pinecate Rocks. She looks to be a happy twelve year old child. She married for the first time just four years later.

Fast forward to the late 1970s or 80s, when she was running her hardest and wildest. After divorce from #8, before #10. I loved her, but couldn't accept her life. Most of what I know from then is what family told me.

The below bizarre photo was taken in that time frame. I found it in one of her photo albums. Brother has no information, except he thinks he gave her that pup.

She's sitting in a rocking chair, on top of a car, facing the rear of the car, near the ocean. She looks a bit sad, while holding a puppy, wearing a *Little House on the Prairie* bonnet, top, jeans, and what she called her "squaw boots". I don't even know if I want to know the story!

Mom bought us matching outfits in the mid 1990s (I think that's when it was!) She had sewn us matching business suits when I was a child, which I really loved. I wasn't so crazy about matching with my mom in my 30s, but she was so excited, I agreed. This might have been a Thanksgiving. Me in my mid 30s, Mom in her mid 50s. Photos of my mother wearing a smile are few and far between. This is an absolute treasure, and worth matching!

Easter Sunday, 1996 ~ at Gran's in Salinas, CA

Mom, Gran, Aunt Pat ~ the three most important women in my life. Easter Sunday was always a big deal in our family; much bigger than Christmas. New outfits, church, and a family meal. Honoring Christ's death, celebrating his resurrection, and the promise of life everlasting.

Grandma Kennedy died a month after this photo, Mom died four years later. Auntie died twelve years after their mother.

I hope I have honored them with my telling of our people's story. They loved me the best the could, as I've loved them the best I'm able.

Cover Photo ~ The Gang 1941

My grandmother and the children she had in 1941 (she had three more in the next five years). Mom's the one with the Trump mugshot face. I've seen this throughout my life, and just, I do mean just, put the pieces together. Mom said she was seven years old and they were living in a tent camp when her mama made her fight those rock throwing girls. I'm guessing this was taken after Mom kicked some little rock throwing girls asses. They lived in that camp for a year. Mom was seven in 1941, which places them in one of the sixteen migrant camps in California that were operated by the Farm Service Administration. This is a professional photo, presumably taken by someone documenting life in the camps. My people were dressed up for the occasion. Judging by the short sleeved, lightweight clothes they were wearing and the size of the youngest daughter, born in October of 1940, I think this was probably in the summer of 1941. I'm guessing one of the southern California camps Sigh. I'll be researching archives to see if I can find this photo, and perhaps a story that went along with it.

ABOUT THE AUTHOR

Geneva Marie Brett

Geneva lives in the Big Valley in Cali with her husband. They have five children, eleven grandchildren, a standard poodle, and two cats.

Prior to becoming a successful real estate broker, Geneva worked as an income tax practitioner, notary public, legal assistant, marketing representative, and loan officer. She even drove a dump truck for a couple weeks to help family!

She is also a volunteer extraordinaire, receiving numerous accolades for her decades of community service, epitomizing "If it is to be, it is up to me" and "WE before me" She currently serves on her County School Board, and USA Adaptive Water Ski and Wake Sports Board of Directors. She remains an advocate for California's Historic Buffalo Soldier Trail and serves on a women's prison ministry team.

Made in the USA
Columbia, SC
02 February 2024

36e663d1-c93b-4c1b-821a-ec2aa5b2e723R02